MACROECONOMICS
STUDY GUIDE

Boyes/Melvin

MACROECONOMICS
STUDY GUIDE

James E. Clark
Wichita State University

Janet L. Wolcutt
Wichita State University

Houghton Mifflin Company   **Boston**

Dallas   Geneva, Illinois   Palo Alto   Princeton, New Jersey

Cover photograph by Ralph Mercer, Boston, MA.

Fundamental Questions, Key Terms, and Idea Maps from William Boyes and Michael Melvin, *Economics*. Copyright © 1991 by Houghton Mifflin Company. Used with permission.

Printed in the U.S.A.

Library of Congress Catalog Card Number: 90–83022

ISBN: 0–395–48275–5

ABCDEFGHIJ-CS-99876543210

CONTENTS

USING THE STUDY GUIDE

WHAT'S IN THE STUDY GUIDE

All Study Guide chapters are organized the same way; each includes the following:

- *Fundamental Questions* are repeated from the text chapter and are briefly answered. The questions and their answers give you an overview of the chapter's main points.
- *Key Terms* from the chapter are listed to remind you of new vocabulary presented in the chapter.
- A *Quick Check Quiz* focuses on vocabulary and key concepts from the chapter. These multiple-choice questions allow you to see whether you understand the material and are ready to move on or whether you need to review some of the text before continuing.
- *Practice Questions and Problems* provide in-depth coverage of important ideas from the chapter and give you the opportunity to apply concepts and work out problems.
- The *Thinking About and Applying* section covers one or more topics in greater depth and will help you learn to apply economics to real-world situations. This section will also show you how various economic concepts are related to one another and, as a result, will help you to think economically.
- The *Answers* section may be the most important part of the Study Guide. Answers to all questions and problems are provided with explanations of how to arrive at the correct answer. In many cases, explanations are given for what you did wrong if you arrived at certain wrong answers.

HOW TO STUDY ECONOMICS

No one ever said that economics is an easy subject, and many students tell us it is the most challenging subject they have studied. Despite the challenge, most students manage to learn a great deal of economics, and we're sure you can too. But doing well in economics requires a commitment from you to *keep up* your studying and to *study properly.*

Keeping up: Although there may be subjects that can be learned reasonably well by cramming the night before an exam, economics is *not* one of them. Learning economics is like building a house: first you need to lay a solid foundation and then you must carefully build the walls. To master economics you must first learn the early concepts, vocabulary, and ideas; if you do not, the later ones will not make any sense.

Studying properly: Listening in class, reading the text, and going through the Study Guide are not enough to really learn economics—you must also organize your studying. The textbook and the Study Guide have been designed to help you organize your thinking and your studying. Used together, they will help you learn.

We recommend following these steps for each chapter:

1. Skim the text chapter before your instructor discusses it in class to get a general idea of what the chapter covers.
   a. Look at the idea map first to see how the chapter fits in with what you've learned already. The idea map is printed in full color in your textbook and is reproduced in black and white in the Study Guide.
   b. Read through the Fundamental Questions and the Preview to get a sense of what is to come.
   c. Skim through the chapter, looking only at the section headings and the section Recaps.
   d. Read the chapter Summary. By this point, you should have a good idea of what topics the chapter covers.

2. Read the text chapter and Study Guide one section at a time. Both the text and the Study Guide break down each chapter into several sections so that you will not need to juggle too many new ideas at once.

   a. Read through one section of the text chapter. Pay attention to the marginal notes containing definitions of Key Terms, highlights of important concepts, and Fundamental Questions.

   b. Study the section Recap. If parts of the Recap are not clear to you, review those parts of the section.

   c. In the Study Guide, read the answers to the Fundamental Questions covered in the section you are studying.

   d. Take the Quick Check Quiz for the section. Write your answers on a separate sheet of paper so that you can use the quiz again later. If you missed any questions, review the applicable section in the text.

   e. Work through the Practice Questions and Problems for the section, writing your answers in the spaces provided. Check your answers; then review what you missed. Read through the explanations in the Answers section, even if you answered the question or problem correctly.

   f. If there are ideas that are not clear or problems you do not understand, talk to your instructor. Economics instructors are interested in helping their students.

3. Review the chapter as a whole. Although each section should initially be studied alone, you will need to put the pieces together.

   a. Read through the chapter again, paying special attention to the idea map, the Fundamental Questions, the section Recaps, the Economic Insight boxes, and the chapter Summary. If you like to outline chapters on paper, now is the time to do so. The section headings and subheadings provide an ideal framework for outlining the text.

   b. In the Study Guide, read through the Fundamental Questions and their answers.

   c. Review the list of Key Terms. Write down the definition of each one at this point, and check your definitions against the marginal notes or the glossary. Study any terms you missed.

   d. Work through the Exercises at the end of the text chapter.

   e. Read through the Economically Speaking section in the text to see how the real world contains examples of economic thinking.

   f. Work through the Thinking About and Applying section of the Study Guide.

4. Ideally, studying for exams should be a repetition of steps 1, 2, and 3 above. However, economists recognize the existence of opportunity costs, and you have many other things to do with your time in addition to studying economics. If you cannot study for an exam as thoroughly as you should, you can use some techniques to help refresh your memory. These techniques assume that you *did* study the materials at least once (there is no magic way to learn economics without doing some serious studying).

   a. Review the Fundamental Questions, the idea maps, the section Recaps, the Key Term lists, and the chapter Summaries in the text.

   b. Read again the Fundamental Questions and their answers in the Study Guide.

   c. Take the Quick Check Quiz again, writing your answers in the Study Guide this time. Questions that you miss will direct you to the areas you need to study most.

If you follow these suggestions, you are sure to meet with success in your study of economics.

This text presents all the key concepts of economics. In addition it explains how people use these concepts—in business, in government, and in ordinary households. In both the world of theory and the real world of application, knowing the relationships of ideas is crucial. No one can move about in either world without knowing the pathways that relationships form. When studying, it helps a great deal to have some picture of these pathways. That is why a map to show you the important conceptual and real-world pathways of macroeconomics is presented on the following pages. Using this map will help you

- pull together and manage a large subject
- learn the process of economic thinking
- improve your own critical thinking.

TAKE MORE THAN ONE VIEW

As you work through the chapters of this book, you will examine in close-up each particular concept. Yet to understand the material, and to get a feel for how economists think, you need to have a second point of view too—an overview. Keeping yourself "up above it" at the same time you are "down in it" will help you remember what you are reading much better and also help you understand and use the concepts you learn more easily. Taking more than one view of your subject has another benefit; it is an ingredient of good critical thinking.

MAKE YOUR OWN CONNECTIONS

To understand economics you need to keep track of how one thing changes in response to another, to see relationships more than fixed ideas. And this requires another ingredient of critical thinking, a sense of independence. With the idea map you can get around on your own (just as different classes may follow different sequences of chapters). Use it to get a feel for how ideas connect and then make your own connections as you read, actively asking yourself questions that cause you to evaluate, structure, and personalize the ideas. Work toward finding your own pathways, from idea to idea and from idea to reality.

USE THIS TEXT AS A SYSTEM

The other features of the text also show pathways, but they do it in a verbal way instead of the visual way the map does. The *Fundamental Questions* point to main issues and help you categorize details, examples, and theories accordingly. Colors in the *graphs* help you classify curves and see relationships to data in the *tables*. The *Recaps* reinforce overarching ideas; they orient you before you go on to the next big section. (Using them, in fact, is a lot like pausing to look at a map.) The *system of referencing* sections and headings by number will help you group concepts and also keep track of what level of ideas you are working with. If you use the idea map and the other features of the text, this text can be more than an authoritative source of information—it can be a system for comprehension. ▶

Making Sense of Macroeconomics

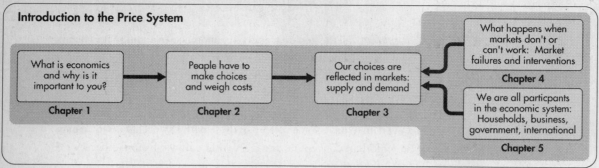

Introduction to the Price System

What is economics and why is it important to you?
Chapter 1

People have to make choices and weigh costs
Chapter 2

Our choices are reflected in markets: supply and demand
Chapter 3

What happens when markets don't or can't work: Market failures and interventions
Chapter 4

We are all particpants in the economic system: Households, business, government, international
Chapter 5

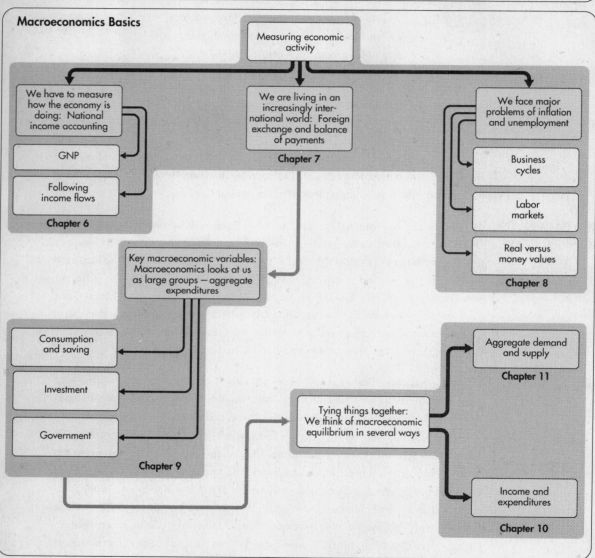

Macroeconomics Basics

Measuring economic activity

We have to measure how the economy is doing: National income accounting

GNP

Following income flows
Chapter 6

We are living in an increasingly international world: Foreign exchange and balance of payments
Chapter 7

We face major problems of inflation and unemployment

Business cycles

Labor markets

Real versus money values
Chapter 8

Key macroeconomic variables: Macroeconomics looks at us as large groups — aggregate expenditures

Consumption and saving

Investment

Government
Chapter 9

Tying things together: We think of macroeconomic equilibrium in several ways

Aggregate demand and supply
Chapter 11

Income and expenditures
Chapter 10

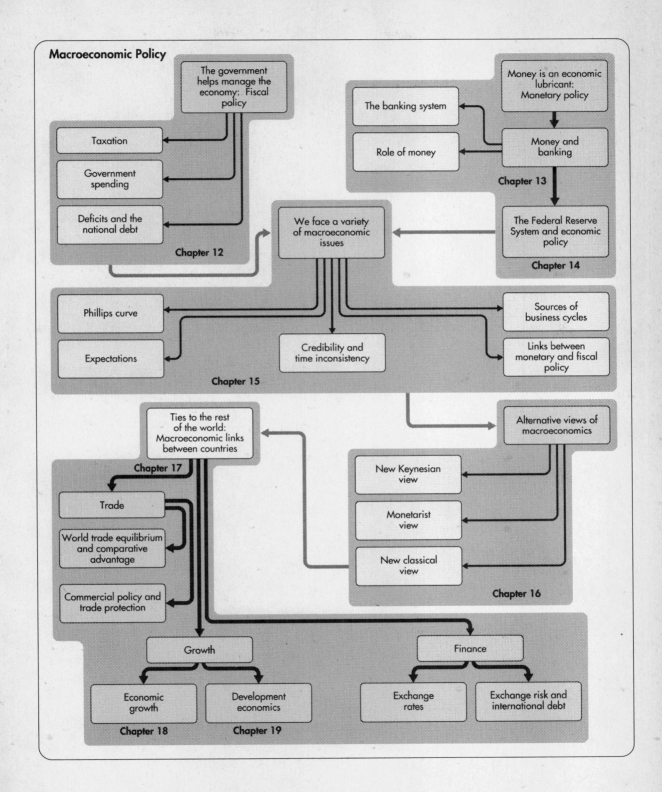

MACROECONOMICS
STUDY GUIDE

CHAPTER 1
Economics: The World Around You

1. What is economics?

   Economics is the study of how people choose to allocate scarce resources to satisfy their unlimited wants. There are several words in this definition that should be emphasized. First, people allocate **scarce** resources. If there were enough of a resource to go around so that everyone could have as much as he or she wanted, there would be no need to allocate.

   The definition states that people have **unlimited wants.** Note that it says "wants," not "needs." People *act* on the basis of their wants, not necessarily on the basis of their needs. (Otherwise they would not buy strawberry sundaes.) If each of us made a list right now of the top ten things we would like to have and our fairy godmother popped out of the air and gave us what we wanted, most of us would immediately find that there are ten *more* things we'd like to have. Since resources are scarce and wants are unlimited, economics studies the best way to allocate these resources so that none of them are wasted.

2. What is scarcity?

   To an economist, a good is scarce if people want more of it than is available when its price is zero. So any item that is not available for free is scarce.

3. What is rational self-interest?

   People acting on the basis of **rational self-interest** will make the choices that, at the time and with the information they have at their disposal, will give them the greatest amount of satisfaction. Economists say "rational" to imply that the self-interest of each individual makes sense or is logical. People do not purposely make themselves less happy. It is important to note that these decisions are made under uncertainty. If you buy a new stereo system and then the same system goes on sale next week, of course you will wish that you had waited. But you didn't know it would go on sale next week—if you had known, you would have waited. People act on the information that they have on hand, which may not be complete or accurate.

4. What is the difference between positive and normative analysis?

   Positive analysis makes no value judgments; it is the study of things the way they are. **Normative analysis** brings value judgments into play; it is the study of what ought to be. Economists usually agree on aspects of positive economics but disagree on issues of normative economics. For example, economists will agree that an increase in the sales tax on cigarettes will reduce the consumption of cigarettes, but they will disagree about whether such a tax ought to be imposed.

KEY TERMS

scarcity
economic good
free good
bad
unlimited wants
rational self-interest
land
labor
capital

entrepreneurial ability
entrepreneur
durables
nondurables
services
microeconomics
macroeconomics
positive analysis
normative analysis

theory
model
test
scientific method
assumptions
ceteris paribus
hypothesis
fallacy of composition
association as causation

QUICK CHECK QUIZ

Section 1: What Is Economics?

1. Which of the following is NOT an economic good?
   a. steaks
   b. houses
   c. cars
   d. garbage
   e. t-shirts

2. Which of the following is NOT one of the four categories of resources?
   a. land
   b. automobiles
   c. capital
   d. entrepreneurial ability
   e. labor

3. The payment for capital is called
   a. rent.
   b. wages.
   c. salaries.
   d. interest.
   e. profit.

4. Which of the following is a durable good?
   a. grapes
   b. wine
   c. refrigerators
   d. disposable razors
   e. bathroom tissue

5. Microeconomics includes the study of
   a. how an individual firm decides the price of its product.
   b. inflation in the United States.
   c. how much output will be produced in the U.S. economy.
   d. how many workers will be unemployed in the U.S. economy.
   e. how the U.S. banking system works.

6. The payment for entrepreneurial ability is called
   a. wages and salaries.
   b. rent.
   c. interest.
   d. profit.
   e. financial capital.

Section 2: The Economic Approach

1. Analysis that does not impose the value judgments of one individual on the decisions of others is called
   _____ analysis.
   a. positive
   b. normative
   c. economic
   d. noneconomic
   e. the scientific method of

2. Which of the following is NOT one of the five steps in the scientific method?
   a. Recognize the problem.
   b. Make assumptions in order to cut away unnecessary detail.
   c. Develop a model of the problem.
   d. Test the hypothesis.
   e. Make a value judgment based on the results of the hypothesis test.

3. If an individual decides to save more, he or she can save more. Therefore, if the society as a whole decides to save more, it will be able to save more. This reasoning is mistaken and as such is an example of
   a. ceteris paribus.
   b. the fallacy of composition.
   c. the interpretation of association as causation.
   d. the scientific method.
   e. none of the above—this reasoning is not mistaken.

4. Tim has noticed that every time he washes his car in the morning, it rains that afternoon. He has therefore decided to sell his services to farmers in drought-stricken areas, since he believes he can cause it to rain by washing his car. Tim's error is called
   a. ceteris paribus.
   b. the fallacy of composition.
   c. the mistaken interpretation of association as causation.
   d. the scientific method.
   e. none of the above—this reasoning is not mistaken.

5. Which of the following is a normative statement?
   a. Lower interest rates encourage people to borrow.
   b. Higher prices for cigarettes discourage people from buying cigarettes.
   c. If the price of eggs fell, people would probably buy more eggs.
   d. There should be a higher tax on cigarettes, alcohol, and other "sin" items to discourage people from buying these products.
   e. A higher interest rate encourages people to save more.

PRACTICE QUESTIONS AND PROBLEMS

Section 1: What Is Economics?

1. _____ exists when people want more of an item than is available when the price of the item is zero.

2. Any good that is scarce is an _____ good.

3. If there is enough of a good available at a zero price to satisfy wants, the good is called a _____ good.

4. A good that people will pay to have less of is called a _____ .

5. People use scarce resources to satisfy their _____ wants.

6. _____ means that people will make the choices that will give them the greatest amount of satisfaction.

7. List the four categories of resources and the payments associated with each.

   _____

   _____

   _____

   _____

8. _____ includes all natural resources, such as minerals, timber, and water, as well as the land itself.

9. _____ refers to the physical and intellectual services of people.

10. _____ is a manufactured or created product used solely to produce goods and services.

11. _____ capital refers to the money value of capital as represented by stocks and bonds.

12. _____ is the ability to recognize a profitable opportunity and the willingness and ability to organize land, labor, and capital and to assume the risk associated with the opportunity.

13. Goods that are used over a period of one or more years are called _____ .

14. _____ are work that is done for others that does not involve the production of goods.

15. _____ is the study of economics at the level of the individual economic entity.

16. The study of the economy at the aggregate level is called _____ .

17. What is economics?

_____

_____

_____

_____

Section 2: The Economic Approach

1. Analysis that does not impose the value judgments of one individual on the decisions of others is called _____ analysis.

2. _____ analysis involves imposing value judgments on the decisions of others.

3. Economists generally agree on the _____ aspects of economics.

4. List the five steps in the scientific method.

_____

_____

_____

_____

_____

5. The role of _____ is to reduce the complexity of a problem.

6. _____ means "other things being equal."

7. A theory, or _____, is a simple, logical story based on positive analysis that is used to explain an event.

8. A _____ is an explanation that accounts for a set of facts and allows us to make predictions in similar situations.

9. The _____ is the error of attributing what applies to one to the case of many.

10. The mistaken interpretation of _____ occurs when unrelated or coincidental events that occur at about the same time are believed to have a cause-and-effect relationship.

THINKING ABOUT AND APPLYING ECONOMICS: THE WORLD AROUND YOU

I. The Relationship Between Speed Limits and Highway Deaths

1. The "Economically Speaking" article in the text states that in twenty-two of the thirty-eight states that chose to raise the speed limit on rural highways, highway deaths jumped 46 percent between May and July over the same three months in 1986. Transportation Committee Chairman James Howard attributes the increase in deaths to the higher speed limit. Can you think of any other reasons that highway deaths might have increased? If states that did not increase rural speed limits experienced a similar increase in highway deaths, what common mistake might Chairman Howard be making?

    _____

    _____

    _____

    _____

ANSWERS

Quick Check Quiz

Section 1: What Is Economics?

1. d; 2. b; 3. d; 4. c; 5. a; 6. d
   If you missed any of these questions, you should go back and review pages 4–7 in Chapter 1.

Section 2: The Economic Approach

1. a; 2. e; 3. b; 4. c; 5. d
   If you missed any of these questions, you should go back and review pages 7–12 in Chapter 1.

Practice Questions and Problems

Section 1: What Is Economics?

1. Scarcity
2. economic
3. free
4. bad
5. unlimited
6. Rational self-interest
7. land; rent
    labor; wages and salaries
    capital; interest
    entrepreneurial ability; profit

8. Land
9. Labor
10. Capital
11. Financial
12. Entrepreneurial ability
13. durables
14. Services
15. Microeconomics
16. macroeconomics
17. Economics is the study of how people choose to use their scarce resources to satisfy their unlimited wants.

Section 2: The Economic Approach

1. positive
2. Normative
3. positive
4. Recognize the problem.
   Make assumptions in order to cut away unnecessary detail.
   Develop a model of the problem.
   Present a hypothesis.
   Test the hypothesis.
5. assumptions
6. Ceteris paribus
7. model
8. hypothesis
9. fallacy of composition
10. association as causation

Thinking About and Applying Economics: The World Around You

I. **The Relationship Between Speed Limits and Highway Deaths**

1. Other factors that might increase highway deaths include the following:

   a. Has there been an increase in population? It seems reasonable to expect more accidents as congestion increases.
   b. Are Americans buying more smaller cars? If so, auto deaths would be expected to increase because smaller cars provide less protection in the event of a crash.
   c. Has there been an increase in the number of people drinking (or being otherwise impaired) and driving? If so, we would expect an increase in the number of traffic fatalities no matter what the speed limit was.

   Perhaps you can think of other factors that might account for the increase in traffic fatalities that Howard attributes to the higher speed limit. If Howard has wrongly attributed the higher death toll to the higher speed limit, he has mistaken association for causation.

APPENDIX TO CHAPTER 1
Working with Graphs

SUMMARY

Most people are visually oriented: they are better able to understand things that they can "picture." The pictures that economists use to explain concepts are called graphs.

There are three commonly used types of graphs: the line graph, the bar graph, and the pie chart. The pie chart is used to show the relative magnitude of the parts that make up a whole. Line graphs and bar graphs are used to show the relationship between two variables. One of the variables, the **independent variable,** has values that do not depend on the values of other variables. The values of **dependent variables** do depend on the values of other variables.

If two variables move in the same direction together, the relationship is called a **direct,** or **positive relationship,** and the **slope** of the line or curve relating the two variables will be positive. If two variables move together but in opposite directions, the relationship is an **inverse,** or **negative relationship,** and the slope of the line or curve relating the two variables will be negative. A curve **shifts** when, for each combination of variables measured on the horizontal and vertical axes, one of the variables changes by a certain amount while the other variable remains the same. Shifts occur when variables other than those on the axes are allowed to change.

The slope of a line or curve is the rise over the run. The **45-degree line** is a special line that bisects the origin and has a slope equal to 1. At every point on the 45-degree line, the variable on the horizontal axis has the same value as the variable on the vertical axis.

We can find the maximum or minimum point on a curve by finding where the slope of the curve is equal to zero. If the slope goes from positive to zero to negative, a maximum occurs. If the slope goes from negative to zero to positive, a minimum occurs.

KEY TERMS

independent variable	positive relationship	shift
dependent variable	inverse relationship	slope
direct relationship	negative relationship	45-degree line

PRACTICE QUESTIONS AND PROBLEMS

1. The owner of a business that sells home heating oil has noticed that the amount of heating oil sold

    increases as the temperature outside decreases. Heating oil is the _____ (depend-

    ent, independent) variable. The relationship between the two variables is _____ (direct,

    inverse), and the slope of the line will be _____ (positive, negative.) Use the graph below to show the nature of the relationship between home heating oil sales and outside temperature. Be sure to label your axes.

2. What might make the curve you drew in question 1 shift?

_____

_____

_____

_____

3. The table below shows the relationship between the quantity of milk that dairy farmers are willing to offer for sale and the price of milk. This relationship is _____ (direct, inverse). The slope of the line will be _____ (positive, negative). Plot the curves on the graph on the following page.

Price of Milk	Quantity of Milk Offered for Sale
$ .50	0
.75	2
1.00	4
1.25	6
1.50	8

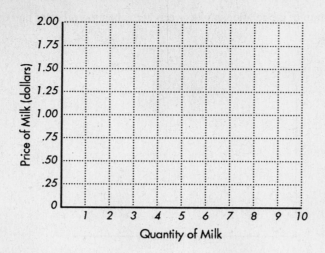

4. Consider the relationship between household spending (called "Consumption") and National Income on the graph below, and answer the following questions.

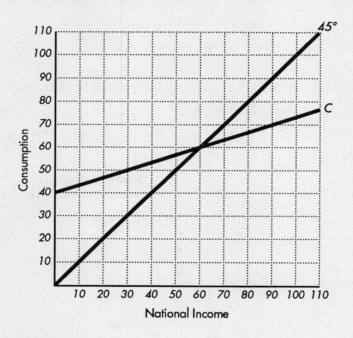

a. The relationship between consumption and income is _____ (direct, inverse).

b. What is the slope of the line? _____

   The intercept? _____

c. What is the equation for this line? _____

d. At what point does consumption equal income? _____

5. The maximum point of the total revenue curve below occurs at the quantity _____ . The slope of the curve is _____ at quantities less than this amount and is _____ at quantities greater than this amount.

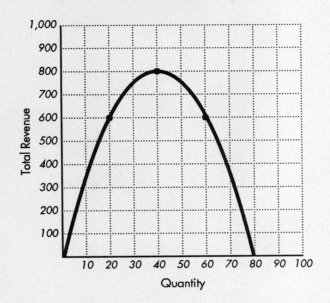

6. The graph below shows the percentages of income that the King family spends, pays in taxes, and saves. What kind of graph is this? _____

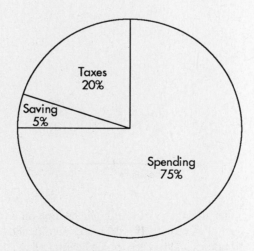

7. The table below shows the relationship between the quantity of airplanes built at a production plant in Wichita and the average cost (cost per airplane). Make up a set of figures that will show that a minimum average cost occurs at 40,000 airplanes.

Quantity of Airplanes	Average Cost per Airplane
10,000	_____
20,000	_____
30,000	_____
40,000	_____
50,000	_____
60,000	_____
70,000	_____
80,000	_____

ANSWERS

1. dependent; inverse; negative

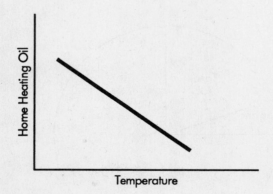

2. Anything other than temperature that affects the sales of home heating oil will cause this curve to shift. One such variable might be the cost of electricity. If it decreases significantly, people may turn to electric space heaters to heat parts of their homes and buy less home heating oil at every price.
3. direct; positive

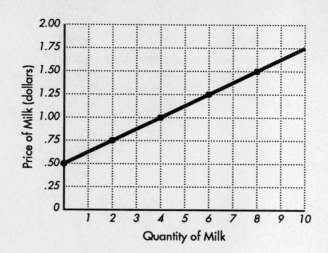

4. a. direct
    b. 1/3; 40
    c. $C = 40 + 1/3Y$
    d. 60
5. 40; positive; negative
6. pie chart
7. There are many possible solutions. The numbers need to decrease until you reach the quantity 40,000, and increase thereafter. Here is one possible solution.

Quantity of Airplanes	Average Cost per Airplane
10,000	40
20,000	30
30,000	20
40,000	10
50,000	20
60,000	30
70,000	40
80,000	50

ADDITIONAL QUESTIONS

1. The demand for Mardi's Tacos in Hammondville is given by the equation $P = \$2.00 - .02Q$, where P is the price of tacos in dollars and Q is the quantity demanded of tacos. Plot the demand for Mardi's Tacos on the graph below.

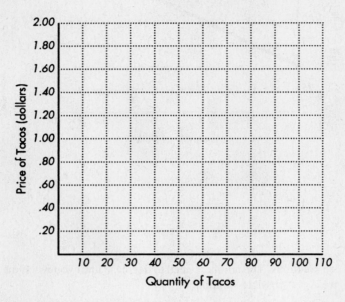

The relationship between price and quantity demanded is _____ (direct, inverse).

2. The supply for tacos in Hammondville is given by the equation $P = \$.40 + .005Q$, where P is the price of tacos in dollars and Q is the quantity supplied of tacos. Plot the supply of tacos on the graph below.

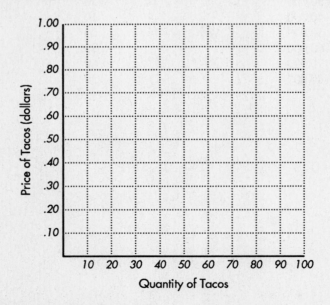

The relationship between price and quantity supplied is _____ (direct, inverse).

3. Plot the total revenue function $TR = -10Q^2 + 600Q$ on the graph below. The maximum total revenue is obtained by selling _____ units.

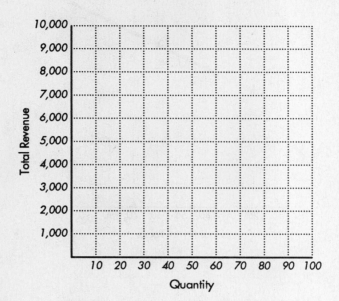

ANSWERS TO ADDITIONAL QUESTIONS

1. inverse

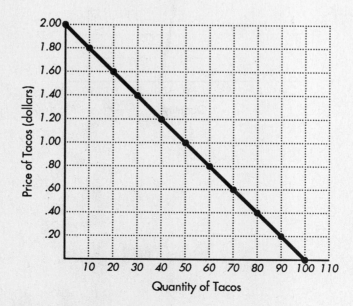

2. direct

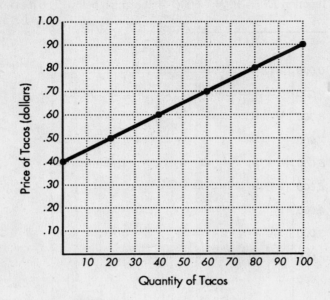

3. 30

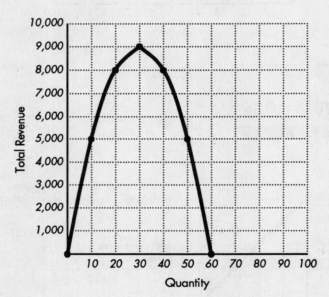

CHAPTER 2
Choice, Opportunity Costs, and Specialization

 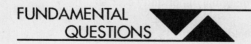

1. What are opportunity costs?

   The **opportunity cost** of something is what you need to give up in order to get it. For example, if you would prefer to be sleeping now instead of studying economics, the opportunity cost of studying is the sleep you could be enjoying.

2. What is the full cost of any purchase?

   The full cost of any purchase is whatever you have to forgo to make the purchase. Part of the cost is the price of the good or service, but it may also include the value of the time you had to give up to stand in line to make the purchase or the time you spent comparing prices and products.

3. What is the production possibilities curve?

   A **production possibilities curve** shows all the combinations of output that could be produced with a given set of resources, assuming that the resources are fully and efficiently used.

4. What accounts for increasing marginal opportunity costs?

   Resources tend to be specialized—that is, better at producing one kind of good or service than another. For example, suppose that Vickeryland can produce either guns or butter. If Vickeryland throws all its resources into producing guns, some resources will not be good at producing guns. If some cows are switched over from making guns to making butter, they will probably be much better at making butter than at making guns. Vickeryland will gain a lot of butter and lose very few guns. But as more and more butter is produced, eventually some resources that were very good at making guns will have to be switched into making butter. If these resources are very good at making guns and not so good at making butter, Vickeryland will give up lots of guns and gain very little butter. If you must give up an increasing number of guns to get each additional unit of butter, then the opportunity cost of each additional unit of butter is increasing. If resources were equally adaptable among uses, the opportunity cost of each additional unit of butter would remain constant. The **marginal opportunity cost** would be constant.

5. What accounts for specialization?

   It pays to specialize whenever opportunity costs are *different*. Two parties can specialize and then trade, which makes both parties better off. Even if one person or nation has an **absolute advantage** over another (does something more efficiently than the other) in the production of a good or service, it does not mean that that person or nation will produce that good or service. Specialization occurs as a result of **comparative,** not absolute, **advantage.** Specialization according to comparative advantage minimizes opportunity cost.

6. What is comparative advantage?

A has a comparative advantage over *B* in the production of a good or service if *A*'s opportunity cost for producing the good or service is lower than *B*'s.

KEY TERMS

opportunity costs
trade off
specialist
production possibilities curve (PPC)
marginal opportunity cost
marginal

constant marginal opportunity cost
increasing marginal opportunity cost
decreasing marginal opportunity cost
sunk costs
comparative advantage
absolute advantage

QUICK CHECK QUIZ

Section 1: Opportunity Costs

1. Janine is an accountant who makes $30,000 a year. Robert is a college student who makes $8,000 a year. All other things being equal, who is more likely to stand in a long line to get a concert ticket?
   a. Janine, because her opportunity cost is lower
   b. Janine, because her opportunity cost is higher
   c. Robert, because his opportunity cost is lower
   d. Robert, because his opportunity cost is higher
   e. Janine, because she is better able to afford the cost of the ticket

2. Which of the following statements is false?
   a. Points inside the production possibilities curve represent combinations where resources are not being fully or efficiently used.
   b. Points outside the production possibilities curve represent combinations that are not attainable with the current level of resources.
   c. If an individual is producing a combination on his or her production possibilities curve, in order to get more of one good, he or she must give up some of the other.
   d. If a nation obtains more resources, the production possibilities curve will shift outward.
   e. Marginal opportunity costs are always constant.

3. At point *A* on a production possibilities curve, there are 50 tons of corn and 60 tons of wheat. At point *B* on the same curve, there are 40 tons of corn and 80 tons of wheat. If the farmer is currently at point *A*, the opportunity cost of moving to point *B* is
   a. 10 tons of corn.
   b. 20 tons of wheat.
   c. 1 ton of corn.
   d. 2 tons of wheat.
   e. 40 tons of corn.

4. President Johnson thought it was possible to spend more resources in Vietnam without having to give up consumer goods at home. President Johnson must have believed that
   a. the American economy was operating at top efficiency.
   b. the American economy was operating at a point inside its production possibilities curve.
   c. the American economy was operating at a point on its production possibilities curve.
   d. the American economy was operating at a point outside its production possibilities curve.
   e. marginal opportunity costs were constant.

Use the table below to answer questions 5 through 8.

Combination	Clothing	Food
A	0	110
B	10	105
C	20	95
D	30	80
E	40	60
F	50	35
G	60	0

5. If the economy is currently producing at point F, the opportunity cost of 10 additional units of clothing is approximately
   a. 25 units of food.
   b. 5 units of food.
   c. 10 units of food.
   d. 35 units of food.
   e. 3.5 units of food.

6. A combination of 20 units of clothing and 80 units of food is
   a. unattainable.
   b. inefficient.
   c. possible by giving up 15 units of food.
   d. possible if the economy obtains more resources.
   e. possible if an improvement in technology makes the production possibilities curve shift in.

7. The marginal opportunity cost of 10 units of clothing is
   a. constant.
   b. decreasing.
   c. increasing.
   d. the same for each 10 units of food.
   e. decreasing for clothing but increasing for food.

8. A combination of 50 units of clothing and 70 units of food is
   a. inefficient.
   b. obtainable by giving up 35 units of food.
   c. a combination where resources are not fully utilized.
   d. unattainable.
   e. possible if an improvement in technology shifts the production possibilities curve in.

Section 2: Specialization

Use the table below to answer questions 1 through 4.

Combination	Alpha Beef	Alpha Microchips	Beta Beef	Beta Microchips
A	0	200	0	300
B	25	150	25	225
C	50	100	50	150
D	75	50	75	75
E	100	0	100	0

1. The opportunity cost of a microchip in Alpha is _____ units of beef, and the opportunity cost of a microchip in Beta is _____ units of beef. The opportunity cost of a unit of beef is _____ units of microchips in Alpha and _____ units of microchips in Beta.
   a. 1/3; 1/2; 3; 2
   b. 2; 3; 1/2; 1/3
   c. 1/2; 1/3; 2; 3
   d. 3; 2; 1/3; 1/2
   e. 1/2; 3; 1/3; 2

2. Marginal opportunity costs are
   a. constant for Alpha but increasing for Beta.
   b. constant for Alpha but decreasing for Beta.
   c. constant for Alpha and for Beta.
   d. increasing for Alpha but decreasing for Beta.
   e. decreasing for Alpha but increasing for Beta.

3. Alpha has a comparative advantage in _____ , and Beta has a comparative advantage in _____ . Alpha should produce _____ , and Beta should produce _____ .
   a. beef; microchips; beef; microchips
   b. beef; microchips; microchips; beef
   c. microchips; beef; microchips; beef
   d. microchips; beef; beef; microchips
   e. There is no basis for specialization and trade between these two countries, since Beta can produce just as much beef and more microchips than Alpha.

4. Which of the following statements is true?
   a. Alpha has an absolute advantage in the production of beef.
   b. Alpha has an absolute advantage in the production of microchips.
   c. Beta has an absolute advantage in the production of beef.
   d. Beta has an absolute advantage in the production of microchips.
   e. Alpha has no absolute advantage over Beta, and Beta has no absolute advantage over Alpha.

5. Which of the following statements is true?
    a. Individuals, firms, and nations will specialize in the production of the good or service that has the highest opportunity cost.
    b. An individual, firm, or nation must first have an absolute advantage in the production of a good or service before it can have a comparative advantage in the production of that good or service.
    c. Comparative advantage exists whenever one person, firm, or nation engaging in an activity incurs lower absolute costs than does some other individual, firm, or nation.
    d. An individual, firm, or nation specializes according to absolute advantage.
    e. An individual, firm, or nation need not have an absolute advantage to have a comparative advantage.

PRACTICE QUESTIONS AND PROBLEMS

Section 1: Opportunity Costs

1. _____ are forgone opportunities or forgone benefits.

2. People purchase items and participate in activities that _____ (maximize, minimize) opportunity costs.

3. A _____ is someone whose opportunity cost of switching to an activity other than the one he or she specializes in is very high relative to the opportunity cost of the activity in which he or she specializes.

4. A _____ is a graph that illustrates the trade-offs facing a society.

5. A point that lies _____ the production possibilities curve indicates that resources are not being fully or efficiently used.

6. Points outside the production possibilities curve represent combinations of goods and services that are _____ .

7. The _____ is the amount of one good or service that must be given up to obtain one additional unit of another good or service.

8. A straight-line production possibilities curve illustrates _____ (increasing, constant, decreasing) marginal opportunity costs.

9. A bowed-out production possibilities curve illustrates _____ (increasing, constant, decreasing) marginal opportunity costs.

10. A bowed-in production possibilities curve illustrates _____ (increasing, constant, decreasing) marginal opportunity costs.

11. Because resources tend to be specialized, the production possibilities curve is likely to be _____ (bowed in, bowed out, straight line), indicating that marginal opportunity costs are _____ (increasing, decreasing, constant).

12. People trade off one activity for another until the marginal opportunity cost of an additional amount of the first activity _____ (is greater than, equals, is less than) the marginal benefits of that additional amount.

13. People make decisions based on the _____ (marginal, total) opportunity cost.

14. Costs borne in the past are known as _____ costs.

15. Opportunity cost is a(n) _____ (objective, subjective) concept.

16. Use the graph below to answer the following questions.

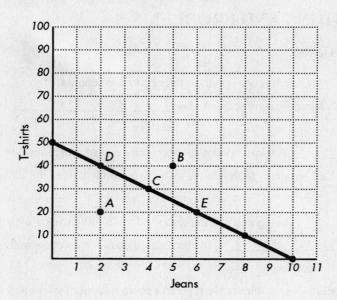

a. The marginal opportunity cost is _____ (increasing, constant, decreasing).

b. Point A represents a combination of t-shirts and jeans that is _____ .

c. Point B represents a combination of t-shirts and jeans that is _____ .

d. If an individual is currently producing the combination of t-shirts and jeans at point C, the marginal opportunity cost of an additional t-shirt is _____ jean(s).

e. If an individual is currently producing the combination of t-shirts and jeans at point D, the marginal opportunity cost of 1 pair of jeans is _____ t-shirt(s).

17. Use the graph below to answer the following questions.

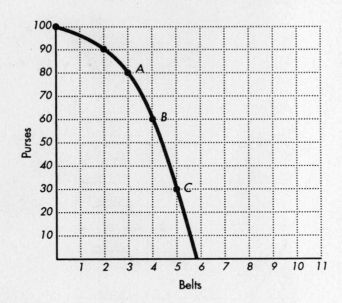

a. The marginal opportunity cost is _____ (increasing, constant, decreasing).

b. If an individual is currently producing the combination of purses and belts at point *B*, the marginal opportunity cost of an additional purse is approximately _____ belt(s).

c. If an individual is currently producing the combination of purses and belts at point *A*, the marginal opportunity cost of an additional purse is approximately _____ belt(s).

d. If an individual is currently producing the combination of purses and belts at Point B, the marginal opportunity cost of an additional belt is _____ purse(s).

18. Use the graph below to answer the following questions.

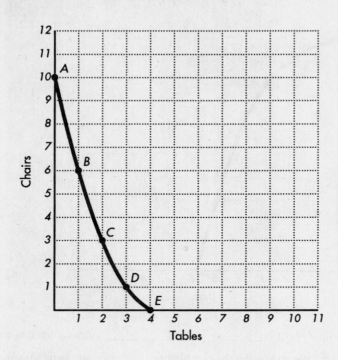

a. The marginal opportunity cost is _____ (increasing, constant, decreasing).

b. If an individual is currently producing the combination of chairs and tables at point *C*, the marginal opportunity cost of an additional chair is approximately _____ table(s).

c. If an individual is currently producing the combination of chairs and tables at point *B*, the marginal opportunity cost of an additional chair is approximately _____ table(s).

d. If an individual is currently producing the combination of chairs and tables at point *B*, the marginal opportunity cost of an additional table is _____ chair(s).

19. Roger Southby was almost finished with his accounting degree when he discovered the wonderful world of marketing. Roger would like to switch majors but does not want to waste the years of schooling he already has. What can you tell Roger to help him make his decision?

_____

_____

_____

_____

20. Mardi and Martin paid $20 each to see a new foreign film. Halfway through the film, Mardi got disgusted and wanted to leave. Martin insisted that they stay, because they paid $40 altogether to see the film, and he wanted to get his money's worth out of it. Can you offer them some economic insight to help them resolve this argument?

_____

_____

_____

_____

Section 2: Specialization

1. It is in your best interest to specialize where your opportunity costs are _____ (highest, constant, lowest).

2. When one person, firm, or nation is more skillful than another person, firm, or nation, that person, firm, or nation has an _____ advantage in producing that good.

3. A nation has a comparative advantage in those activities in which it has _____ (the highest, constant, the lowest) opportunity costs.

4. People specialize according to their _____ (absolute, comparative) advantage.

5. If a country specializes in the production of goods and services in which it has a comparative advantage, it can trade with other countries and enjoy a combination of goods and services that lies _____ its production possibilities curve.

6. Use the table below to answer the following questions.

Combination	Robinson Crusoe		Man Friday	
	Coconuts	Fish	Coconuts	Fish
A	5	0	10	0
B	4	1	8	1
C	3	2	6	2
D	2	3	4	3
E	1	4	2	4
F	0	5	0	5

a. The marginal opportunity costs for Robinson Crusoe and his Man Friday are _____ (increasing, constant, decreasing).

b. The marginal opportunity cost of a coconut is _____ fish for Robinson Crusoe and _____ fish for his Man Friday.

c. The marginal opportunity cost of a fish is _____ coconut(s) for Robinson Crusoe and _____ coconut(s) for his Man Friday.

d. His Man Friday has an absolute advantage in the production of _____ . Robinson Crusoe has an absolute advantage in _____ .

e. Robinson Crusoe has a comparative advantage in _____ , and Friday has a comparative advantage in _____ .

f. Robinson Crusoe should specialize in producing _____ , and Friday should specialize in producing _____ .

THINKING ABOUT AND APPLYING CHOICE, OPPORTUNITY COSTS, AND SPECIALIZATION

I. More on Opportunity Costs

Marc and Shelly Colby are a couple in their thirties with two children. Marc owns his own company and makes $70,000 a year, and Shelly has been responsible for raising their children. Now that the children are in school all day, Shelly is considering going back to school to finish her degree. She estimates that tuition will cost about $3,000. Marc likes carpentry and is thinking about going to a special school for a year to learn more about it. He estimates that the school will cost about $1,500. After they discuss it, they decide that Shelly should go back to school but that it costs too much for Marc to go to carpentry school. Explain.

_____

_____

_____

_____

II. Still More on Opportunity Costs

The "Economically Speaking" article in your text suggests that some entrepreneurs may actually increase their incomes by selling their firms. The text presents an example of an entrepreneur who could earn $330,310 per year by selling his company as opposed to $125,000 per year by continuing to run it. If money were the only consideration, the entrepreneur would clearly be better off to sell.

What if the situation were reversed, and the entrepreneur would make $125,000 by selling the company and $330,310 per year by continuing to run the company? Why might the entrepreneur sell the company?

_____

_____

_____

_____

ANSWERS

Quick Check Quiz

Section 1: Opportunity Costs

1. c; 2. e; 3. a; 4. b; 5. d; 6. b; 7. c; 8. d
   If you missed any of these questions, you should go back and review pages 34–44 in Chapter 2.

Section 2: Specialization

1. c; 2. c; 3. a; 4. d; 5. e
   If you missed any of these questions, you should go back and review pages 44–48 in Chapter 2.

Practice Questions and Problems

Section 1: Opportunity Costs

1. Opportunity costs
2. minimize
3. specialist
4. production possibilities curve (PPC)
5. inside
6. unattainable
7. marginal opportunity cost
8. constant
9. increasing
10. decreasing
11. bowed out; increasing
12. equals
13. marginal
14. sunk
15. subjective
16. a. constant
    b. inefficient (or does not fully utilize all resources)
    c. unattainable
    d. .2 (We must move to point D to get additional t-shirts. Moving from C to D, we get 10 t-shirts by giving up 2 pairs of jeans. To get 1 t-shirt, we must give up 2/10 jean, or .2 jean.)
    e. 5 (We must move toward point C to get additional jeans. Moving from D to C, we get 2 pairs of jeans by giving up 10 t-shirts. For 1 pair of jeans, we must give up 10/2 t-shirts, or 5 t-shirts.)
17. a. increasing
    b. .05 (We must move toward point A to get additional purses. Moving from B to A, we give up 1 belt for 20 purses. For 1 purse, we give up approximately 1/20 or .05 belt.)
    c. .1 (We must move up the curve to get additional purses. At point A we have 80 purses and 3 belts. Moving up the curve, we have 90 purses and 2 belts. We gave up 1 belt for 10 purses. For 1 purse, we give up approximately 1/10 or .1 belts.) Note that as we make more purses, the opportunity cost in terms of belts increases.
    d. 30 (To get an additional belt, we must move from B to C. At B, we had 60 purses and 4 belts. At C, we have 30 purses and 5 belts. We gave up 30 purses for 1 belt.)

18. a. decreasing
    b. 1/3 (To get more chairs, we must move toward point *B*. At point *C* we had 2 tables and 3 chairs. At point *B* we have 1 table and 6 chairs. We gave up 1 table for 3 chairs. To get 1 chair, we give up approximately 1/3 table.)
    c. 1/4 (To get more chairs, we must move toward point *A*. At point *B* we had 1 table and 6 chairs. At point *A* we have no tables and 10 chairs. We gave up 1 table for 4 chairs. To get 1 chair, we give up approximately 1/4 table.)
    d. 3 (To get more tables, we must move from *B* to *C*. At *B*, we had 6 chairs and 1 table. At *C*, we have 3 chairs and 2 tables. we gave up 3 chairs for 1 table.)
19. The years of schooling Roger already has are a *sunk* cost—he cannot get them back whether he continues as an accounting major or switches to marketing. These costs should have no effect on his decision to change majors, since he cannot change what has already happened. The relevant costs are the opportunity costs of continuing his accounting major versus the opportunity costs of switching to marketing.
20. Whether they stay or leave, they cannot get their $40 back. It is a sunk cost and should not enter the decision-making process. The relevant costs are the opportunity costs of staying versus the opportunity costs of leaving.

Section 2: Specialization

1. lowest
2. absolute
3. the lowest
4. comparative
5. outside
6. a. constant
   b. 1; 1/2
   c. 1; 2
   d. coconuts; neither fish nor coconuts
   e. fish; coconuts
   f. fish; coconuts

Thinking About and Applying Choice, Opportunity Costs, and Specialization

I.   More on Opportunity Costs

Tuition isn't the only cost. If Marc has to give up $70,000 a year to go to carpentry school for a year, he and Shelly may feel that the benefits from carpentry school are not worth $70,000. Carpentry school costs too much. Since Shelly is not working outside the home, her major cost is the leisure time she will have now that their children are in school. She may feel that the benefits of having her degree are worth giving up her leisure time.

II.   Still More Opportunity Costs

There are nonmonetary costs to running your own business: the hours you put in, the strain and worry of being in charge of the business, and so forth. An entrepreneur may feel that it is worth giving up some income to get more leisure time and peace of mind.

CHAPTER 3
Markets, Demand and Supply, and the Price System

FUNDAMENTAL
QUESTIONS

1. What is a market?

   A **market** is a place or service that allows buyers and sellers to exchange goods and services. A market may refer to a specific place or may be the exchange of a particular good or service at many different locations. Market transactions may involve the use of money or **barter.** Markets dealing with illegal goods and services are called **black markets.** Markets whose transactions are not recorded are known as **underground markets.** In all markets, goods and services are exchanged and prices are determined.

2. What is demand?

   Demand is a schedule showing the quantities of a good or service that consumers are willing and able to buy at each possible price during a specific period of time, all other things being equal. People often confuse *demand* with *quantity demanded. Demand* refers to a list of prices and corresponding quantities. It is similar to a bus schedule in that it gives many price and quantity options, just as a bus schedule gives many time and location options. *Quantity demanded* indicates how much of a good or service will be bought at *one* particular price. It is correct to say "If the price of a hair dryer is $15, the *quantity demanded* is 20." It is not correct to say "If the price of a hair dryer is $15, the *demand* is 20." Quantity demanded would be analogous to one particular time on the bus schedule: "At 1:10 the bus will be at Lion's Head."

   The **law of demand** states that as the price of a good decreases, people will buy more. That's why stores have sales to get rid of merchandise they can't sell: they know that if they lower the price, people will buy more.

   When economists construct a **demand schedule,** they hold everything except the price of the good constant and determine what quantity consumers will buy at all the possible prices. However, things other than price affect how much of a good or service people are willing to buy. These other **determinants of demand** are income, tastes, prices of related goods or services, expectations, and number of buyers. When one of these determinants of demand changes, the whole demand schedule changes.

   Economists take seriously the adage "A picture is worth a thousand words," so they draw pictures of demand schedules. Such pictures are called **demand curves.** Price is put on the vertical axis and quantity on the horizontal axis. Demand curves slope down from left to right because of the **substitution** and **income effects.** When one of the five determinants of demand (income, tastes, etc.) changes, the demand curve shifts to the left or the right. Increases in demand shift the curve to the right, and decreases in demand shift the curve to the left. A change in the price of a good or service does not shift the demand curve but instead is represented by a movement from one point to another along the same curve.

3. What is supply?

Supply is a schedule showing the quantities of a good or service that producers are willing and able to offer at each possible price during a specific period of time, all other things being equal. People often confuse *supply* with *quantity supplied*. *Supply* refers to a list of prices and corresponding quantities. *Quantity supplied* indicates how much of a good or service will be offered for sale at *one* particular price. It is correct to say "If the price of a hair dryer is $15, the *quantity supplied* will be 10." It is not correct to say "If the price of a hair dryer is $15, the *supply* is 10."

The **law of supply** states that as the price of a good increases, producers will offer more for sale. That's why people offer a seller a higher price for the product when there is a shortage: they know the higher price will entice the producer to produce more.

When economists construct a **supply schedule,** they hold everything except the price of the good constant, and determine what quantity producers will offer for sale at all the possible prices. However, things other than price affect how much of a good or service producers are willing to supply. These other **determinants of supply** are prices of resources, technology and **productivity,** expectations of producers, number of producers, and prices of related goods or services. When one of these determinants of supply changes, the whole supply schedule changes.

A picture of a supply schedule is called a **supply curve.** As before, price goes on the vertical axis and quantity on the horizontal axis. Supply curves slope up from left to right. When one of the five determinants of supply (prices of resources, etc.) changes, the supply curve shifts to the left or the right. Increases in supply shift the curve to the right and decreases in supply shift the curve to the left. A change in the price of a good or service does not shift the supply curve but instead is represented by a movement from one point to another along the same curve.

4. How is price determined by demand and supply?

The price of a good or service will change until the equilibrium price is reached. **Equilibrium** occurs when the quantity demanded is equal to the quantity supplied at a particular price. At prices above the equilibrium price, quantity supplied is greater than quantity demanded, so a **surplus** develops. Sellers must lower their prices to get rid of the goods and services that accumulate. At prices below the equilibrium price, quantity demanded is greater than quantity supplied, and a **shortage** develops. Sellers see the goods and services quickly disappear and realize they could have asked a higher price. The price goes up until the shortage disappears. The price continues to adjust until quantity demanded and quantity supplied are equal.

5. What causes price to change?

The price may change when demand, supply, or both change. A change in demand causes price to change in the same direction: an increase in demand causes price to increase. A change in supply causes price to change in the opposite direction: an increase in supply causes price to decrease. If supply and demand both change, the direction of the change in price depends on the relative sizes of the changes in demand and supply. For example, if demand and supply both increase but the demand change is larger, price will increase: it will act as if the only change had been a change in demand. If demand and supply both increase but the supply change is larger, price will decrease: it will act as if the only change had been a change in supply.

KEY TERMS

market	law of demand	law of supply
black market	determinants of demand	supply schedule
underground market	substitution effect	supply curve
barter	income effect	determinants of supply
double coincidence of wants	demand schedule	productivity
transaction costs	demand curve	equilibrium
relative price	substitute goods	surplus
nominal price	complementary goods	shortage
purchasing power	supply	disequilibrium
demand		

QUICK CHECK QUIZ

Section 1: Markets

1. Which of the following is an example of an underground market activity?
   a. A trader buys IBM stock on the New York Stock Exchange.
   b. The United Mine Workers negotiate a wage contract with a mine owner.
   c. A hair stylist cuts a manicurist's hair in exchange for a manicure.
   d. The Mertzes have lunch at the Dew Drop Inn.
   e. The Federal Reserve buys bonds from the public.

2. Which of the following is NOT a black market activity?
   a. A street addict buys cocaine from a drug dealer.
   b. A yuppie stockbroker buys marijuana from a neighbor.
   c. A fifteen-year-old girl does not report her paper route earnings to the IRS.
   d. A liquor store sells whiskey to a minor.
   e. A prostitute performs her services in a major hotel.

3. In Mongoverna this year, apples cost fifty cents each and oranges cost thirty-five cents each. Suppose that next year, inflation runs rampant in Mongoverna. The price of apples increases to one dollar each, and the price of oranges increases to seventy cents each. Which of the following statements is true?
   a. The relative price of an apple has not changed.
   b. The relative price of an orange has changed.
   c. The absolute price of an apple has not changed.
   d. The absolute price of an orange has not changed.
   e. Both c and d are correct.

4. Which of the following statements is true?
   a. The transaction costs of finding a double coincidence of wants in order to barter are usually quite low.
   b. Money reduces transaction costs.
   c. People base economic decisions on nominal prices.
   d. If all money prices doubled, nominal prices would not change.
   e. A double coincidence of wants is necessary to conduct money transactions.

5. If the price of a t-shirt is $12 and the price of a pair of designer jeans is $66, the relative price of a pair of designer jeans is
   a. 5 1/2 t-shirts.
   b. 2/11 t-shirts.
   c. 5 1/2 jeans.
   d. 2/11 jeans.
   e. $66.

Section 2: Demand

1. Which of the following will NOT cause a decrease in the demand for bananas?
   a. Reports surface that imported bananas are infected with a deadly virus.
   b. Consumers' incomes drop.
   c. The price of bananas rises.
   d. A deadly virus kills monkeys in zoos across the United States.
   e. Consumers expect the price of bananas to decrease in the future.

2. An increase in demand
   a. shifts the demand curve to the left.
   b. causes an increase in equilibrium price.
   c. causes a decrease in equilibrium price.
   d. causes a decrease in equilibrium quantity.
   e. does not affect equilibrium quantity.

3. Which of the following is NOT a determinant of demand?
   a. incomes
   b. tastes
   c. prices of resources
   d. prices of complements
   e. consumers' expectations about future prices

4. If demand decreases,
   a. price and quantity increase.
   b. price and quantity decrease.
   c. price increases and quantity decreases.
   d. price decreases and quantity increases.
   e. the supply will decrease.

5. A decrease in quantity demanded could be caused by
   a. a decrease in consumers' incomes.
   b. a decrease in the price of a substitute good.
   c. an increase in the price of a complementary good.
   d. a decrease in the price of the good.
   e. an increase in the price of the good.

6. A consumer buys more of a good or service when its price falls because it becomes cheaper relative to other goods. This is called
   a. the income effect.
   b. the substitution effect.
   c. a decrease in quantity demanded.
   d. a decrease in quantity supplied.
   e. a change in tastes.

7. The law of demand states that
   a. as the price of a good rises, the quantity demanded will fall, ceteris paribus.
   b. as the price of a good rises, the quantity supplied will fall, ceteris paribus.
   c. as the price of a good rises, the quantity demanded will rise, ceteris paribus.
   d. as the price of a good rises, the quantity supplied will rise, ceteris paribus.
   e. as the price of a good falls, the quantity demanded will fall, ceteris paribus.

8. Which of the following will cause an increase in the demand for eggs?
   a. The price of eggs drops.
   b. The price of bacon rises.
   c. A government report indicates that eating eggs three times a week increases the chances of having a heart attack.
   d. A decrease in the cost of chicken feed makes eggs less costly to produce.
   e. None of the above will increase the demand for eggs.

9. When the price of a good that a consumer typically buys goes up, the purchasing power of that consumer's income goes down. The consumer will buy less of that good and all other goods. This is called
   a. the substitution effect.
   b. the income effect.
   c. a decrease in quantity demanded.
   d. a decrease in quantity supplied.
   e. a change in tastes.

10. A freeze in Peru causes the price of coffee to skyrocket. Which of the following will happen?
   a. The demand for coffee will increase, and the demand for tea will increase.
   b. The demand for coffee will increase, and the quantity demanded of tea will increase.
   c. The quantity demanded of coffee will increase, and the demand for tea will increase.
   d. The quantity demanded of coffee will increase, and the quantity demanded of tea will increase.
   e. The quantity demanded of coffee will decrease, and the demand for tea will increase.

Section 3: Supply

1. According to the law of supply,
   a. as the price of a good or service rises, the quantity supplied will decrease, ceteris paribus.
   b. as the price of a good or service rises, the quantity supplied will increase, ceteris paribus.
   c. as the price of a good or service rises, the quantity demanded will increase, ceteris paribus.
   d. as the price of a good or service rises, the quantity demanded will decrease, ceteris paribus.
   e. as the price of a good or service falls, the quantity supplied of the good or service will increase.

2. Which of the following is NOT a determinant of supply?
   a. prices of resources
   b. technology and productivity
   c. prices of complements
   d. expectations of producers
   e. the number of producers

3. Japanese producers of a type of microchip offered such low prices that U.S. producers of the chip were driven out of business. As the number of producers decreased,
   a. the market supply of microchips increased; that is, the supply curve shifted to the right.
   b. the market supply of microchips increased; that is, the supply curve shifted to the left.
   c. the market supply of microchips decreased; that is, the supply curve shifted to the right.
   d. the market supply of microchips decreased; that is, the supply curve shifted to the left.
   e. there was no change in the supply of microchips; this event is represented by a movement from one point to another on the same supply curve.

4. Electronics firms can produce more than one type of good. Suppose that electronics firms are producing both military radios and microchips. A war breaks out, and the price of military radios skyrockets. The electronics firms throw more resources into making military radios and fewer resources into making microchips. Which of the statements below is true?
   a. The supply of microchips has decreased, and the quantity supplied of military radios has increased.
   b. The supply of microchips has decreased, and the supply of military radios has increased.
   c. The quantity supplied of microchips has decreased, and the supply of military radios has decreased.
   d. The quantity supplied of microchips has decreased, and the quantity supplied of military radios has decreased.
   e. There has been no change in the supply of microchips or in the supply of military radios.

5. Suppose that a change in technology makes car phones cheaper to produce. Which of the following will happen?
   a. The supply curve will shift to the left.
   b. The supply curve will shift to the right.
   c. The supply of car phones will increase.
   d. The supply of car phones will decrease.
   e. Both b and c are correct.

6. If supply decreases,
   a. the supply curve shifts to the right.
   b. equilibrium price increases.
   c. equilibrium price decreases.
   d. equilibrium price decreases and equilibrium quantity increases.
   e. equilibrium price increases and equilibrium quantity decreases.

7. Suppose that automakers expect car prices to be lower in the future. What will happen now?
   a. Supply will increase.
   b. Supply will decrease.
   c. Supply will not change.
   d. Demand will increase.
   e. Demand will decrease.

8. Which of the following will NOT cause an increase in the supply of milk?
   a. an increase in the number of dairy farmers
   b. a change in technology that reduces the cost of milking cows
   c. a decrease in the price of cheese
   d. a decrease in the price of milk
   e. a decrease in the price of cow feed

9. Which of the following will NOT change the supply of beef?
   a. The U.S. government decides to give a subsidy to beef producers.
   b. An epidemic of cow flu renders many cattle unfit for slaughter.
   c. The price of fish increases.
   d. A new hormone makes cows fatter and requires less feed.
   e. Beef producers expect lower beef prices next year.

Section 4: Equilibrium: Putting Demand and Supply Together

1. If demand increases and supply does not change,
   a. equilibrium price and quantity increase.
   b. equilibrium price and quantity decrease.
   c. equilibrium price increases and equilibrium quantity decreases.
   d. equilibrium price decreases and equilibrium quantity increases.
   e. the demand curve shifts to the left.

2. If supply decreases and demand does not change,
   a. equilibrium price and quantity increase.
   b. equilibrium price and quantity decrease.
   c. equilibrium price increases and equilibrium quantity decreases.
   d. equilibrium price decreases and equilibrium quantity increases.
   e. the supply curve shifts to the right.

3. Prices above the equilibrium price
   a. cause a shortage to develop and drive prices up.
   b. cause a shortage to develop and drive prices down.
   c. cause a surplus to develop and drive prices up.
   d. cause a surplus to develop and drive prices down.
   e. cause an increase in supply.

4. Prices below the equilibrium price
   a. cause a shortage to develop and drive prices up.
   b. cause a shortage to develop and drive prices down.
   c. cause a surplus to develop and drive prices up.
   d. cause a surplus to develop and drive prices down.
   e. cause an increase in demand.

5. Utility regulators in some states are considering forcing operators of coal-fired generators to be responsible for cleaning up air and water pollution resulting from the generators. Utilities in these states do not currently pay the costs of the cleanup. If this law goes into effect,
   a. demand for electricity will increase, and price and quantity will increase.
   b. demand for electricity will decrease, and price and quantity will decrease.
   c. the supply of electricity will decrease, and price and quantity will decrease.
   d. the supply of electricity will increase, the price will decrease, and the quantity will decrease.
   e. the supply of electricity will decrease, the price of electricity will increase, and the quantity will decrease.

6. Medical research from South Africa indicates that vitamin A may be useful in treating measles. If the research can be substantiated,
   a. the supply of vitamin A will increase, causing equilibrium price and quantity to increase.
   b. the supply of vitamin A will increase, causing equilibrium price to fall and quantity to increase.
   c. the demand for vitamin A will increase, causing equilibrium price and quantity to increase.
   d. the demand for vitamin A will increase, causing equilibrium price to rise and quantity to fall.
   e. the supply of vitamin A will increase, causing equilibrium price to rise and quantity to fall.

7. Since 1900, changes in technology have greatly reduced the costs of growing wheat. The population has also increased since then. If you know that the changes in technology had a greater effect than the increase in population, then since 1900
   a. the price of wheat has increased and the quantity of wheat has decreased.
   b. the price and quantity of wheat have increased.
   c. the price and quantity of wheat have decreased.
   d. the price of wheat has decreased and the quantity of wheat has increased.
   e. the quantity of wheat has increased, and you haven't got the faintest idea what happened to the price.

8. Which of the following statements is false?
   a. Disequilibrium may persist in some markets because it is too costly to change prices rapidly.
   b. Most concert promoters believe it is better to have low ticket prices and long lines rather than high ticket prices and empty seats.
   c. Money prices set by governments are typically lower than equilibrium prices.
   d. Part of the cost of a restaurant meal is the opportunity cost of the time spent waiting for a table.
   e. All of the above are true.

Use the table below to answer questions 9 through 12.

Price	Quantity Demanded	Quantity Supplied
$0	24	0
1	20	2
2	16	4
3	12	6
4	8	8
5	4	10
6	0	12

9. The equilibrium price is
   a. $1.
   b. $2.
   c. $3.
   d. $4.
   e. $5.

10. The equilibrium quantity is
   a. 2.
   b. 4.
   c. 6.
   d. 8.
   e. 10.

11. If the price is $2, a _____ of _____ units will develop, causing the price to _____ .
   a. shortage; 12; increase
   b. shortage; 12; decrease
   c. surplus; 12; increase
   d. surplus; 12; decrease
   e. surplus; 19; decrease

12. If the price is $5, a _____ of _____ units will develop, causing the price to _____ .
   a. shortage; 6; increase
   b. shortage; 6; decrease
   c. surplus; 6; increase
   d. surplus; 6; decrease
   e. shortage; 12; increase

Use the graph below to answer questions 13 through 16.

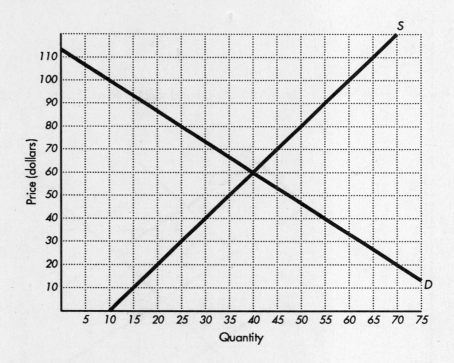

13. The equilibrium price is
   a. $20.
   b. $40.
   c. $60.
   d. $80.
   e. $100.

14. The equilibrium quantity is
    a. 25.
    b. 30.
    c. 35.
    d. 40.
    e. 45.

15. A price of $80 would cause a _____ of _____ units to develop, driving the price _____ .
    a. shortage; 6; up
    b. shortage; 25; up
    c. surplus; 6; down
    d. surplus; 25; down
    e. surplus; 25; up

16. A price of $20 would result in a _____ of _____ units, driving the price _____ .
    a. shortage; 10; up
    b. shortage; 50; up
    c. surplus; 10; down
    d. surplus; 50; down
    e. shortage; 50; down

Use the graph below to answer questions 17 through 20. The original supply curve is S_1, and the original demand curve is D_1.

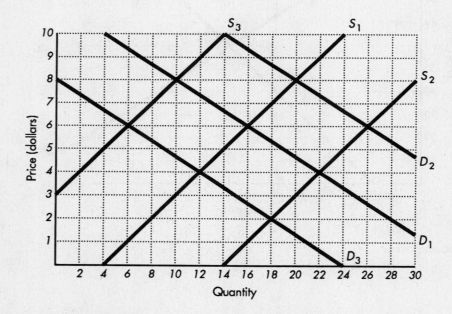

17. The original equilibrium price is _____ , and the original equilibrium quantity is _____ units.
    a. $6; 6
    b. $4; 12
    c. $8; 20
    d. $6; 16
    e. $8; 20

18. An increase in the price of a resource causes _____ to shift to _____ . The new equilibrium price is _____ , and the new equilibrium quantity is _____ units.
    a. demand; D_2; $8; 20
    b. demand; D_3; $4; 12
    c. supply; S_2; $4; 22
    d. supply; S_3; $8; 10
    e. supply; S_3; $10; 14

19. Begin at the original equilibrium position at the intersection of D_1 and S_1. Now a decrease in the price of a complementary good causes the _____ to shift to _____ . The new equilibrium price is _____ , and the equilibrium quantity is _____ units.
    a. demand; D_2; $8; 20
    b. demand; D_3; $4; 12
    c. supply; S_2; $4; 22
    d. supply; S_3; $8; 10
    e. supply; S_3; $10; 14

20. Begin at the original equilibrium position at the intersection of D_1 and S_1. An increase in income occurs at the same time as a change in technology decreases the costs of production. The new equilibrium price will be _____ , and the new equilibrium quantity will be _____ units.
    a. $6; 26
    b. $$4; 22
    c. $8; 20
    d. $10; 14
    e. $6; 8

PRACTICE QUESTIONS AND PROBLEMS

Section 1: Markets

1. A _____ is a place or service that enables buyers and sellers to exchange goods and services.

2. Another name for exchanges that violate the law is the _____ market.

3. The name given to unrecorded transactions, whether legal or illegal, is the _____ market.

4. The exchange of goods and services directly, without money, is called _____ .

5. In a barter economy, trade cannot occur unless there is a _____ of wants.

6. Another name for the money price of a good or service is the _____ price.

7. _____ prices, as opposed to money prices, affect economic behavior.

8. A person who chooses not to report his or her earnings to the IRS in order to avoid paying taxes would be part of the _____ market.

9. _____ occurs when an auto mechanic tunes up an accountant's car in exchange for the accountant doing the mechanic's income taxes.

10. The costs involved in making a barter exchange are called _____ costs.

11. The price established when an exchange occurs is called the _____ price.

12. If all nominal prices double, relative prices _____ (do, do not) change.

Section 2: Demand

1. _____ refers to the quantities of a well-defined commodity that consumers are willing and able to buy at each possible price during a given time period, ceteris paribus.

2. According to the law of demand, if you _____ your price, people will buy more, ceteris paribus.

3. _____ is Latin for "other things being equal."

4. List the five determinants of demand.

   _____

   _____

   _____

   _____

   _____

5. Demand curves slope down because of the _____ and _____ effects.

6. Suppose that an increase in the price of Nohr Cola causes you to switch to Sooby Cola. You therefore buy less Nohr Cola. This is an example of the _____ effect.

7. Suppose that the price of steak decreases and your income does not change. You therefore can buy more steak than you did before. This is an example of the _____ effect.

8. A _____ is a graph of a demand schedule.

9. _____ goods can be used in place of each other; such goods would not be consumed at the same time.

10. Goods that are used together are called _____ goods.

11. Mardi, Dot, and Diane are college students who share an apartment. Dot loves strawberries and will buy them whenever they are available. Diane is a fair-weather strawberry eater: she only buys them if she thinks she is getting a good price. Mardi will eat strawberries for their vitamin C content but isn't crazy about them. The table on the following page shows the individual demand schedules for Mardi, Dot, and Diane. Suppose that these three are the only consumers in the local market for strawberries. Sum their individual demands to get the market demand schedule.

Price per Quart	Quantity for Dot	Quantity for Diane	Quantity for Mardi	Market
$0	6.00	4.00	2.00	_____
1	5.00	3.50	1.50	_____
2	4.00	3.00	1.00	_____
3	3.25	2.00	0.75	_____
4	2.00	1.50	0.50	_____
5	1.25	0.50	0.25	_____
6	0	0	0	_____

Plot the market demand for strawberries on the graph below.

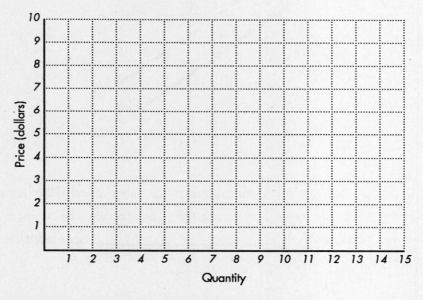

12. Suppose that the price of strawberries increases from $2 to $3 per quart. The increase in price would cause a decrease in the _____ (demand, quantity demanded) of strawberries. Show the effect of a change in the price of strawberries on the graph above.

13. Suppose that Dot reads in the paper that eating strawberries increases the sexual attractiveness of females. As a group, Dot and her friends decide to buy twice as many strawberries as they did before at every price. Plot the new market demand curve in the graph above, and label it D_2. This change in tastes has caused a/an _____ (increase, decrease) in _____ (demand, quantity demanded).

14. An increase in income _____ (increases, decreases) the _____ (demand, quantity demanded) for haircuts.

15. Many Americans have decreased their consumption of beef and switched to chicken in the belief that eating chicken instead of beef will lower their cholesterol. This change in tastes has

_____ (increased, decreased) the _____ (demand, quantity demanded) for beef and _____ (increased, decreased) the _____ (demand, quantity demanded) for chicken.

16. In the graph below, the price of good X increased, causing the demand for good Y to change from D_1 to D_2. The demand for good Y _____ (increased, decreased). X and Y are _____ (substitutes, complements).

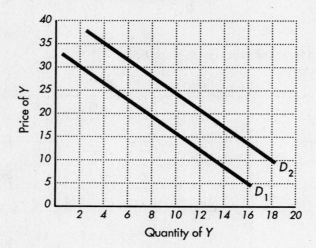

17. Mr. and Mrs. Gertsen are retiring next year and expect that their future income will be less than it is now. If D_1 is their current demand for bacon, show the effect of these expectations on the graph below. Label your new curve D_2. Demand for bacon has _____ (increased, decreased).

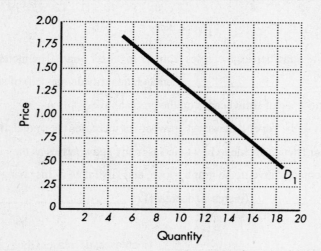

18. In the year 2000, one out of every five Americans will be over 65 years old. The demand for healthcare facilities for the elderly will _____ (increase, not change, decrease).

19. A crisis in the Middle East causes people to expect the price of gasoline to increase in the future. The demand for gasoline today will _____ (increase, not change, decrease).

20. If the price of Pepsi increases, the demand for Coke and other substitutes will

_____ .

Section 3: Supply

1. _____ is the amount of a good or service that producers are willing and able to offer for sale at each possible price during a period of time, ceteris paribus.

2. According to the law of supply, as the price _____, the quantity supplied decreases.

3. A table or list of the prices and corresponding quantity supplied of a well-defined good or service is called a _____ .

4. A _____ is a graph of a supply schedule.

5. Market supply curves have _____ slopes.

6. There are only two strawberry producers in the little town where Dot, Diane, and Mardi live. Their individual supply schedules are shown below. Sum the individual supplies to get market supply, and plot market supply on the graph on the following page.

Price per Quart	Quantity Supplied by Farmer Dave	Quantity Supplied by Farmer Ruth	Market
$0	2	2	_____
1	3	3	_____
2	4	4	_____
3	5	5	_____
4	6	6	_____
5	7	7	_____
6	8	8	_____

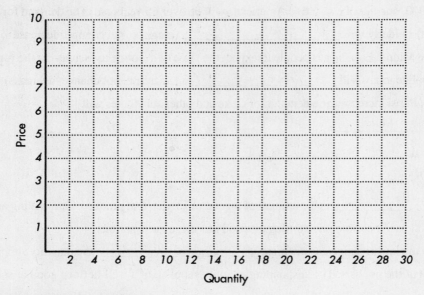

7. List the five determinants of supply.

_____

_____

_____

_____

_____

8. Suppose that a crisis in the Middle East cuts off the supply of oil from Saudi Arabia. If S_1 is the original market supply of oil, draw another supply curve, S_2, on the graph below to show the effect of Saudi Arabia's departure from the market. The _____ (quantity supplied, supply) has _____ (increased, decreased).

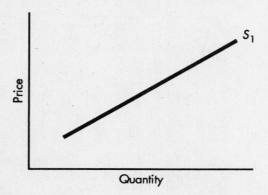

9. If the price of tomato sauce increases, the _____ (supply, quantity supplied) of pizza will _____ (increase, decrease).

10. _____ is the quantity of output produced per unit of resource.

11. A new process for producing microchips is discovered that will decrease the cost of production by 10 percent. The supply of microchips will _____ (increase, decrease, not change), causing the supply curve to _____ (shift to the right, shift to the left, not change).

12. A paper manufacturer can produce notebook paper or wedding invitations. If the price of wedding invitations skyrockets, we can expect the supply of _____ (notebook paper, wedding invitations) to _____ (increase, decrease).

13. A real estate developer who specializes in two-bedroom homes believes that the incomes of young couples will decline in the future. We can expect the supply of this realtor's two-bedroom homes to _____ (increase, decrease).

14. Changes in quantity supplied are caused by changes in the _____ of the good.

Section 4: Equilibrium: Putting Demand and Supply Together

1. The point at which the quantity demanded equals the quantity supplied at a particular price is known as the point of _____ .

2. Whenever the price is greater than the equilibrium price, a _____ arises.

3. A _____ arises when the quantity demanded is greater than the quantity supplied at a particular price.

4. Shortages lead to _____ in price and quantity supplied and _____ in quantity demanded.

5. Surpluses lead to _____ in price and quantity supplied and _____ in quantity demanded.

6. The only goods that are not scarce are _____ goods.

7. The change in equilibrium price and quantity is in the _____ (same, opposite) direction as the change in demand.

8. Balloon manufacturers are nervous about a children's movement that may affect their product. The children are lobbying state legislatures to ban launchings of more than ten balloons at a time, citing the danger that balloons can do to wildlife. If the children are successful, we can expect the _____ (demand for, supply of) balloons to _____ (increase, decrease), causing the equilibrium price to _____ and the equilibrium quantity to _____ .

9. If design changes in the construction of milk cartons cause the cost of production to decrease, we can expect the _____ (demand for, supply of) such cartons to _____ (increase, decrease), and the equilibrium price to _____ and the equilibrium quantity to _____ .

10. A decrease in supply leads to a(n) _____ in price and a(n) _____ in quantity.

11. Remember Dot, Diane, and Mardi and the strawberry farmers Dave and Ruth? The local market for strawberries (before Dot read about the effects of strawberries on sexual attractiveness) is reproduced on the graph below. The original demand is D_1, and the original supply is S. The equilibrium price is _____, and the equilibrium quantity is _____.

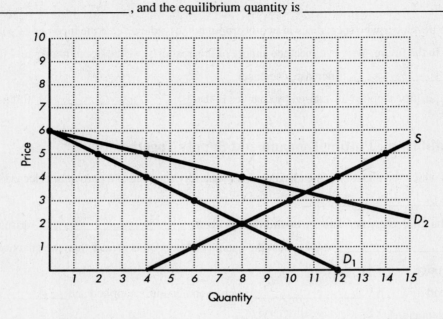

After Dot read the article on strawberries and sexual attractiveness, the market demand curve shifted to D_2. The new equilibrium price is _____, and the equilibrium quantity is _____. There was also a change in _____ (supply, quantity supplied).

12. _____ occurs when the quantity demanded and the quantity supplied are not equal.

13. The graph on the following page shows the market for corn. The equilibrium price is _____, and the equilibrium quantity is _____.

   If the price of corn is $14, the quantity demanded will be _____, and the quantity supplied will be _____. A _____ of _____ units will develop, causing the price and quantity supplied to _____ and the quantity demanded to _____.

   If the price is $4, the quantity demanded will be _____, and the quantity supplied will be _____. A _____ of _____ units will develop, causing the price and quantity supplied to _____ and the quantity demanded to _____.

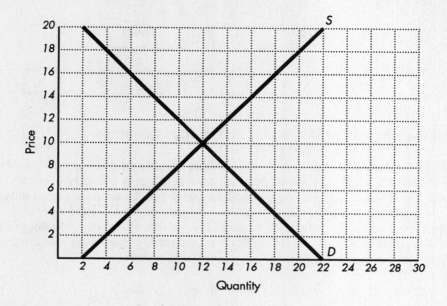

14. List three reasons why markets do not clear all the time.

_____

_____

_____

THINKING ABOUT AND APPLYING MARKETS, DEMAND AND SUPPLY, AND THE PRICE SYSTEM

I. Wooden Bats Versus Metal Bats

1. The "Economically Speaking" section in Chapter 3 suggests an exercise for you to do. The supply of wooden bats is shown as S_w on the graph below. It has a steeper slope than the supply of metal bats, S_m, reflecting the fact that it is easier to produce additional metal bats than additional wooden bats. Suppose that D_m is the demand for metal bats. If baseball purists are willing to pay more for a "sweet crack" sound than for a dull metallic "ping" when they connect with a fastball, draw a demand curve for wooden bats and label it D_w. What are the consequences for the relative prices of wooden and metal bats?

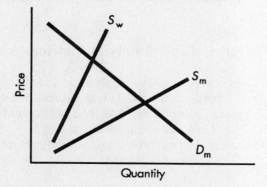

_____

_____

_____

_____

II. Distinguishing Changes in Demand from Changes in Supply

It is important that you be able to distinguish between factors that affect demand and factors that affect supply. For each event below, indicate whether the event affects the demand or supply of battery-operated dancing flowers and the direction of the change. Also indicate what will happen to equilibrium price and quantity. Remember, the determinants of demand are income, tastes, prices of related goods or services, expectations (of consumers), and number of buyers. The determinants of supply are prices of resources, changes in technology or productivity, producers' expectations, number of producers, and prices of related goods or services (goods that are substitutes in production).

1. There is a change in tastes toward battery-operated dancing gorillas.
2. The price of plastic rises.
3. A technological breakthrough makes it cheaper to produce plastic flowers.
4. Consumers' incomes rise.
5. The price of battery-operated dancing gorillas rises.
6. The price of batteries skyrockets.
7. A fire destroys a major production facility for dancing flowers.
8. Consumers expect lower prices for dancing flowers in the future.

	Demand	Supply	Price	Quantity
1.	_____	_____	_____	_____
2.	_____	_____	_____	_____
3.	_____	_____	_____	_____
4.	_____	_____	_____	_____
5.	_____	_____	_____	_____
6.	_____	_____	_____	_____
7.	_____	_____	_____	_____
8.	_____	_____	_____	_____

III. Simultaneous Shifts in Demand and Supply: A Shortcut Approach

What do you do if events occur that shift both demand and supply at the same time? If you know the relative magnitudes of the shifts in demand and supply, you can predict both the equilibrium price and the equilibrium quantity. If you do not know the relative magnitudes of the shifts, you will be able to predict either equilibrium price or equilibrium quantity, but not both. Let's look at a quick way to do this.

Suppose demand and supply both increase. In the chart on the following page, consider what will happen to price and quantity if you consider ONLY an increase in demand.

	D↑
Price	↑
Quantity	↑

Now consider what will happen to price and quantity if you consider ONLY an increase in supply.

	D↑	S↑
Price	↑	↓
Quantity	↑	↑

It's easy to see now that the quantity will increase but that the effect on price will be uncertain. If the demand change is larger than the supply change, price will increase. If the supply change is larger than the demand change, price will decrease.

Let's try it again. Suppose demand increases and supply decreases. First, consider what will happen to price and quantity if you consider ONLY an increase in demand.

	D↑
Price	↑
Quantity	↑

Now consider what will happen to price and quantity if you consider ONLY a decrease in supply.

	D↑	S↓
Price	↑	↑
Quantity	↑	↓

Can you see that the price will increase but that the effect on quantity will be uncertain? If the demand change is larger than the supply change, quantity will increase. If the supply change is larger than the demand change, quantity will decrease.

1. In the chart below, indicate a decrease in demand coupled with an increase in supply.

	D	S
Price		
Quantity		

2. Now try a decrease in demand coupled with a decrease in supply.

	D	S
Price		
Quantity		

3. Now let's try a more concrete example. We are analyzing the market for home computers. We foresee three main events coming up that will affect this market:
   a. Consumers' incomes are likely to increase.
   b. There will be an increase in the number of buyers as more schoolchildren become familiar with home computers in the classroom.
   c. We expect improvements in technology that will decrease the costs of production.

   Use the chart to determine what will happen to the equilibrium price and equilibrium quantity of home computers.

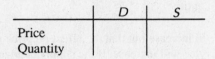

	D	S
Price		
Quantity		

ANSWERS

Quick Check Quiz

Section 1: Markets

1. c; 2. c (This is an underground market activity and not necessarily illegal.); 3. a; 4. b; 5. a
   If you missed any of these questions, you should go back and review pages 56–60 in Chapter 3.

Section 2: Demand

1. c (A change in the price of a good causes a movement along the curve—a change in quantity demanded—not a change in demand.); 2. b; 3. c; 4. b; 5. e (Items a, b, and c are determinants of demand and cause the demand curve to shift. Item d causes an *increase* in quantity demanded.); 6. b; 7. a; 8. e (Item a causes an increase in quantity demanded. Items b and c cause decreases in demand. Item d affects the *supply* of bacon.); 9. b; 10. e (The demand for coffee is designed to tell us the quantity demanded when the price changes, so it does not shift when price changes: you move from one price to another on the same curve. Coffee and tea are substitutes in consumption. When the price of coffee rises, people buy less coffee and substitute tea. They buy more tea at every price, so the demand for tea increases.)
   If you missed any of these questions, you should go back and review pages 60–68 in Chapter 3.

Section 3: Supply

1. b; 2. c; 3. d; 4. a (The supply of military radios exists to tell us the quantity supplied of military radios when the price of radios changes. Supply doesn't change when the price changes: you simply move from one price to another on the same curve. Since microchips and military radios are substitutes in production, when the price of military radios increases, the supply of microchips decreases.); 5. e; 6. e; 7. a; 8. d (A change in the price of a good causes a change in quantity supplied, not a change in supply. Cheese and milk are substitutes in production, so if the price of cheese decreases, the supply of milk increases.); 9. c
   If you missed any of these questions, you should go back and review pages 68–74 in Chapter 3.

Section 4: Equilibrium: Putting Demand and Supply Together

1. a; 2. c; 3. d; 4. a; 5. e; 6. c; 7. d (Item e would be correct if you did not know that the supply change was greater than the demand change.), 8. b; 9. d; 10. d; 11. a; 12. d; 13. c; 14. d; 15. d; 16. b; 17. d; 18. d; 19. a; 20. a
   If you missed any of these questions, you should go back and review pages 74–80 in Chapter 3.

Practice Questions and Problems

Section 1: Markets

1. market
2. black
3. underground
4. barter
5. double coincidence
6. nominal
7. Relative
8. underground
9. Barter
10. transaction
11. relative
12. do not

Section 2: Demand

1. Demand
2. lower
3. Ceteris paribus
4. income
    tastes
    prices of related goods or services
    expectations (of consumers)
    number of buyers
5. income; substitution
6. substitution
7. income
8. demand curve
9. Substitute
10. complementary

11.

Price per Quart	Market
$0	12
1	10
2	8
3	6
4	4
5	2
6	0

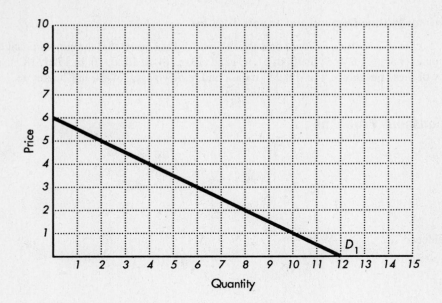

12. quantity demanded

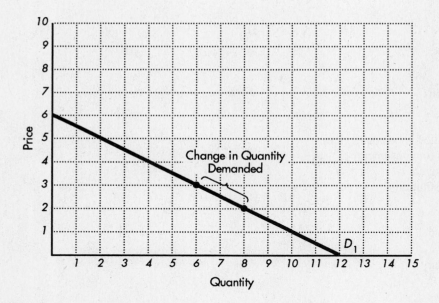

13. increase; demand

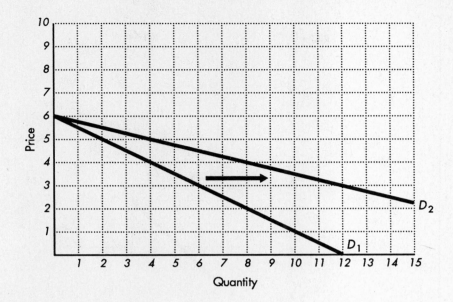

14. increases; demand
15. decreased; demand; increased; demand
16. increased; substitutes
17. decreased

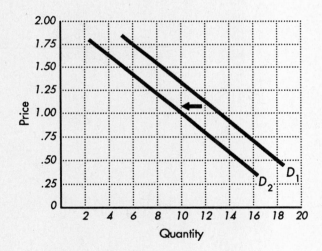

18. increase
19. increase
20. increase

Section 3: Supply

1. Supply
2. decreases
3. supply schedule
4. supply curve
5. positive

6.

Price per Quart	Market
$0	4
1	6
2	8
3	10
4	12
5	14
6	16

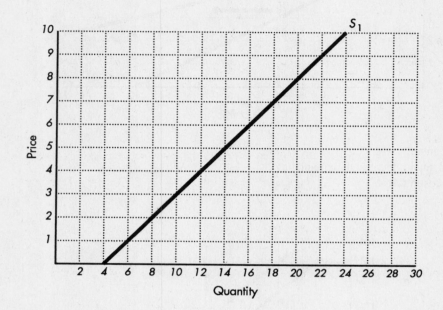

7. prices of resources
   technology and productivity
   expectations of producers
   number of producers
   prices of related goods or services

8. supply; decreased

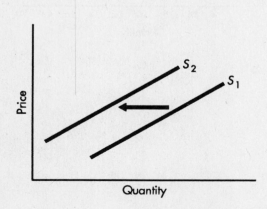

9. supply; decrease
10. Productivity
11. increase; shift to the right
12. notebook paper; decrease
13. increase (The real estate developer will try to offer as many homes for sale *now*, before incomes drop and the prices of houses drop.)
14. price

Section 4: Equilibrium: Putting Demand and Supply Together

1. equilibrium
2. surplus
3. shortage
4. increases; decreases
5. decreases; increases
6. free
7. same
8. demand for; decrease; decrease; decrease
9. supply of; increase; decrease; increase
10. increase; decrease
11. $2; 8; $3 1/3; 10 2/3 (These two values are eyeballed from the graph.); quantity supplied
12. Disequilibrium
13. $10; 12; 8; 16; surplus; 8; decrease; increase; 18; 6; shortage; 12; increase; decrease
14. Price changes can be costly.
    Buyers and sellers may not want price changes.
    Government intervention affects prices.

Thinking About and Applying Markets, Demand and Supply, and the Price System

I. Wooden Bats Versus Metal Bats

1.

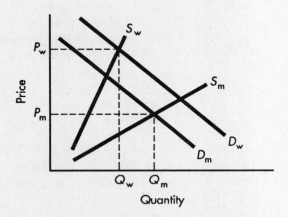

If baseball purists prefer wooden bats to metal bats, the demand for wooden bats will be to the right of the demand for metal bats. The price of wooden bats will be higher than the price of metal bats.

II. Distinguishing Changes in Demand from Changes in Supply

	Demand	Supply	Price	Quantity
1.	decrease	no change	decrease	decrease
2.	no change	decrease	increase	decrease
3.	no change	increase	decrease	increase
4.	increase	no change	increase	increase
5.	increase	no change	increase	increase
6.	no change	decrease	increase	decrease
7.	no change	decrease	increase	decrease
8.	decrease	no change	decrease	decrease

III. Simultaneous Shifts in Demand and Supply: A Shortcut Approach

1.

	D↓	S↑
Price	↓	↓
Quantity	↓	↑

Price will surely decrease, but the effect on quantity is uncertain. If the demand change is larger than the supply change, quantity will decrease. If the supply change is larger than the demand change, quantity will increase.

2.

	D↓	S↓
Price	↓	↑
Quantity	↓	↓

Quantity will surely decrease, but the effect on price is uncertain. If the demand change is larger than the supply change, price will decrease. If the supply change is larger than the demand change, price will increase.

3. An increase in consumers' incomes is one of the five determinants of demand, so this factor will cause demand to increase. Likewise, an increase in the number of buyers will increase demand. Improvements in technology are one of the five determinants of supply. Since these improvements lower costs, supply will increase. We are therefore looking at an increase in demand coupled with an increase in supply. Our chart looks like this:

	D↑	S↑
Price	↑	↓
Quantity	↑	↑

The quantity of home computers will surely increase, but whether the price rises or falls depends on whether the demand shifts outweigh the supply shift. If the shifts in demand overwhelm the shift in supply, prices will increase. If the supply change is larger than the demand change, prices will decrease.

CHAPTER 4
The Price System, Market Failures, and Alternatives

FUNDAMENTAL
QUESTIONS

1. In a market system, who decides what goods and services are produced?

    In a **market system,** consumers decide what goods and services are produced by means of their purchases. If consumers want more of a good or service and are able to pay for it, demand increases and the price of the good or service increases. Higher profits then attract new producers to this industry. If consumers want less of an item, demand decreases and the price of the item decreases. Resources are attracted away from this industry.

    Under **socialism** and **communism,** central planners decide what goods and services are to be produced. In **traditional economies,** the same goods and services are produced now and in the same way as they were produced in the past.

2. How are goods and services produced?

    In a market system, the search for profit leads firms to use the least-cost combinations of resources to produce goods and services.

3. Who obtains the goods and services that are produced?

    In a market system, income and prices determine who gets what. Income is determined by the ownership of resources: those who own highly valued resources get more income. Output is then allocated to whoever is willing to pay the price.

4. What is a market failure?

    A **market failure** occurs when the price of a good or service does not fully reflect all the costs or benefits associated with the production or consumption of that good or service. It may result from imperfect information, **externalities,** the existence of **public goods,** or the existence of common ownership.

5. How do different economic systems answer the *what, how,* and *for whom* questions?

    Capitalist economies rely on prices to allocate resources and output. Socialist and communist economies rely on central planning boards. **Mixed economies** rely on a mixture of prices and government planning. Traditional societies produce the goods they have always produced and allocate output in the way it has always been allocated.

KEY TERMS

market system
price system
centrally planned system
consumer sovereignty
technical efficiency
economic efficiency
market failure

market price
market imperfection
long run
externalities
public goods
private property right
free ride

capitalism
laissez faire
socialism
communism
mixed economies
traditional economies

QUICK CHECK QUIZ

Section 1: What Is Produced

1. In a market system, _____ decide what will be produced.
   a. producers
   b. consumers
   c. politicians
   d. government authorities
   e. central planning boards

2. Many fitness educators are advocating step exercise as a way to improve cardiovascular fitness. Special boxes are used by participants, who step up and down, from side to side, and so on. If these boxes catch on, the (demand for, supply of) these boxes will (increase, decrease), their price will (increase, decrease), and (more, fewer) boxes will be produced.
   a. demand for; increase; increase; more
   b. supply of; increase; increase; more
   c. supply of; increase; decrease; more
   d. demand for; increase; decrease; more
   e. supply of; increase; decrease; fewer

Section 2: How Goods and Services Are Produced

1. Assume that labor costs $3/unit, capital costs $2/unit, land costs $1/unit, and entrepreneurial ability costs $4/unit. All of the following combinations of resources will produce 35 units of good X. Which is the technically efficient way to produce good X?
   a. 3 units of land, 4 units of labor, 2 units of capital, and 1 unit of entrepreneurial ability
   b. 2 units of land, 1 unit of labor, 2 units of capital, and 1 unit of entrepreneurial ability
   c. 4 units of land, 1 unit of labor, 1 unit of capital, and 1 unit of entrepreneurial ability
   d. 1 unit of land, 2 units of labor, 3 units of capital, and 2 units of entrepreneurial ability
   e. 2 units of land, 2 units of labor, 3 units of capital, and 1 unit of entrepreneurial ability

2. Economic efficiency refers to
   a. the combination of inputs that result in the lowest costs.
   b. the allocation of resources in their most highly valued uses.
   c. the role of central planning boards in determining what goods and services are to be produced.
   d. the role of government in providing public goods.
   e. the role of government in imposing taxes on those goods and services that produce negative externalities.

Section 3: The Distribution of Goods and Services: For Whom

1. About 60 percent of national income comes from
   a. rent.
   b. wages and salaries.
   c. interest.
   d. profit.
   e. dividends.

2. Which of the following statements is true?
   a. In a communist system, income and prices allocate goods and services.
   b. Incomes are more equally distributed in less developed countries than in developed countries.
   c. About 26 percent of national income in the United States comes from profit, the return for entrepreneurial ability.
   d. In a market system, incomes are evenly distributed.
   e. Government-directed answers to the questions of what to produce, how to produce, and for whom to produce lead to a more equal distribution of income.

Section 4: Evaluating the Price System

1. Which of the following does NOT involve negative externalities?
   a. cigarette smoke in a crowded restaurant
   b. acid rain
   c. Amazon rain forests, which help to neutralize the effects of air pollution
   d. a blaring stereo
   e. the use of a highway by an additional vehicle

2. A lighthouse is an example of
   a. a negative externality.
   b. a positive externality.
   c. a public good.
   d. a commonly owned good.
   e. a private property right.

3. If negative externalities are involved in the production or consumption of a good, (too little, too much) of the good is produced or consumed. The government should (impose taxes, grant subsidies) to encourage producers to produce (more, less) of the good.
   a. too little; grant subsidies; more
   b. too little; impose taxes; less
   c. too much; impose taxes; more
   d. too much; impose taxes; less
   e. too much; grant subsidies; less

4. Which of the following statements is false?
   a. It is not possible to exclude people from the benefits of public goods.
   b. Education is an example of a good with positive externalities.
   c. People have an incentive to try for a free ride when goods are public goods.
   d. If a good has positive externalities, too little of the good is produced.
   e. The price system ensures that the appropriate amount of public goods will be produced.

5. Which of the following is an example of market failure?
   a. Lana hates her new haircut.
   b. Stan's new car turns out to be a clunker.
   c. Jan's neighbor blasts her out of bed with his new stereo at 4 A.M.
   d. Dan's new sweater falls apart the first time he washes it.
   e. Tim buys expensive basketball shoes that hurt his feet.

Section 5: Alternative Economic Systems

1. Which country(ies) come(s) closest to a purely socialist form of economic system?
   a. Cuba
   b. Italy
   c. Canada
   d. Vietnam
   e. Cuba and Vietnam

2. Laissez faire is associated with
   a. capitalist economies.
   b. socialist economies.
   c. communist economies.
   d. mixed economies.
   e. traditional economies.

3. Central planners answer the questions of *what, how,* and *for whom* to produce in
   a. capitalist economies.
   b. socialist economies.
   c. communist economies.
   d. traditional economies.
   e. socialist and communist economies.

4. _____ economies exist because people lack the opportunities or incentives to learn new ways.
   a. Capitalist
   b. Socialist
   c. Communist
   d. Traditional
   e. Mixed

PRACTICE QUESTIONS AND PROBLEMS

Section 1: What Is Produced

1. The _____ , or price, system is an economic system in which supply and demand determine what goods and services are produced and the prices at which they are sold.

2. An economic system in which the government determines what goods and services are produced and the prices at which they are sold is called a _____ system.

3. _____ is the supreme authority of consumers to determine, by means of their purchases, what is produced.

4. Resources tend to flow from _____ -valued uses to _____ - valued uses as firms seek to make a profit.

5. If consumers' tastes change in favor of a good, _____ (demand, supply) will _____ (increase, decrease). A _____ (higher, lower) price will attract new firms to the production of that good.

6. If consumers' tastes change away from a good, _____ (demand, supply) will _____ (increase, decrease). A _____ (higher, lower) price will cause firms to leave the industry.

7. In a market system, _____ dictate what is to be produced by means of their purchases of goods and services.

Section 2: How Goods and Services Are Produced

1. _____ efficiency is the combination of inputs that results in the lowest cost.

2. _____ efficiency is the employment of resources in their most highly valued use in order to maximize the value of the output.

3. The search for _____ induces firms to use resources in their most efficient manner.

4. A small company continues to use an old mimeograph machine even though a new personal copier would cut the company's copying costs by 50 percent. This is an example of _____ inefficiency.

5. A black man is repeatedly passed over for promotion because of his race. This is an example of _____ inefficiency.

Section 3: The Distribution of Goods and Services: For Whom

1. Most income comes from _____ .

2. The most unequal distribution of income occurs in _____ (developed, less developed) countries.

3. _____ and _____ determine for whom to produce.

4. The price system _____ (does, does not) guarantee an equal distribution of income.

Section 4: Evaluating the Price System

1. _____ is the failure of the market system to achieve economic and technical efficiency.

2. The _____ price is the equilibrium price.

3. Situations in which the least-cost combination of resources is not used or in which a resource is not used where it has its highest value are called _____.

4. The _____ is a period of time in which something once believed to be fixed becomes variable.

5. _____ are the costs or benefits of a market activity borne by someone who is not a party to the market transaction.

6. When negative externalities exist, the market price _____ (overstates, understates) the full cost of the activity.

7. _____ are goods whose consumption benefits more than the person who purchased the good.

8. The limitation of ownership to an individual is called a _____.

9. A producer or consumer who enjoys the benefits of a good without having to pay for it is getting a

   _____.

10. Common ownership results in _____ (overutilization, underutilization).

11. Market imperfections may result from _____ or inaccurate information.

12. Once streetlights exist, people who have not paid for them cannot be excluded from their benefits. Streetlights are _____ goods.

Section 5: Alternative Economic Systems

1. _____ is an economic system characterized by private ownership of most resources, goods, and services.

2. _____ is a French phrase meaning "leave alone."

3. _____ is an economic system characterized by government ownership of resources other than labor and centralized economic decision making.

4. In socialist systems, incomes tend to be _____ (more, less) evenly distributed than in capitalist countries.

5. _____ is an economic system in which all resources are commonly owned and economic decision making is centrally planned.

6. _____ economies have the characteristics of more than one economic system.

7. In _____ economies, long-established customs provide answers to the *what, how,* and *for whom* questions.

THINKING ABOUT AND APPLYING THE PRICE SYSTEM, MARKET FAILURES, AND ALTERNATIVES

I. The Demand for Services in the Travel Industry

The "Economically Speaking" selection in the text looks at the economic incentives for travel firms to add services. These services add costs to the expenses of the firm but may also increase demand. If the demand shift is greater than the supply shift, it pays the firm to add the service. If the supply shift is greater than the demand shift, it does not pay the firm to add the service.

The graph below represents the demand for hotel rooms without daily delivery of newspapers. Plot new demand and supply curves that show the effects of providing daily newspapers, and construct your curves to make it profitable for hotels to provide the newspapers.

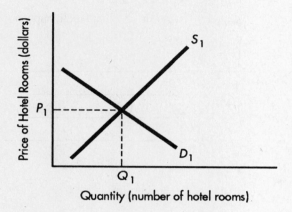

What happened to the price of hotel rooms?

_____

_____

_____

_____

II. Government Response to Externalities

The graph on the following page shows the demand and supply of an industry's product. This industry currently spews pollution into the air but bears no costs for its actions. If the industry is made responsible for the cleanup, show the effect on the market for this firm's product.

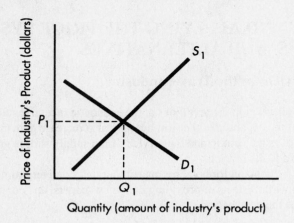

How could the government make this cost internal to the firm? What would happen to the price of the firm's output?

_____

_____

_____

_____

ANSWERS

Quick Check Quiz

Section 1: What Is Produced

1. b; 2. a

If you missed any of these questions, you should go back and review pages 86–90 in Chapter 4.

Section 2: How Goods and Services Are Produced

1. b; 2. b

If you missed any of these questions, you should go back and review page 91 in Chapter 4.

Section 3: The Distribution of Goods and Services: For Whom

1. b; 2. c

If you missed any of these questions, you should go back and review pages 92–94 in Chapter 4.

Section 4: Evaluating the Price System

1. c; 2. c; 3. d; 4. e; 5. c

If you missed any of these questions, you should go back and review pages 94–99 in Chapter 4.

Section 5: Alternative Economic Systems

1. e; 2. a; 3. e; 4. d
   If you missed any of these questions, you should go back and review pages 99–104 in Chapter 4.

Practice Questions and Problems

Section 1: What Is Produced

1. market
2. centrally planned
3. Consumer sovereignty
4. low; higher
5. demand; increase; higher
6. demand; decrease; lower
7. consumers

Section 2: How Goods and Services Are Produced

1. Technical
2. Economic
3. profit
4. technical
5. economic

Section 3: The Distribution of Goods and Services: For Whom

1. wages and salaries
2. less developed
3. Income; price
4. does not

Section 4: Evaluating the Price System

1. Market failure
2. market
3. market imperfections
4. long run
5. Externalities
6. understates
7. Public goods
8. private property right
9. free ride
10. overutilization
11. incomplete
12. public

Section 5: Alternative Economic Systems

1. Capitalism
2. *Laissez faire*
3. Socialism
4. more
5. Communism
6. Mixed
7. traditional

Thinking About and Applying the Price System, Market Failures, and Alternatives

I.   The Demand for Services in the Travel Industry

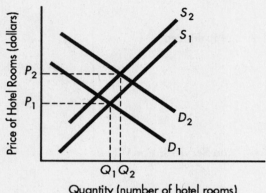

If your graph is correct, the demand shift will be greater than the supply shift. If the new equilibrium price and quantity are greater than the original price and quantity, you have done it correctly.

The price of hotel rooms increased.

II.   Government Response to Externalities

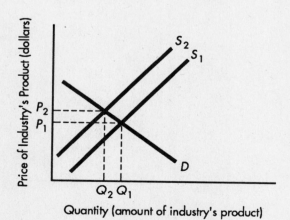

If the industry is forced to pay for the cleanup, costs will rise, shifting the supply curve to the left. The government could achieve this effect by imposing a tax on the industry or by setting quotas on its output.

CHAPTER 5
Households, Businesses, Government, and the International Sector

1. What is a household, and what is household income and spending?

   A **household** consists of one or more persons who occupy a unit of housing. Householders derive their incomes from ownership of the factors of production: land, labor, capital, and entrepreneurial ability. Household spending is called **consumption** and is the largest component of total spending in the economy.

2. What is a firm, and what is business spending?

   A firm is a business organization controlled by a single management. **Business firms** may be organized as **sole proprietorships, partnerships,** or **corporations.** Business spending by firms is called **investment** and consists of expenditures on capital goods to be used in producing goods and services.

3. What is the economic role of government?

   The economic role of government may be divided into two categories: microeconomic policy and macroeconomic policy. Microeconomic policy deals with providing public goods, correcting externalities, promoting competition, and redistributing income. Macroeconomic policy is divided into two categories, **fiscal policy** and **monetary policy**. Monetary policy is directed toward control of the money supply and credit. Fiscal policy deals with government spending and taxation.

4. How does the international sector affect the economy?

   The economies of industrialized nations are highly interdependent. As business conditions change in one country, business firms shift resources between countries so that economic conditions in one country spread to other countries.

   The international trade of the United States occurs primarily with the industrial countries, especially Canada and Japan. **Exports** are products the United States sells to foreign countries. **Imports** are products it buys from other countries. The United States had **trade surpluses** after World War II up until the 1980s.

5. How do the four sectors interact in the economy?

   Households own the **factors of production** and sell them to firms, the government, and the international sector in return for income. Business firms combine the factors of production into goods and services and sell them to households, the international sector, and the government in exchange for total revenue. The government receives income from households and firms in the form of taxes and uses these taxes to provide certain goods and services. The international sector buys and sells goods and services to business firms. The **circular flow diagram** is used to illustrate these relationships.

KEY TERMS

household	venture capital	imports
consumption	investment	exports
business firm	monetary policy	trade surplus (deficit)
sole proprietorship	Federal Reserve	net exports
partnership	fiscal policy	factors of production
corporation	budget surplus (deficit)	circular flow diagram
multinational business		

QUICK CHECK QUIZ

Section 1: Households

1. Householders _____ years old make up the largest number of households.
   a. 15–24
   b. 25–34
   c. 35–44
   d. 45–54
   e. 55–64

2. Householders _____ years old have the largest median income.
   a. 15–24
   b. 25–34
   c. 35–44
   d. 45–54
   e. 55–64

3. The largest percentage of households consists of _____ person(s).
   a. one
   b. two
   c. three
   d. four
   e. five

4. Household spending, or consumption, is the _____ component of total spending in the economy.
   a. largest
   b. second largest
   c. third largest
   d. fourth largest
   e. smallest

Section 2: Business Firms

1. In _____ , the owners of the business are responsible for all the debts incurred by the business and may have to pay these debts from their personal wealth.
   a. sole proprietorships
   b. partnerships
   c. corporations
   d. sole proprietorships and partnerships
   e. sole proprietorships, partnerships, and corporations

2. _____ are the most numerous form of business organization, and _____ account for the largest share of total revenues.
   a. Sole proprietorships; partnerships
   b. Sole proprietorships; corporations
   c. Partnerships; corporations
   d. Corporations; sole proprietorships
   e. Partnerships; sole proprietorships

3. Investment, as used in the text, is NOT
   a. a financial transaction such as buying bonds or stock.
   b. business spending on capital goods.
   c. equal to about one-fourth of household spending.
   d. extremely volatile.
   e. All of the above describe investment.

4. The largest percentage of the cash needed to start new businesses comes from
   a. bank loans.
   b. relatives.
   c. friends.
   d. SBA loans.
   e. personal assets.

Section 3: Government

1. Which of the following is NOT a microeconomic function of government?
   a. provision of public goods
   b. control of money and credit
   c. correction of externalities
   d. promotion of competition
   e. redistribution of income

2. Which of the following is a macroeconomic function of government?
   a. redistribution of income
   b. promotion of competition
   c. determining the level of government spending and taxation
   d. provision of public goods
   e. correction of externalities

3. The _____ is/are responsible for fiscal policy, and the _____ is/are responsible for monetary policy.
   a. Federal Reserve; Congress
   b. Federal Reserve; Congress and the president
   c. Congress; Federal Reserve
   d. Congress and the president; Federal Reserve
   e. Congress; Federal Reserve and the president

Section 4: The International Sector

1. The United States tends to import primary products such as agricultural products or minerals from
   a. low-income countries.
   b. medium-income countries.
   c. high-income countries.
   d. industrialized countries.
   e. developing countries.

2. The United States does most of its trading with
   a. the United Kingdom and Germany.
   b. Eastern Europe.
   c. Canada and Japan.
   d. oil exporters.
   e. Western Europe.

Section 5: Linking the Sectors

1. Which of the following statements is false?
   a. Households own the factors of production.
   b. Firms buy the factors of production from households.
   c. The value of output must equal the value of income.
   d. The value of private production must equal the value of household income.
   e. Households receive income from the government in exchange for providing the factors of production for the government.

PRACTICE QUESTIONS AND PROBLEMS

Section 1: Households

1. A _____ consists of one or more persons who occupy a unit of housing.

2. Household spending is called _____ .

3. Householders between _____ and _____ years old have the largest median incomes.

4. A household is most likely to consist of _____ persons.

Section 2: Business Firms

1. A _____ is a business organization controlled by a single management.

2. A _____ is a business owned by one person.

3. A _____ is a business owned by two or more individuals who share both the profits of the business and the responsibility for the firm's losses.

4. A _____ is a legal entity owned by shareholders whose liability for the firm's losses is limited to the value of the stock they own.

5. A _____ business is a firm that owns and operates producing units in foreign countries.

6. In the United States, the most common form of business organization is the _____.

7. _____ refers to a loan provided by an individual or firm that specializes in lending to new, unproven businesses.

8. The _____ is a government agency that assists small firms.

9. _____ is the expenditure by business firms for capital goods.

10. _____ account for the largest fraction of business revenue.

Section 3: Government

1. a. List the four microeconomic functions of government.

   _____

   _____

   _____

   _____

   b. Who is responsible for microeconomic policies? _____

2. The macroeconomic functions of government are _____ and _____ policy.

3. The _____ is the central bank of the United States.

4. Monetary policy is directed toward control of the _____.

5. Fiscal policy is directed toward _____ and _____.

6. Who is responsible for monetary policy? _____

7. Who is responsible for fiscal policy? _____

8. The _____ usually initiates major policy changes.

9. If federal government spending is less than tax revenue, a budget _____ exists.

10. If federal government spending is greater than tax revenue, a budget _____ exists.

Section 4: The International Sector

1. The _____ is an international organization that makes loans to developing countries.

2. Low-income economies are heavily concentrated in _____ and _____ .

3. Products that a country buys from another country are called _____ .

4. Products that a country sells to another country are called _____ .

5. The United States trades mainly with two countries, _____ and _____ .

6. A trade _____ exists when exports exceed imports.

7. A trade _____ exists when imports exceed exports.

8. _____ equal exports minus imports.

9. _____ net exports signal a trade surplus; _____ net exports signal a trade deficit.

Section 5: Linking the Sectors

1. List the four factors of production.

   _____

   _____

   _____

   _____

2. _____ own the factors of production.

3. The _____ is a model showing the flow of output and income from one sector of the economy to another.

THINKING ABOUT AND APPLYING HOUSEHOLDS, BUSINESSES, GOVERNMENT, AND THE INTERNATIONAL SECTOR

I. The Circular Flow Diagram

Use the diagram below to see if you understand how the four sectors of the economy are linked together. Fill in the appropriate labels. Money flows are represented by broken lines. Flows of physical goods and services are represented by solid lines.

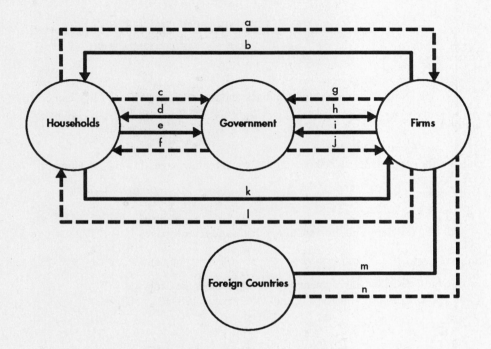

II. Student Entrepreneurs

The "Economically Speaking" article in your text describes some successful and not so successful ventures by student entrepreneurs. Consider student entrepreneurs as a group and compare them with entrepreneurs in general. What advantages might student entrepreneurs have because they are students? What disadvantages are they likely to have?

_____

_____

_____

_____

ANSWERS

Quick Check Quiz

Section 1: Households

1. b; 2. d; 3. b; 4. a
   If you missed any of these questions, you should go back and review pages 110–112 in Chapter 5.

Section 2: Business Firms

1. d; 2. b; 3. a; 4. e
   If you missed any of these questions, you should go back and review pages 112–117 in Chapter 5.

Section 3: Government

1. b (It's a macroeconomic function.); 2. c; 3. d
   If you missed any of these questions, you should go back and review pages 117–123 in Chapter 5.

Section 4: The International Sector

1. e; 2. c
   If you missed either of these questions, you should go back and review pages 123–127 in Chapter 5.

Section 5: Linking the Sectors

1. d (This must be true only when the government and foreign sectors are excluded.)
   If you missed this question, you should go back and review pages 128–132 in Chapter 5.

Practice Questions and Problems

Section 1: Households

1. household
2. consumption
3. 45; 54
4. two

Section 2: Business Firms

1. business firm
2. sole proprietorship
3. partnership
4. corporation
5. multinational
6. sole proprietorship
7. Venture capital
8. Small Business Administration (SBA)
9. Investment
10. Corporations

Section 3: Government

1. a. provision of public goods
       correction of externalities
       promotion of competition
       redistribution of income
    b. Congress and the president
2. fiscal; monetary
3. Federal Reserve
4. money supply
5. government spending; taxation
6. Federal Reserve
7. Congress and the president
8. president
9. surplus
10. deficit

Section 4: The International Sector

1. World Bank
2. Africa; Asia
3. imports
4. exports
5. Canada; Japan
6. surplus
7. deficit
8. Net exports
9. Positive; negative

Section 5: Linking the Sectors

1. land
   labor
   capital
   entrepreneurial ability
2. Households
3. circular flow diagram

Thinking About and Applying Households, Businesses, Government, and the International Sector

I. The Circular Flow Diagram

line a—payments for goods and services
line b—goods and services
line c—taxes
line d—government services
line e—factors of production
line f—payments for factors of production
line g—taxes
line h—government services
line i—factors of production
line j—payments for factors of production

line k—factors of production
line l—payments for factors of production ($)
line m—net exports
line n—payments for net exports ($)

II. Student Entrepreneurs

Student entrepreneurs may be more in touch with the campus market than entrepreneurs as a group. It may be less expensive for students to get information about the student market (demographics, tastes, and so forth) and what products or services might appeal to that market. It may also be easier for them to disseminate information about their product or service and to find reliable, cheap employees. Finally, most students have not yet taken on family responsibilities, so they are at a point in their life cycle where they are the only ones who are hurt if the risk of opening their own business does not pay off.

Probably the biggest disadvantage in being a student entrepreneur is financing the firm. Students generally do not have many personal assets, and they may find that youth and inexperience hamper them in getting loans.

CHAPTER 6
National Income Accounting

1. How is the total output of an economy measured?

   Suppose you read an article in the financial section of today's newspaper in which the president argues that the Federal Reserve should lower interest rates because of recent slow growth in the economy. How did the president know that the economy was growing slowly?

   We want to be able to compare the condition of the economy across different points in time and also against the economies of other countries. How can we tell whether the economy is better or worse than before? If we are producing more goods and services than before, the economy is growing. In order to combine dissimilar items like apples and oranges, economists use the market value of goods and services. The **gross national product (GNP)** is the market value of all final goods and services produced in a year by domestic resources. We use final goods and services to avoid double counting. If a tire is to be sold directly to a consumer, the value of the tire is included in the GNP. But if the tire is sold as part of an automobile, its value is already included in the value of the automobile, so we do not count it separately.

2. Who produces the nation's goods and services?

   Economists divide producers into four categories: households, firms, government, and the international sector. Business firms produce the largest part of the U.S. GNP.

3. Who purchases the goods and services produced?

   The same groups that produce the GNP also purchase the GNP: households, firms, government, and the international sector. Household spending is called consumption; business spending is called investment; government spending is spending by the government for goods and services; and spending by the international component is called net exports. In the United States, households are the largest purchasers of goods and services. A shorthand way of expressing the GNP as the sum of expenditures is $GNP = C + I + G + X$.

4. Who receives the income from the production of goods and services?

   Income is received by the factors of production, which economists divide into four categories: land, labor, capital, and entrepreneurial ability. The payment to land is called rent, the payment to labor is called wages, the payment to capital is called interest, and the payment to entrepreneurial ability is called profits. Two income categories that are not payments to the factors of production are included in the GNP: **capital consumption allowance** and **indirect business taxes**. For GNP as output to be equal to GNP as income, we must include all the expenses producers incur in the production of output. A shorthand way to write GNP as income is GNP = wages + interest + rent + profits + capital consumption allowance + indirect business taxes.

5. What is the difference between nominal and real GNP?

Nominal GNP measures output in terms of its current dollar value. A rise in nominal GNP can be from an increase in physical goods and services, a rise in prices, or both. **Real GNP** measures output in constant dollars. Real GNP can only increase if the production of physical goods and services increases. Real GNP is thus a better indicator of economic activity than nominal GNP.

6. What is a price index?

A **price index** measures the level of average prices and shows how prices, on average, have changed. If a pair of running shoes costs $75 this year, then 10 pairs of running shoes have a market value of $750. If the same shoes cost $80 next year, then 10 pairs have a market value of $800. The nominal value has increased, but we still have only 10 pairs of running shoes. A price index adjusts nominal values for price changes.

KEY TERMS

national income accounting	gross investment	real GNP
gross national product (GNP)	net investment	price index
intermediate good	national income (NI)	base year
value added	personal income (PI)	implicit GNP deflator
inventory	transfer payment	consumer price index (CPI)
capital consumption allowance	disposable personal income	cost of living adjustment
depreciation	(DPI)	(COLA)
indirect business tax	gross domestic product (GDP)	producer price index (PPI)
net national product (NNP)	nominal GNP	

QUICK CHECK QUIZ

Section 1: Measures of Output and Income

1. Gross national product is
   a. the market value of all goods and services produced in the United States in a year.
   b. the market value of all final goods and services produced in a year.
   c. the market value of all final goods and services produced in a year by domestic resources.
   d. the market value of all final goods and services sold in a year.
   e. the total number of final goods and services produced in a year by domestic resources.

2. GNP as expenditures can be expressed as
   a. $C + I + G + X$.
   b. wages + interest + rent + profits + capital consumption allowance + indirect business taxes.
   c. the sum of the values added at each stage of production.
   d. NI + indirect business taxes.
   e. NI + capital consumption allowance.

3. Which of the following is incorrect?
   a. PI = DPI – personal taxes.
   b. GDP = GNP – net factor income from abroad.
   c. DPI = PI – personal taxes.
   d. NI = NNP – indirect business taxes.
   e. NNP = GNP – capital consumption allowance.

4. Unplanned inventory
   a. is a cushion above expected sales.
   b. is gross investment – capital consumption allowance.
   c. is the difference between the value of the output and the value of the intermediate goods used in the production of that output.
   d. is unsold goods that the firm had expected to be able to sell when it placed the order.
   e. is the market value of the goods and services produced by a firm in one year.

5. The largest component of total expenditures is
   a. consumption.
   b. investment.
   c. government spending.
   d. net exports.
   e. rent.

6. To get disposable personal income from GNP, we must subtract all of the following except
   a. indirect business taxes.
   b. net factor income from abroad.
   c. capital consumption allowance.
   d. income earned but not received.
   e. personal taxes.

7. To get NNP from GNP, we subtract
   a. capital consumption allowance.
   b. net factor income from abroad.
   c. capital consumption allowance and indirect business taxes.
   d. capital consumption allowance, indirect business taxes, and personal taxes.
   e. capital consumption allowance, indirect business taxes, net transfer payments, and personal taxes.

8. National income equals
   a. GNP – capital consumption allowance.
   b. GNP – net factor income from abroad.
   c. GNP – capital consumption allowance – indirect business taxes.
   d. NNP – indirect business taxes.
   e. Both c and d above are correct.

9. Which of the following is a transfer payment?
   a. profits that are retained by corporations rather than paid out to stockholders
   b. Social Security benefits
   c. FICA taxes
   d. estimated in-kind wages
   e. barter and cash transactions in the underground economy

10. Which of the following is counted in the GNP?
    a. the value of homemaker services
    b. estimated illegal drug transactions
    c. the value of oil used in the production of gasoline
    d. estimated in-kind wages
    e. the sale of a used automatic dishwasher

Section 2: Nominal and Real Measures

1. Nominal GNP
   a. is real GNP divided by the price level.
   b. measures output in constant prices.
   c. decreases when the price level increases.
   d. measures output in terms of its current dollar value.
   e. is real GNP multiplied by the consumer price index.

2. The producer price index (PPI)
   a. is the price index given by the ratio of nominal GNP to real GNP.
   b. measures the average price of consumer goods and services that a typical household purchases.
   c. measures average prices received by producers.
   d. was originally known as the COLA.
   e. is used to get real GNP from nominal GNP.

3. The real GNP
   a. is calculated by multiplying the implicit GNP deflator by nominal GNP.
   b. measures the average level of prices in the economy and shows, on average, how prices have changed.
   c. measures output in constant dollars.
   d. is calculated by dividing nominal GNP by the CPI.
   e. is calculated by dividing nominal GNP by the PPI.

4. A price index equal to 90 in a given year
   a. indicates that prices were lower than prices in the base year.
   b. indicates that the year in question was a year previous to the base year.
   c. indicates that prices were 10 percent higher than prices in the base year.
   d. is inaccurate—price indexes cannot be lower than 100.
   e. indicates that real GNP was lower than GNP in the base year.

5. Social Security payments are tied to the
   a. implicit GNP deflator.
   b. CPI.
   c. PPI.
   d. wholesale price index.
   e. nominal GNP.

Section 3: Flows of Income and Expenditures

1. Total expenditures on final goods and services
   a. equal NNP.
   b. equal the total value of goods and services produced.
   c. equal total income from selling goods and services.
   d. Items b and c above are correct.
   e. All of the above are correct.

PRACTICE QUESTIONS AND PROBLEMS

Section 1: Measures of Output and Income

1. Gross national product is the _____ value of all _____ goods and services produced in a year by domestic resources.

2. _____ are goods that are used in the production of a final product.

3. _____ is the difference between the value of output and the value of the intermediate goods used in the production of that output.

4. _____ is a firm's stock of unsold goods.

5. The estimated value of capital goods used up or worn out in a year plus the value of accidental damage to capital goods is called _____, or depreciation.

6. Excise taxes and sales taxes are forms of _____.

7. List the four factors of production and the name of the payments each factor receives. What two items must be added to these factor payments to equal gross national product?

   _____

   _____

   _____

   _____

8. GNP minus net factor income from abroad yields _____.

9. A lei maker buys flowers from a nursery for $125. She makes 50 leis from the flowers and sells each lei for $3.99. What is the value added for the lei maker? _____

10. A Kansas farmer sells wheat to a craftsperson to make into decorative ornaments. The farmer sells his wheat to the craftsperson for $300. The craftsperson adds labor, valued at $200, and some ribbons, valued at $50, and produces 110 ornaments. What is the final market value of each ornament?

_____

11. Unplanned inventory _____ (is, is not) included in the GNP.

12. Government spending on goods and services _____ (is, is not) the largest component of GNP as expenditures.

13. Use the information below to calculate GNP, NNP, and NI. All figures are in billions of dollars.

Capital consumption allowance	328	Wages and salaries	1,803
Corporate profits	124	Personal taxes	398
Rents	6	Indirect business taxes	273
Interest	264	Proprietor's income	248

GNP _____   NNP _____   NI _____

Section 2: Nominal and Real Measures

1. The table below shows nominal GNP and the implicit GNP deflator for 3 years. Use this information to calculate the real GNP and to answer the following questions.

Year	Nominal GNP	Implicit GNP Deflator	Real GNP
1	206	98	_____
2	216	100	_____
3	228	115	_____

a. Which year is the base year? _____

b. Prices in year 3 were _____ (higher, lower) than prices in the base year.

c. In year 3, nominal GNP _____ (increased, did not change, decreased) and real GNP _____ (increased, did not change, decreased).

2. If the real GNP this year is 232 and the nominal GNP is 256, calculate the implicit GNP deflator.

_____

_____

_____

_____

3. An increase in the _____ index can indicate a coming change in the CPI.

4. Why isn't nominal GNP a good measure of the strength or weakness of the economy? What measure would be better?

_____

_____

_____

_____

5. If the price index in the current year is 212, then prices have _____ (increased, not changed, decreased) by _____ percent from the base year.

Section 3: Flows of Income and Expenditures

1. Fill in the diagram below with the terms listed below. Dollar flows are represented by broken lines. The flow of physical goods and services is represented by solid lines.

payments for goods and services	goods and services
taxes	government services
factors of production	wages, rent, interest, and profits
net exports	payments for net exports

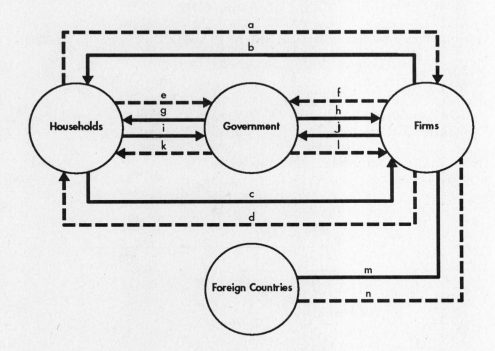

THINKING ABOUT AND APPLYING NATIONAL INCOME ACCOUNTING

I. Difficulties in Measuring GNP

GNP is used to measure economic performance and to determine whether the overall standard of living is improving or declining. But does GNP really measure the total output of the economy? Decide if each item listed below is counted as part of GNP. If the item is NOT counted but is productive activity, indicate whether its omission overstates or understates GNP.

1. cocaine sold by Colombians to U.S. consumers
2. your parent's service to the family doing housework
3. a college textbook published this year
4. the fee for your cat's yearly rabies vaccine
5. intermediate goods
6. $10 paid for a 3-year-old infant car seat purchased at a garage sale
7. your teacher's salary this year
8. this year's rental income from an office building
9. the services of a homeowner painting his or her own house
10. pollution produced as a result of steel production

II. The Expenditures Approach for Calculating GNP

1. Use the information below to calculate GNP, NNP, NI, PI, and DPI. All figures are in billions of dollars.

Income earned but not received	110
Personal taxes	198
Government purchases of goods and services	396
Capital consumption allowance	684
Personal consumption expenditures	1,326
Imports	800
Gross private domestic investment	296
Income received but not earned	225
Exports	670
Indirect business taxes	515

GNP _____   NNP _____   NI _____

PI _____   DPI _____

III. Understanding Price Indexes

Suppose the economy of Strandasville produces only four goods: trolls, pizza, desk chairs, and sweaters. The table below shows the dollar value of output for three different years.

Year	Number of Trolls	Price per Troll	Number of Pizzas	Price per Pizza
1	1,000	$5	8,000	$6.00
2	1,000	$6	8,000	$6.60
3	4,000	$7	10,000	$6.80

Year	Number of Desk Chairs	Price per Chair	Number of Sweaters	Price per Sweater
1	3,000	$20	5,000	$20
2	3,000	$25	5,000	$18
3	3,500	$25	4,900	$15

1. Calculate the total dollar value of output for year 1, year 2, and year 3.

_____

_____

_____

_____

2. The dollar value of output in year 2 is higher than the dollar value of output in year 1
    a. entirely because of price changes.
    b. entirely because of output changes.
    c. because of both price and output changes.

3. The dollar value of output in year 3 is higher than the dollar value of output in year 1
    a. entirely because of price changes.
    b. entirely because of output changes.
    c. because of both price and output changes.

ANSWERS

Quick Check Quiz

Section 1: Measures of Output and Income

1. c; 2. a; 3. a; 4. d; 5. a; 6. b; 7. a; 8. e; 9. b; 10. d
   If you missed any of these questions, you should go back and review pages 143–153 in Chapter 6.

Section 2: Nominal and Real Measures

1. d; 2. c; 3. c; 4. a; 5. b
   If you missed any of these questions, you should go back and review pages 153–158 in Chapter 6.

Section 3: Flows of Income and Expenditures

1. d
   If you missed any of these questions, you should go back and review page 159 in Chapter 6.

Practice Questions and Problems

Section 1: Measures of Output and Income

1. market; final
2. Intermediate goods
3. Value added
4. Inventory
5. capital consumption allowance
6. indirect business taxes
7. land   rent
   labor   wages
   capital   interest
   entrepreneurial ability   profits
   You must add capital consumption allowance and indirect business taxes to get GNP.
8. gross domestic product
9. $74.50
   The lei maker gets $3.99 for each of her 50 leis, for a total of $199.50. Since her cost for the flowers was $125, her value added is $199.50 – $125 = $74.50.
10. $5
    The total of the values added is $300 + $200 + $50 = $550. The 110 ornaments are worth $550, or $5 each.
11. is
12. is not—Consumption is the largest expenditure component.
13. GNP = wages + rent + interest + profits (corporate profits + proprietor's income) + capital consumption allowance + indirect business taxes = 1,803 + 6 + 264 + (124 + 248) + 328 + 273 = 3,046
    NNP = GNP – capital consumption allowance = 3,046 – 328 = 2,718
    NI = NNP – indirect business taxes = 2,718 – 273 = 2,445

Section 2: Nominal and Real Measures

1. | Year | Real GNP |
    |------|----------|
    | 1 | $206/98 \times 100 = 210.20$ |
    | 2 | 216 (this is the base year) |
    | 3 | $228/115 \times 100 = 198.26$ |

    a. Year 2. You can tell because the price index is 100 for that year.
    b. higher
    c. increased; decreased
2. Implicit GNP deflator = nominal GNP/real GNP $\times 100 = 256/232 \times 100 = 110.34$
3. producer price
4. Increases in nominal GNP can come about from a rise in prices, an increase in output, or both. To know if the economy is performing better than before, we need to know if output has increased. Real GNP is a better measure, since it rises only when output has increased.
5. increased; 112

Section 3: Flows of Income and Expenditures

line a—payments for goods and services
line b—goods and services
line c—factors of production
line d—wages, rent, interest, and profits
line e—taxes
line f—taxes
line g—government services
line h—government services
line i—factors of production
line j—goods and services
line k—wages, rent, interest, and profits
line l—payments for goods and services
line m—net exports
line n—payments for net exports

Thinking About and Applying National Income Accounting

I. Difficulties in Measuring GNP

1. The Colombians' sale of cocaine to U.S. consumers is an illegal activity and therefore not represented in the GNP. If the resources used to produce cocaine are domestically owned and production occurred this year, then this activity should be included in the GNP. Its omission would understate the GNP.
2. This activity does not involve a market transaction and therefore is not included in the GNP. It is productive activity, however, and its omission understates the GNP.
3. A college textbook published this year would be included in the GNP.
4. The fee for your cat's yearly rabies vaccine would be included in the GNP.
5. Intermediate goods are not counted in the GNP. To do so would be double-counting.
6. A 3-year-old car seat was not produced this year. It is not and should not be counted in the GNP.
7. Your teacher's salary this year is for productive activity and is included in the GNP.
8. This year's rental income from an office building represents productive activity—the use of the space over a period of time. It is included in the GNP.
9. The services of a homeowner painting his or her own house would not be included in the GNP, since no market transaction is involved. However, it does represent productive activity and should be included. GNP is understated by its omission.

10. Some economists feel that the production of "bads" such as pollution should be included in GNP if we are to get a true picture of economic well-being. Production of "bads" such as pollution is not currently included in GNP.

II. The Expenditures Approach for Calculating GNP

1. GNP $= C + I + G + X = 1,326 + 296 + 396 + (670 - 800) = 1,888$
   NNP = GNP – capital consumption allowance $= 1,888 - 684 = 1,204$
   NI = NNP – indirect business taxes $= 1,204 - 515 = 689$
   PI = NI – income earned but not received + income received but not earned $= 689 - 110 + 225 = 804$
   DPI = PI – personal taxes $= 804 - 198 = 606$

III. Understanding Price Indexes

1. The dollar value of output for year 1 is $1,000(5) + 8,000(6) + 3,000(20) + 5,000(20) = 213,000$. For year 2 the value is $1,000(6) + 8,000(6.6) + 3,000(25) + 5,000(18) = 223,800$. For year 3 the value is $4,000(7) + 10,000(6.80) + 3,500(25) + 4,900(15) = 257,000$.
2. a
3. c

CHAPTER 7
An Introduction to the Foreign Exchange Market and the Balance of Payments

FUNDAMENTAL
QUESTIONS

1. How do individuals of one nation trade money with individuals of another nation?

   People trade one currency for another in **foreign exchange markets.** It is not necessary for large traders to go to a specific place to conduct such transactions. They call a bank that deals in foreign currency and ask the bank to convert some of their dollars to the currency they want. The amount of foreign currency exchanged for dollars depends on the **exchange rate**—the price of one country's money in terms of another. If the dollar appreciates against a foreign currency, you will get more of that currency per dollar. If the dollar depreciates against a foreign currency, you will get less of that currency per dollar.

2. How do changes in exchange rates affect international trade?

   If a country's currency appreciates in value, international demand for its product falls, all other things being equal. This is because that country's goods become more expensive in terms of other currencies. If a country's currency depreciates, the prices of its goods and services in terms of other countries' currencies fall, and international demand for its products increases.

3. How do nations record their transactions with the rest of the world?

   The record of a nation's transactions with the rest of the world is called its **balance of payments.** The balance of payments is divided into two categories: the **current account** and the **capital account.** The current account is the sum of the balances for goods, services, and unilateral transfers. The capital account records the transactions necessary to move goods, services, and unilateral transfers into and out of the country. The net balance in the balance of payments must be zero, so a **deficit** (or surplus) in the current account must be offset by a **surplus** (or deficit) in the capital account. A country becomes a larger net debtor (or smaller net creditor) if it shows a deficit in its current account (or surplus in its capital account).

KEY TERMS

foreign exchange	balance of payments	surplus
foreign exchange market	double-entry bookkeeping	deficit
exchange rate	current account	capital account

QUICK CHECK QUIZ

Section 1: The Foreign Exchange Market

1. The foreign exchange market, like the New York Stock Exchange, is located in a specific building in New York City. (true or false?) _____

2. Most foreign exchange transactions involve the movement of currency. (true or false?)

   _____

3. In the foreign exchange market, the smaller the quantity of foreign currency purchased, the

   _____ (higher, lower) the price.

4. As a country's currency depreciates, international demand for its products _____

   (rises, falls), all other things being equal.

5. If one U.S. dollar sells for 147.30 yen, then the price of the Japanese yen in terms of dollars is
   a. $.0067888.
   b. $.6788866.
   c. $.006780.
   d. $.006801.
   e. $1.4730.

6. Suppose that a cassette recorder costs 226.44 Norwegian krone and that the current exchange rate between the U.S. dollar and the Norwegian krone is $.1590. What is the price of the cassette recorder in U.S. dollars?
   a. $1424.15
   b. $36.00
   c. $181.15
   d. $283.05
   e. $212.99

7. Suppose that the exchange rate between the U.S. dollar and the Australian dollar is $.7985 (1A$ = $.7985). If the exchange rate tomorrow is $.7975, then the Australian dollar has _____ against the U.S. dollar. Australian goods will be _____ in the United States.
   a. appreciated; more expensive
   b. appreciated; less expensive
   c. depreciated; more expensive
   d. depreciated; less expensive
   e. depreciated; the same price as before

8. If an Austrian schilling is equivalent to $.088677 U.S. dollars, then $1 is equal to _____ schillings, and an opal ring costing 1,700 schillings would have a U.S. dollar value of _____ .
   a. 11.28; $19,170.70
   b. 11.28; $150.75
   c. .09; $19,170.70
   d. .09; $150.76
   e. 1; $1,700

9. If the U.S. dollar drops to 1.6310 German marks from 1.6609 German marks, then
   a. the dollar has appreciated against the mark, and the prices of German cars will increase in the United States.
   b. the dollar has appreciated against the mark, and the prices of German cars will decrease in the United States.
   c. the dollar has depreciated against the mark, and the prices of German cars will increase in the United States.
   d. the dollar has depreciated against the mark, and the prices of German cars will decrease in the United States.
   e. the dollar has depreciated against the mark, and the prices of American cars will increase in Germany.

10. The great majority of transactions in the foreign exchange market involve
    a. foreign coins.
    b. foreign paper money.
    c. bank deposits denominated in foreign currency.
    d. foreign currency.
    e. items b and c above.

Section 2: The Balance of Payments

1. Which of the following is NOT included in the current account?
   a. merchandise balances
   b. services balances
   c. unilateral transfer accounts
   d. purchases of stocks and bonds
   e. All of the above are included in the current account.

2. The largest component of the services account is
   a. travel and tourism.
   b. royalties.
   c. insurance premiums.
   d. return on investments.
   e. transportation costs.

3. The United States traditionally shows a _____ (deficit, surplus) in its services account because of its large investments in the rest of the world.

4. GNP net exports is the sum of
   a. merchandise balances and unilateral transfers.
   b. services balances and unilateral transfers.
   c. merchandise balances and services balances.
   d. merchandise balances, services balances, and unilateral transfers.
   e. merchandise balances, services balances, unilateral transfers, and the statistical discrepancy account.

5. If export goods exceed import goods, the (merchandise, services, unilateral transfers) account will show a (deficit, surplus).
   a. merchandise; deficit
   b. merchandise; surplus
   c. services; deficit
   d. services; surplus
   e. unilateral transfers; surplus

6. Which account contains all of the activities involving goods and services?
   a. merchandise
   b. services
   c. unilateral transfers
   d. current
   e. capital

7. In the terminology of the balance of payments, capital refers to all of the following except
   a. bank deposits.
   b. purchases of stocks.
   c. purchases of bonds.
   d. loans.
   e. purchases of equipment.

8. A country with a deficit in its current account
   a. exports more goods and services than it imports.
   b. is running a deficit in its capital account.
   c. is a net lender to the rest of the world.
   d. is a net borrower from the rest of the world.
   e. is running a surplus in its merchandise account.

9. The net balance in the balance of payments
   a. is positive if a country is a net creditor to the rest of the world.
   b. is negative if a country imports more goods and services than it exports.
   c. is negative if the country is a net debtor to the rest of the world.
   d. is positive if a country exports more goods and services than it imports.
   e. must be zero.

10. The United States
    a. has always run a surplus in its merchandise account.
    b. typically runs a surplus in its unilateral transfers account.
    c. typically runs a deficit in its services account.
    d. was an international creditor from the end of World War I until the mid-1980s.
    e. had large capital account deficits in the 1980s.

PRACTICE QUESTIONS AND PROBLEMS

Section 1: The Foreign Exchange Market

1. _____ is another expression for foreign money.

2. A global market in which people trade one currency for another is called a _____ .

3. An _____ is the price of one country's money in terms of another.

4. A rise in the value of a currency is called _____ , and a decrease in the value of a currency is called _____ .

5. What is the price of one U.S. dollar given the following exchange rates?

   a. 1 Canadian dollar = $.86610 _____
   b. 1 Swiss franc = $.70597 _____
   c. 1 Italian lira = $.00083 _____
   d. 1 Japanese yen = $.00677 _____
   e. 1 British pound = $1.8155 _____

Country	U.S. Dollar Equivalent	Currency per U.S. Dollar
France (franc)	.18086	5.5290
Greece (drachma)	.006196	161.40
Netherlands (guilder)	.5379	1.8590
Pakistan (rupee)	.0463	21.61
Philippines (peso)	.04413	22.66

6. A 35-mm camera manufactured in the United States costs $150. Using the exchange rates listed in the table above, what would the camera cost in each of the following countries?

   a. France _____

   b. Greece _____

   c. Netherlands _____

   d. Pakistan _____

   e. Philippines _____

7. Suppose the dollar ended at 1.4165 Swiss francs today, well above 1.4045 francs yesterday.

   a. The dollar has _____ (appreciated, depreciated) against the franc.

   b. Swiss goods are now _____ (more expensive, cheaper) in the United States.

   c. As a result of the change in exchange rates, U.S. exports to Switzerland will

   _____ (increase, decrease), all other things being equal.

8. You read in the paper that the Finnish markka is expected to depreciate against the dollar. Therefore, the price of a Finnish sweater sold in the United States will _____ (increase, decrease), and the price of U.S. blue jeans sold in Finland will _____ (increase, decrease).

Section 2: The Balance of Payments

1. The _____ is a record of a country's trade in goods, services, and financial assets with the rest of the world.

2. _____ record activities that bring payments into a country, and _____ record activities that involve payments to the rest of the world.

3. _____ means that for every transaction there is a credit entry and a debit entry.

4. When exports exceed imports, the merchandise account shows a _____ .

5. GNP net exports is the sum of the _____ and the _____ balances.

6. A net _____ owes more to the rest of the world than it is owed.

7. The sum of the balances in the merchandise, services, and unilateral transfers accounts is called the _____ account.

8. Use the table below to calculate the current account, capital account, and statistical discrepancy for the mythical country of Dimmenland.

Account	Credit	Debit	Net Balance
Merchandise	412.68	212.89	199.79
Services	142.52	108.37	34.15
Unilateral transfers	8.24	180.56	−100.32
Capital account	170.36	308.72	_____
Statistical discrepancy			_____

9. Refer to problem 8. Dimmenland is running a _____ (deficit, surplus) in its current account and a _____ (deficit, surplus) in its capital account. Dimmenland is becoming a greater net _____ (debtor, creditor) to the rest of the world.

10. Refer to problem 8. Calculate Dimmenland's GNP net exports. If consumption = $2,490, investment = $58.48, and government spending = $540.12, what is Dimmenland's GNP? _____

11. A government-tolerated alternative to the official exchange market is called a _____ market rather than a black market.

THINKING ABOUT AND APPLYING THE FOREIGN EXCHANGE MARKET AND THE BALANCE OF PAYMENTS

I.   The Balance of Payments as an Indicator

A surplus in the merchandise account means that a nation is exporting more goods than it is importing. This is often interpreted as a sign that a nation's producers can produce at a lower cost than their foreign counterparts. A trade deficit may indicate that a nation's producers are less efficient than their foreign counterparts.

1.   Interpret these statements in terms of what you have read about the United States as the world's largest debtor nation. Can you explain why many analysts viewed the U.S. balance of payments accounts with concern in 1985?

   _____

   _____

   _____

   _____

II.   The Balance of Payments and Exchange Rates

If U.S. residents lend and invest less in foreign countries than foreigners lend and invest in the United States, the capital account will be in surplus. If U.S. purchases of foreign stocks and bonds exceed foreign purchases of U.S. stocks and bonds, then more funds are leaving the country than entering it, and the capital account will be in deficit. Pretend that you are willing to sell your stereo system to a French resident. Would you prefer to be paid in U.S. dollars or French francs? Since you can't easily spend francs in this country, you would prefer to be paid in U.S. dollars. So if the French buy more U.S. goods and services, they will need dollars to pay for them and the dollar will appreciate against the franc. Similarly, if U.S. investors demand more French bonds and stocks, the franc will appreciate.

1.   In view of what you have read about U.S. and foreign lending in 1985, what impact will a capital account surplus have on a domestic currency? If U.S. federal budget deficits continue, what will be the impact on the dollar?

   _____

   _____

   _____

   _____

III.   Black Markets in Foreign Exchange

1.   Consider the market for dollars in terms of the borg, the domestic currency of Dimmenland. The government of Dimmenland has set an artificially low official exchange rate of 5 borgs per U.S. dollar.

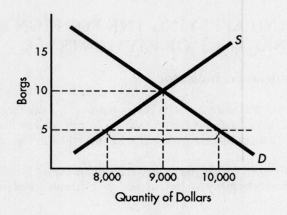

The demand for dollars is D, and the supply is S. The free market price is 10 borgs, but the government has set an artificial exchange rate of 5 borgs per dollar. At this low rate, only 8,000 dollars will be supplied, but 10,000 will be demanded. A shortage develops, spawning a black market. How high will the black market price be bid up?

_____

_____

_____

_____

2. In August 1982, the Mexican government banned the sale of U.S. dollars by Mexican banks. Use the graph below to illustrate how the black market developed.

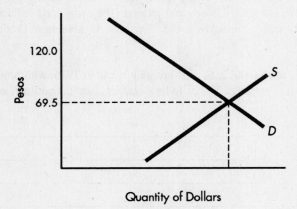

ANSWERS

Quick Check Quiz

Section 1: The Foreign Exchange Market

1. false; 2. false; 3. higher; 4. rises; 5. a; 6. b; 7. d; 8. b; 9. c; 10. c
   If you missed any of these questions, you should go back and review pages 166–169 in Chapter 7.

Section 2: The Balance of Payments

1. d; 2. d; 3. surplus; 4. c; 5. b; 6. d; 7. e; 8. d; 9. e; 10. d
   If you missed any of these questions, you should go back and review pages 170–176 in Chapter 7.

Practice Questions and Problems

Section 1: The Foreign Exchange Market

1. Foreign exchange
2. foreign exchange market
3. exchange rate
4. appreciation; depreciation
5. a. 1/.86610 = C$1.154601
   b. 1/.70597 = SF1.4164907
   c. 1/.00083 = Lit1,204.8192
   d. 1/.00677 = ¥147.71048
   e. 1/1.8155 = £.5508124
6. a. $150 × FF5.5290/$ = FF829.35
   b. $150 × Dr161.40/$ = Dr24,210
   c. $150 × FL1.8590/$ = FL278.85
   d. $150 × RS21.61/$ = RS3,241.5
   e. $150 × 22.66 pesos/$ = 3,399 pesos
7. a. appreciated
   b. cheaper
   c. decrease
8. decrease; increase

Section 2: The Balance of Payments

1. balance of payments
2. Credits; debits
3. Double-entry bookkeeping
4. surplus
5. merchandise; services
6. debtor
7. current

8. Current account = merchandise balance + services balances + unilateral transfers = 199.79 + 34.15 + −100.32 = 133.62

   Capital account = capital credits − capital debits = 170.36 − 308.72 = −138.36

   Current account + capital account + statistical discrepancy = 0

   133.62 + −138.36 + Statistical discrepancy = 0

   Statistical discrepancy = 4.74

9. surplus; deficit; creditor

10. GNP net exports = merchandise balance + services balance = 199.79 + 34.15 = 233.94

    GNP = C + I + G + E = 2,490 + 58.48 + 540.12 + 233.94 = 3,322.54

11. parallel

Thinking About and Applying the Foreign Exchange Market and the Balance of Payments

I. The Balance of Payments as an Indicator

1. A merchandise deficit such as the United States had in 1985 may indicate that domestic producers have higher costs than their foreign competitors. Many analysts viewed the 1985 current account deficit as a sign that U.S. manufacturers had lost their competitive edge.

II. The Balance of Payments and Exchange Rates

1. A capital account surplus means that there are more foreign purchases of U.S. stocks and bonds than U.S. purchases of foreign stocks and bonds. Foreign purchasers therefore need to acquire U.S. dollars, so the dollar will appreciate. U.S. federal budget deficits may signal higher domestic interest rates. Foreign investors will be attracted to the high U.S. interest rates, and the dollar will appreciate.

III. Black Markets in Foreign Exchange

1. The demand curve indicates that consumers will be willing to pay 15 borgs per dollar for 8,000 dollars. As the black market exchange rate rises above the official rate, however, more dollars will be supplied so that the exchange rate is less than 15.

2.

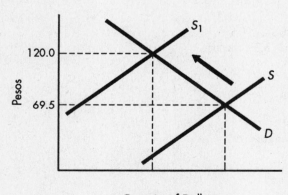

A decrease in the number of suppliers shifts the supply curve to the left and increases the price of the dollar.

CHAPTER 8
Unemployment and Inflation

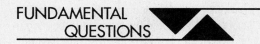
1. What is a business cycle?

    Business cycles are recurring patterns of ups and downs in economic activity. A typical cycle has four stages: expansion, peak, contraction, and trough. During an economic expansion (boom), output, employment, incomes, and prices all rise. A peak is reached, after which economic activity declines. During the contraction (**recession**) phase, output, employment, and income all drop. If the contraction is severe enough, prices may also decline. The trough marks the end of a contraction and the beginning of a new expansion.

2. How is the unemployment rate defined and measured?

    The **unemployment rate** is the percentage of the labor force that is not working. Economists do not include the entire population in the labor force: it is of little consequence, for example, that a newborn baby is unemployed. To be in the U.S. labor force, an individual must be working or actively seeking work.

    Some types of unemployment have more impact on the economy than others. *Frictional unemployment* occurs when previously employed workers change jobs or new workers seek their first jobs. *Seasonal unemployment* is a product of regular, recurring changes in the hiring needs of certain industries. Both these types of unemployment tend to be short term. *Structural unemployment*, on the other hand, results from fundamental changes in the structure of the economy, and can be long term. Structurally unemployed persons can't find *any* job they can do. Likewise, *cyclically unemployed* persons who are out of work because the economy is in a recession may be unemployed for a long time.

    Economists do not advocate a zero unemployment rate. Some unemployment is necessary so that workers may be channeled to their most productive employment as their skills change. Economists use the term **natural rate of unemployment** to describe the unemployment rate that would exist in the absence of cyclical unemployment. It describes the labor market when the economy is producing what it realistically can produce. Estimates of the natural rate of unemployment vary from 4 percent to around 7 percent.

3. What is the cost of unemployed resources?

    The cost of unemployed resources is lost output. **Potential GNP** is the level of output that can be produced if all nonlabor resources are fully utilized and unemployment is at its natural rate—that is, if the economy is producing the level of output it can realistically produce. To measure lost output, one subtracts the actual GNP from potential GNP. The resulting figure indicates the GNP gap—the cost of unemployed resources.

4. What is inflation?

Inflation is a sustained rise in the average level of prices. This does not mean that *all* prices will rise. Some may rise and some may fall, but inflation occurs when the *average* level of prices rises.

5. Why is inflation a problem?

Inflation is not a problem if prices and incomes rise at the same rate. But if incomes rise more slowly than prices, households will not be able to buy as many goods and services as they did before. Unanticipated inflation redistributes income away from those who receive fixed incomes toward those who make fixed expenditures. Suppose that your mother agrees to lend you $1,000 for school and that prices unexpectedly double between the time you receive the money and the time you repay your mother. Your mother has lost half of her purchasing power: the $1,000 that you paid back can only buy what $500 bought at the time she lent you the money. Your mother, like other creditors, has lost purchasing power to inflation.

KEY TERMS

business cycle
recession
depression
leading indicator
coincident indicator
lagging indicator

unemployment rate
discouraged workers
underemployment
underground economy
potential GNP

natural rate of unemployment
inflation
nominal interest rate
real interest rate
hyperinflation

QUICK CHECK QUIZ

Section 1: Business Cycles

1. All of the following are leading economic indicators except
   a. the average workweek.
   b. unemployment claims.
   c. new plant and equipment orders.
   d. the prime interest rate.
   e. All of the above are leading indicators.

2. All of the following change at the same time real output changes except
   a. inventories.
   b. personal income.
   c. payroll employment.
   d. industrial production.
   e. All of the above are coincident indicators.

3. Which of the following does NOT change its value until after the value of real GNP has changed?
   a. outstanding commercial loans
   b. the prime interest rate
   c. the labor cost per unit of output
   d. unemployment duration
   e. All of the above are lagging indicators.

4. The four stages of the business cycle are
   a. peak, boom, expansion, and contraction.
   b. peak, contraction, trough, and expansion.
   c. recession, expansion, peak, and boom.
   d. contraction, trough, expansion, and boom.
   e. recession, contraction, peak, and boom.

5. Which of the following statements is true?
   a. Leading indicators are infallible predictors of future changes in real GNP.
   b. Business fluctuations are called business cycles because they tend to follow regular and predictable patterns.
   c. Real GNP has risen over the long term.
   d. According to the NBER, there have been eight recessions since 1929.
   e. The average time workers are unemployed is a coincident indicator.

6. Which of the following statements is false?
   a. The value of outstanding business and consumer credit is a leading indicator.
   b. The inventories to sales ratio is a lagging indicator.
   c. Manufacturing and trade sales are a coincident indicator.
   d. Materials prices are a coincident indicator.
   e. Delivery times of goods are a leading indicator.

Section 2: Unemployment

1. To arrive at the number in the U.S. labor force, we subtract all of the following from the number of all U.S. residents except
   a. residents under 16 years old.
   b. institutionalized adults.
   c. adults who are not looking for work.
   d. unemployed adults.
   e. All of the above must be subtracted from the number of U.S. residents to arrive at the number in the labor force.

2. Which of the following cause(s) the unemployment rate to be overstated?
   a. discouraged workers
   b. underground economic activities
   c. part-time employment
   d. underemployment
   e. students who are not looking for work

3. A graduating college basketball star who has one month off before reporting to his new NBA team is an example of
   a. frictional unemployment.
   b. structural unemployment.
   c. cyclical unemployment.
   d. technological unemployment.
   e. a rich, employed person.

4. Unemployed migrant workers are examples of
   a. frictional unemployment.
   b. seasonal unemployment.
   c. structural unemployment.
   d. discouraged workers.
   e. cyclical unemployment.

5. A person who finds that her skills are no longer needed because she has been replaced by a machine is an example of
   a. frictional unemployment.
   b. seasonal unemployment.
   c. cyclical unemployment.
   d. search unemployment.
   e. structural unemployment.

6. A steelworker who has been laid off during a recession is an example of
   a. frictional unemployment.
   b. seasonal unemployment.
   c. cyclical unemployment.
   d. search unemployment.
   e. structural unemployment.

7. Job training and counseling are policy measures used to fight primarily
   a. frictional unemployment.
   b. seasonal unemployment.
   c. cyclical unemployment.
   d. structural unemployment.
   e. both a and d.

8. Which of the following statements is false?
   a. The GNP gap widens during recessions and narrows during expansions.
   b. The influx of women and baby boomers into the labor force has increased the natural rate of unemployment in recent decades.
   c. Men have higher unemployment rates than women because women move out of the labor force to have children.
   d. Teenagers have the highest unemployment rates in the economy.
   e. Nonwhites have higher unemployment rates than whites.

Section 3: Inflation

1. If a college professor's income has increased by 3 percent at the same time that prices have risen by 5 percent, the professor's real income has
   a. decreased by 2 percent.
   b. increased by 2 percent.
   c. increased by 7 percent
   d. decreased by 7 percent.
   e. not changed.

2. Which of the following groups benefit from unanticipated inflation?
    a. creditors
    b. retirees on fixed incomes
    c. debtors
    d. workers whose salaries are tied to the CPI
    e. suppliers who have contracted to supply a fixed amount of their product for a fixed price

3. Which of the following could be a cause of demand-pull inflation?
    a. war in the Middle East, which can increase oil prices
    b. drought in the Midwest, which can cause crop failures
    c. suppliers who increase their profit margins by raising prices faster than their costs increase
    d. increased government spending in the absence of increased taxes
    e. labor unions, which can force wage increases that are not justified by increases in productivity

4. Which of the following statements is true?
    a. The higher the price level, the higher the purchasing power of money.
    b. Demand-pull inflation can be a result of increased production costs.
    c. High rates of inflation are generally caused by rapid growth of the money supply.
    d. Unexpectedly high inflation redistributes income away from those who make fixed dollar payments toward those who receive fixed dollar payments.
    e. The real interest rate increases as the rate of inflation increases.

5. A lender who does not expect any change in the price level is willing to make a mortgage loan at a 10 percent rate of interest. If that same lender anticipates a future inflation rate of 5 percent, she will charge the borrower
    a. 5 percent interest.
    b. 10 percent interest.
    c. 15 percent interest.
    d. 2 percent interest.
    e. 1/2 percent interest.

PRACTICE QUESTIONS AND PROBLEMS

Section 1: Business Cycles

1. The recurring pattern of real GNP rising and then falling is called a _____ .

2. When real GNP is growing, the economy is in the _____ phase, or boom period, of the business cycle.

3. The _____ marks the end of a contraction and the start of a new business cycle.

4. The _____ marks the end of the expansion phase of a business cycle.

5. Real GNP falls during the contraction, or _____ , phase of the business cycle.

6. The _____ has the responsibility of officially dating recessions in the United States.

7. A _____ is a prolonged period of severe economic contraction.

8. _____ change before real GNP changes.

9. _____ are economic variables that tend to change at the same time real output changes.

10. Variables that do not change their value until after the value of real GNP has changed are called _____.

Section 2: Unemployment

1. The _____ is the percentage of the labor force that is not working.

2. _____ have given up looking for work because they believe that no one will hire them.

3. The employment of workers in tasks that do not fully utilize their productive potential is called _____.

4. _____ unemployment is a product of business-cycle fluctuations.

5. _____ unemployment is a product of regular, recurring changes in the hiring needs of certain industries over the months or seasons of the year.

6. _____ unemployment is a product of short-term movements of workers between jobs, and of first-time job seekers.

7. _____ unemployment is a product of technological change and other changes in the structure of the economy.

8. The level of output produced when nonlabor resources are fully utilized and unemployment is at its natural rate is called _____.

9. The _____ is the unemployment rate that would exist in the absence of cyclical unemployment.

10. Potential GNP minus real GNP equals the _____.

11. The existence of _____ and _____ causes the official unemployment rate in the United States to be understated.

12. The existence of the underground economy causes the official unemployment rate in the United States to be _____.

13. Economists measure the cost of unemployment in terms of _____.

Section 3: Inflation

1. _____ is a sustained rise in the average level of prices.

2. The higher the price level, the _____ the purchasing power of the dollar.

3. The observed rate of interest in the market is called the _____ rate of interest.

4. The nominal interest rate minus the rate of inflation equals the _____ interest rate.

5. Unexpectedly high inflation hurts _____ and benefits _____ because it lowers real interest rates.

6. _____ inflation is the result of increased spending that is not offset by increases in the supply of goods and services.

7. Increases in prices caused by increases in production costs characterize _____ inflation.

8. A very high rate of inflation is called a _____.

THINKING ABOUT AND APPLYING UNEMPLOYMENT AND INFLATION

I. Economic Indicators

A clumsy economist has dropped his basket of the following economic indicators, and now they are all jumbled together. Try to use economic reasoning to sort them out in the table that follows.

Labor cost per unit of output
Money supply
Stock prices
Prime interest rate
Payroll employment
Average workweek
Outstanding commercial loans
Inventories
New plant and equipment orders
Unemployment duration
Materials prices
Unemployment claims
Manufacturing and trade sales
New building permits
Personal income
Consumer credit to personal income ratio
Manufacturers' new orders
Inventories to sales ratio
Delivery time of goods
Industrial production
Outstanding business and commercial credit
New businesses formed

Leading Indicators	Coincident Indicators	Lagging Indicators
_____	_____	_____
_____	_____	_____
_____	_____	_____
_____	_____	_____
_____		_____
_____		_____
_____		
_____		
_____		
_____		
_____		

II. Unemployment Rates and Discouraged Workers

1. The tiny country of Lanastan has a civilian labor force of 40,000, of whom 38,000 are employed. There are _____ unemployed persons in Lanastan, and the unemployment rate is _____ percent.

2. Five hundred of the unemployed people become discouraged and quit looking for a job. Now the official unemployment rate in Lanastan is _____ percent. These discouraged workers have _____ the unemployment rate.

III. Inflation and the Elderly

Thanks to the late congressman Claude Pepper, most of us immediately think of elderly people living on fixed incomes when we think of people who are hurt by unexpected inflation. Social Security payments are now indexed to the CPI, but elderly people still say they are hurt by unexpected inflation: the inflation adjustment does not cover the rising prices of things they must buy. What do elderly people buy that is inadequately represented by the CPI?

_____

_____

_____

_____

IV. Structural Unemployment and Retraining

The "Economically Speaking" section for this chapter describes GE's efforts to retrain its laid-off workers. Many factory workers who had been making good money for years were not able to meet entry-level requirements for other jobs. The job-specific skills they had learned over the years were not easily transferable to other firms.

You do not read about people with college degrees being laid off and undergoing retraining: this problem seems to be largely connected with factory workers. Why? What kind of training or skills do college grads have that factory workers do not have?

_____

_____

_____

_____

ANSWERS

Quick Check Quiz

Section 1: Business Cycles

1. d; 2. a; 3. e; 4. b; 5. c; 6. d
   If you missed any of these questions, you should go back and review pages 182–186 in Chapter 8.

Section 2: Unemployment

1. d; 2. b; 3. a; 4. b; 5. e; 6. c; 7. e; 8. c
   If you missed any of these questions, you should go back and review pages 186–195 in Chapter 8.

Section 3: Inflation

1. a; 2. c; 3. d; 4. c; 5. c
   If you missed any of these questions, you should go back and review pages 195–203 in Chapter 8.

Practice Questions and Problems

Section 1: Business Cycles

1. business cycle
2. expansion
3. trough
4. peak
5. recession
6. NBER (National Bureau of Economic Research)
7. depression
8. Leading indicators
9. Coincident indicators
10. lagging indicators

Section 2: Unemployment

1. unemployment rate
2. Discouraged workers
3. underemployment
4. Cyclical
5. Seasonal
6. Frictional
7. Structural
8. potential GNP
9. natural rate of unemployment
10. GNP gap
11. discouraged workers; underemployment
12. overstated
13. lost output (or the GNP gap)

Section 3: Inflation

1. Inflation
2. lower
3. nominal
4. real
5. creditors; debtors
6. Demand-pull
7. cost-push
8. hyperinflation

Thinking About and Applying Unemployment and Inflation

I. Economic Indicators

Leading Indicators

Money supply
Stock prices
Average workweek
Inventories
New plant and equipment orders
Materials prices
Unemployment claims
New building permits
Manufacturers' new orders
Delivery time of goods
Outstanding business and commercial credit
New businesses formed

Coincident Indicators

Payroll employment
Manufacturing and trade sales
Personal income
Industrial production

Lagging Indicators

Labor cost per unit of output
Prime interest rate
Outstanding commercial loans
Unemployment duration
Consumer credit to personal income ratio
Inventories to sales ratio

II. Unemployment Rates and Discouraged Workers

1. 2,000; 5

   To find the number of unemployed persons, we subtract the number employed from the number in the labor force: $40,000 - 38,000 = 2,000$. The unemployment rate is the number unemployed divided by the labor force: $2,000/40,000 = .05$, or 5 percent.

2. 3.8; understated

   If 500 unemployed people drop out of the labor force, the labor force becomes $40,000 - 500 = 39,500$. We still have 38,000 employed, so the number of "unemployed" people is $39,500 - 38,000 = 1,500$. The official unemployment rate becomes $1,500/39,500 = .0379746$, or about 3.8 percent. Thus the existence of discouraged workers understates the true unemployment rate.

III. Inflation and the Elderly

Elderly people spend a greater proportion of their incomes on health-care costs than the "typical" family represented in the CPI market basket. Since health-care costs have been rising faster than the CPI, increases in Social Security payments linked to the CPI do not keep up with increases in health-care costs.

IV. Structural Unemployment and Retraining

Colleges and universities are mainly interested in teaching transferable skills, skills that can be easily adapted from job to job. If college graduates lose one job, their skills are not so tied to that job or industry that they can't find another job. Factory workers amass considerable job-specific skills. When they lose their jobs, their skills cannot be adapted to new work settings.

CHAPTER 9
Aggregate Expenditures

1. How are consumption and saving related?

Households do three things with their income: spend it, save it, and pay taxes on it. Since households have no choice about paying taxes, economists usually look at after-tax, or disposable, income. **Consumption** and **saving** are the two components of disposable income. So if we know that disposable income is $1,000 and saving is $200, then we know that consumption must be $800.

It is possible to spend more than your disposable income by borrowing or using past saving. If disposable income is again $1,000 and consumption is $1,100, then saving is –$100: you borrowed $100 or used $100 of past saving. Negative saving is called **dissaving.**

Because consumption and saving together equal disposable income, any change (Δ) in disposable income equals the change in consumption plus the change in saving:

$$\Delta C + \Delta S = \Delta Yd$$

If we divide both sides by the change in disposable income, we have

$$\Delta C/\Delta Yd + \Delta S/\Delta Yd = \Delta Yd/\Delta Yd \quad \text{or}$$

$$\text{MPC} + \text{MPS} = 1$$

The change in consumption divided by the change in disposable income is called the **marginal propensity to consume (MPC).** It tells us how much consumption changes when income changes. If the MPC is .80, when disposable income changes by $100, consumption changes by $80. Likewise, the change in saving divided by the change in disposable income is called the **marginal propensity to save (MPS).** It tells us how much saving changes when income changes. If the MPS is .20, when disposable income changes by $100, saving changes by $20. Since the only thing households can do with disposable income is save it or spend it, MPC + MPS = 1.

There is another relationship between consumption and saving. Start with

$$C + S = Yd$$

and divide both sides by disposable income:

$$C/Yd + S/Yd = Yd/Yd \quad \text{or} \quad \text{APC} + \text{APS} = 1$$

Consumption divided by disposable income is the **average propensity to consume (APC).** It tells us the proportion of disposable income that is consumed. Likewise, saving divided by disposable income is the **average propensity to save (APS)** and tells us the proportion of income saved. Since disposable income can only be spent or saved, the two proportions must sum to 1.

2. What are the determinants of consumption?

The determinants of consumption are income, **wealth,** expectations, demographics, and taxation. Consumption is a positive function of income, wealth, positive expectations about the economy, and population. If any of these determinants increase, consumption increases. Consumption is negatively related to negative expectations about the economy and taxes. If either of these factors increases, consumption decreases.

3. What are the determinants of investment?

The determinants of investment are the interest rate, profit expectations, technological change, the cost of capital goods, and the rate at which capacity is utilized. Investment is a positive function of expected profit, technological change that reduces costs, and the rate at which capacity is utilized. If any of these factors increase, investment will increase. Investment is a negative function of interest rates and the cost of capital goods. If either of these determinants increases, investment will decrease. Because these determinants of investment are so variable over the business cycle, investment is the most volatile component of aggregate spending.

4. What are the determinants of government spending?

Government spending is assumed to be autonomous of income. The government authorities set government spending according to political and other considerations at whatever level they choose.

5. What are the determinants of net exports?

Net exports are exports minus imports. The determinants of net exports are foreign and domestic income, tastes, trade restrictions, and exchange rates. Net exports are a positive function of *foreign* income, tastes that favor exports, favorable changes in government restrictions on trade, and depreciation of the domestic currency. Net exports are negatively related to *domestic* income, tastes that favor imports, unfavorable changes in government restrictions on trade, and appreciation of the domestic currency.

6. What is the aggregate expenditures function?

The aggregate expenditures function is the sum of the spending components in the economy: consumption plus investment plus government spending plus net exports.

$$AE = C + I + G + X$$

The aggregate expenditures function has a flatter (smaller) slope than $C + I + G$ because the net exports function has a negative slope.

KEY TERMS

consumption function	marginal propensity to save (MPS)	wealth
saving function		rate of return
dissaving	average propensity to consume (APC)	marginal propensity to import (MPI)
autonomous consumption		
marginal propensity to consume (MPC)	average propensity to save (APS)	

QUICK CHECK QUIZ

Section 1: Consumption and Saving

1. Consumption accounts for _____ percent of total expenditures in the U.S. economy.
   a. 20
   b. 15
   c. 66
   d. −1
   e. 35

2. Which of the following is a stock concept?
   a. GNP
   b. savings
   c. consumption
   d. investment
   e. net exports

3. Which of the following is NOT a determinant of consumption?
   a. disposable income
   b. wealth
   c. expectations
   d. the cost of capital goods
   e. taxation

4. Which of the following is the equation for the marginal propensity to consume?
   a. change in consumption/change in income
   b. consumption/income
   c. change in consumption/change in disposable income
   d. consumption/disposable income
   e. 1 + MPS

5. Which of the following is the equation for the average propensity to save?
   a. change in saving/change in income
   b. saving/income
   c. change in saving/change in disposable income
   d. saving/disposable income
   e. 1 − MPC

Use the table below to answer questions 6 through 11.

Disposable Income	Consumption
$ 0	$1,000
2,000	2,700
4,000	4,400
6,000	6,100
8,000	7,800
10,000	9,500

6. Dissaving occurs at levels of income below
   a. $10,000.
   b. $8,000.
   c. $6,000.
   d. $4,000.
   e. $2,000.

7. Autonomous consumption is
   a. $1,000.
   b. $2,700.
   c. $4,400.
   d. $6,100.
   e. $7,800.

8. When disposable income is $6,000, saving is
   a. $–100.
   b. $100.
   c. $200.
   d. $500.
   e. $1,000.

9. The MPC is
   a. 1.35.
   b. 1.10.
   c. .975.
   d. .95.
   e. .85.

10. The MPS is
    a. .35.
    b. .15.
    c. .105.
    d. .05.
    e. .025.

11. If disposable income is $10,000, the APC is
    a. 1.11.
    b. 1.35.
    c. .975.
    d. .95.
    e. .85.

12. Which of the following will increase consumption?
    a. a decrease in disposable income
    b. an increase in wealth
    c. gloomy expectations about the economy
    d. a decrease in population
    e. an increase in expected profits

13. Which of the following do/does NOT shift the consumption function?
    a. increases in wealth
    b. optimistic expectations about the economy
    c. an increase in disposable income
    d. an increase in taxes
    e. an increase in population

Section 2: Investment

1. Which of the following is NOT a determinant of investment?
   a. the interest rate
   b. profit expectations
   c. disposable income
   d. the cost of capital goods
   e. capacity utilization

2. A firm must borrow $1,000 to buy a bottling machine and must pay 10 percent interest on the funds. The firm expects the machine to yield $1,188 in output. The rate of return on the investment is
   a. 1.188.
   b. 1.08.
   c. 1.088.
   d. .08.
   e. .088.

3. Which of the following will increase investment?
   a. an increase in the rate of capacity utilization
   b. an increase in interest rates
   c. an increase in disposable income
   d. an increase in the cost of capital goods
   e. a decrease in expected profits

4. Which of the following will NOT decrease investment?
   a. an increase in the cost of capital goods
   b. an improvement in technology
   c. an increase in interest rates
   d. unfavorable changes in tax policy
   e. rumors that the government will nationalize firms.

5. Which of the following is NOT a volatile component of investment?
   a. interest rates
   b. expectations
   c. technological change
   d. rate of capacity utilization
   e. All of the above are volatile components of investment spending.

Section 3: Government Spending

1. Government spending accounts for ____ percent of total spending.
   a. 20
   b. 15
   c. 66
   d. –1
   e. 35

2. Which of the following does the text cite as a determinant of government spending?
   a. population
   b. disposable income
   c. interest rates
   d. taxes
   e. The text does not cite any of these as determinants of government policy; it assumes that government authorities set government spending at whatever level they choose.

3. When plotted against disposable income, the government expenditures function has a/an ____ slope.
   a. positive
   b. negative
   c. zero
   d. increasing
   e. decreasing

Section 4: Net Exports

1. Which of the following is NOT a determinant of exports?
   a. foreign income
   b. domestic disposable income
   c. tastes
   d. government trade restrictions
   e. exchange rates

2. Which of the following will NOT cause an increase in exports?
   a. an increase in foreign incomes
   b. domestic currency depreciation
   c. a favorable change in tastes
   d. domestic currency appreciation
   e. a lowering of trade restrictions

3. Which of the following is the equation for the marginal propensity to import?
   a. change in imports/change in income
   b. imports/income
   c. change in imports/change in disposable income
   d. imports/disposable income
   e. 1 – MPS

4. Which of the following will NOT shift the net exports function?
    a. changes in foreign income
    b. changes in tastes
    c. changes in domestic disposable income
    d. changes in exchange rates
    e. changes in government trade restrictions

Section 5: The Aggregate Expenditures Function

1. Which of the following is NOT a component of aggregate expenditures?
    a. consumption
    b. saving
    c. investment
    d. government spending
    e. net exports

2. Which of these functions is NOT drawn parallel to the others?
    a. C
    b. $C + I$
    c. $C + I + G$
    d. $C + I + G + X$
    e. All of the above are parallel lines.

3. Net exports
    a. are autonomous of disposable income.
    b. increase aggregate expenditures at relatively low levels of income.
    c. increase aggregate expenditures at relatively high levels of income.
    d. increase with disposable income.
    e. have the same slope as consumption.

PRACTICE QUESTIONS AND PROBLEMS

Section 1: Consumption and Saving

1. _____ equals consumption plus saving.

2. _____ is "not consuming" and is defined over a unit of time.

    _____ are an amount accumulated at a particular point in time.

3. GNP, consumption, saving, investment, government spending, and net exports are all

    _____ (stock, flow) concepts.

4. The primary determinant of consumption over any given period of time is _____.

5. The _____ is the relationship between disposable income and consumption.

6. The _____ is the relationship between disposable income and saving.

7. _____ occurs when a household spends more than it earns in income, either by

    borrowing or by using savings.

8. Consumption and saving are _____ (positive, negative) functions of disposable income.

9. The level of consumption that does not depend on income is called _____.

10. The relationship between change in consumption and change in disposable income is the _____.

11. The _____ is equal to the change in saving divided by the change in disposable income.

12. MPC + MPS = _____.

13. The MPC is the _____ of the consumption function.

14. The steeper the consumption function, the _____ the MPC.

15. The slope of the saving function is the _____.

16. The _____ the saving function, the larger the MPS.

17. The _____ equals consumption divided by disposable income.

18. The APS equals _____ divided by _____.

19. APC + APS = _____.

20. The APS _____ (rises, falls) as disposable income rises.

21. Fill in the table below and answer the following questions.

Disposable Income	Consumption	Saving	APC	APS
$ 0	$1,000	$_____	_____	_____
1,000	1,800	_____	_____	_____
2,000	2,600	_____	_____	_____
3,000	3,400	_____	_____	_____
4,000	4,200	_____	_____	_____
5,000	5,000	_____	_____	_____
6,000	5,800	_____	_____	_____
7,000	6,600	_____	_____	_____
8,000	7,400	_____	_____	_____
9,000	8,200	_____	_____	_____
10,000	9,000	_____	_____	_____

a. What is the MPC? _____ the MPS? _____

b. Plot the consumption function on the graph below. Show on the graph the level of saving when disposable income is $9,000.

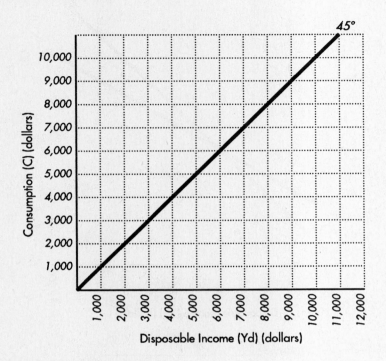

c. Plot the saving function on the graph below.

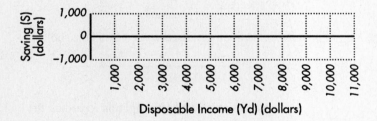

22. Use the graph below to answer the following questions.

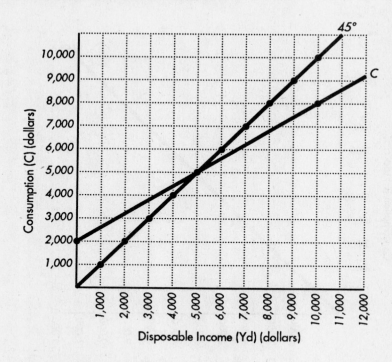

a. What is autonomous consumption? _____

b. What is the MPC? _____

c. What is savings when disposable income equals $10,000? _____

23. Disposable income is _____ income.

24. _____ is the value of all the assets owned by a household.

25. As household wealth increases, consumption _____ (increases, decreases) at every level of income.

26. The _____ is a measure of consumer opinion regarding the outlook for the economy.

27. When consumers expect future income to increase, autonomous consumption _____ (increases, decreases, does not change).

28. Ceteris paribus, economists expect consumption to _____ (rise, fall, not change) as the population increases.

29. Young households have _____ (larger, smaller, the same) MPCs than/as older households.

30. As taxation increases, autonomous consumption _____ (rises, falls, does not change).

31. List the five determinants of consumption.

_____

_____

_____

_____

_____

32. Changes in the nonincome determinants of consumption affect the _____ (slope, intercept) of the consumption function.

Section 2: Investment

1. _____ is business spending on capital goods and inventories and is the most variable component of total spending.

2. The text assumes that investment is _____ of current income.

3. _____ investment combines with consumer, government, and foreign-sector spending to determine national income.

4. The higher the interest rate, the _____ (higher, lower) the rate of investment.

5. _____ is the profit from an investment divided by its cost.

6. As the interest rate falls, the rate of return from an investment _____ (rises, falls).

7. As the cost of capital goods rises, the amount of investment _____ (rises, falls).

8. When capacity utilization is high, investment tends to _____ (rise, fall).

9. List the five determinants of investment.

_____

_____

_____

_____

_____

Section 3: Government Spending

1. Government spending on goods and services is the _____ largest component of aggregate expenditures in the United States.

2. The text assumes that government spending, like investment, is _____ of disposable income.

Section 4: Net Exports

1. _____ equal exports minus imports.

2. When net exports are positive, there is a _____ (deficit, surplus) on the merchandise and services accounts.

3. The text assumes that exports are _____ of current domestic income.

4. List the factors that affect exports.

   _____

   _____

   _____

   _____

5. When the domestic currency appreciates, exports _____ (rise, fall).

6. The greater domestic incomes, the _____ domestic imports.

7. The _____ equals the change in imports divided by the change in income.

8. When the domestic currency depreciates, imports _____ (rise, fall).

9. The higher domestic income, the _____ (higher, lower) net exports.

10. List the four determinants of net exports.

    _____

    _____

    _____

    _____

Section 5: The Aggregate Expenditures Function

1. _____ equals $C + I + G + X$.

2. $Yd =$ _____ , and Y equals _____ or

   _____ .

3. Net exports _____ (increase, decrease) aggregate expenditures at relatively low levels of domestic income and _____ (increase, decrease) aggregate expenditures at relatively high levels of domestic income.

4. The aggregate expenditures function has a _____ (larger, smaller) slope than the consumption function.

5. The components of aggregate expenditures that are NOT autonomous are _____ and _____ .

6. Complete the table below and answer the following questions.

Y	C	I	G	X	AE
$1,000	$1,000	$30	$70	$100	$_____
2,000	1,900	30	70	0	_____
3,000	2,800	30	70	-100	_____
4,000	3,700	30	70	-200	_____
5,000	4,600	30	70	-300	_____
6,000	5,500	30	70	-400	_____

a. What is the MPC? _____

b. What is the MPS? _____

c. What is the MPI? _____

THINKING ABOUT AND APPLYING AGGREGATE EXPENDITURES

I.   Aggregate Expenditures and Its Determinants

Now that you have finished this chapter, you should be able to predict the effect on aggregate expenditures when one of its determinants changes. In the exercise below, decide which of the spending components each event affects, whether it increased or decreased the component, and whether it increased or decreased aggregate expenditures. Remember the determinants of each component of expenditures:

Consumption: disposable income, wealth, expectations, demographics, taxation
Investment: interest rate, profit expectations, technological change, cost of capital goods, rate of capacity
    utilization
Government spending: set by government authorities
Net exports: foreign and domestic income, tastes, trade restrictions, exchange rates

Events

1. Interest rates increase.
2. The dollar depreciates against foreign currencies.
3. The government increases its spending.
4. Foreign incomes rise.
5. The population increases more quickly.
6. Factories note a decline in the rate of capacity utilization.
7. The government imposes a nationwide sales tax on retail goods and services.
8. The cost of capital goods decreases.

	Component	Effect on Component	Effect on Aggregate Expenditures
1.	Investment	Decrease	Decrease
2.			
3.			
4.			
5.			
6.			
7.			
8.			

II. Determinants of Saving

Your text emphasizes that the determinants of saving are the same as the determinants of consumption, since saving is "not consuming." The "Economically Speaking" article in your text cites reasons why Americans don't save. Translate its wording into the determinants of consumption (wealth, expectations, demographics, taxation). Here are some examples for you to try:

1. President Bush is pushing a proposal to allow families to put money into a savings plan tax free.

   _____

2. Tax laws generally benefit borrowing more than saving. _____

3. The spread of pension plans, Social Security benefits, and other items has reduced the need felt by many Americans to save. (Why?) _____

4. Edward Yardeni says that the aging population will cause an increase in saving.

   _____

ANSWERS

Quick Check Quiz

Section 1: Consumption and Saving

1. c; 2. b; 3. d; 4. c; 5. d; 6. b; 7. a; 8. a; 9. e; 10. b; 11. d; 12. b; 13. c (An increase in disposable income would be reflected in a movement along the consumption function, not a shift in the curve.)

If you missed any of these questions, you should go back and review pages 210–221 in Chapter 9.

Section 2: Investment

1. c; 2. d (Rate of return = profit/cost. The cost is $1,000 + $100 in interest, so the rate of return is $88/$1,100 = .08.); 3. a; 4. b; 5. e

If you missed any of these questions, you should go back and review pages 221–227 in Chapter 9.

Section 3: Government Spending

1. a; 2. e; 3. c

If you missed any of these questions, you should go back and review page 228 in Chapter 9.

Section 4: Net Exports

1. b; 2. d; 3. c; 4. c (A change in domestic disposable income would be represented by a movement along the curve, not a shift in the curve.)

If you missed any of these questions, you should go back and review pages 228–233 in Chapter 9.

Section 5: The Aggregate Expenditures Function

1. b; 2. d; 3. b

If you missed any of these questions, you should go back and review pages 233–235 in Chapter 9.

Practice Questions and Problems

Section 1: Consumption and Saving

1. Disposable income
2. Saving; Savings
3. flow
4. disposable income
5. consumption function
6. saving function
7. Dissaving
8. positive
9. autonomous consumption
10. marginal propensity to consume (MPC)
11. marginal propensity to save (MPS)
12. 1
13. slope
14. larger

15. marginal propensity to save (MPS)
16. steeper
17. average propensity to consume (APC)
18. saving; disposable income
19. 1
20. rises
21. Note: The APC + APS will not always equal 1 due to rounding.

Disposable Income	Consumption	Saving	APC	APS
$ 0	$1,000	$–1,000	—	—
1,000	1,800	–800	1.8	–.8
2,000	2,600	–600	1.3	–.3
3,000	3,400	–400	1.13	–.13
4,000	4,200	–200	1.05	–.05
5,000	5,000	0	1.00	0
6,000	5,800	200	.97	.03
7,000	6,600	400	.94	.06
8,000	7,400	600	.93	.07
9,000	8,200	800	.91	.09
$10,000	9,000	1,000	.90	.10

a. MPC = change in consumption/change in disposable income
    = $800/$1,000 = .8
  MPS = change in saving/change in disposable income
    = $200/$1,000 = .2 (or MPS = 1 – MPC = 1 – .8 = .2)

b.

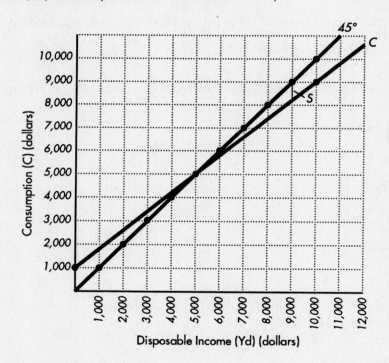

c.

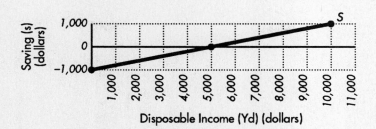

22. a. $2,000
    b. 3/5, or .6
    c. $2,000
23. after-tax
24. Wealth
25. increases
26. consumer confidence index
27. increases
28. rise
29. larger
30. falls
31. disposable income
    wealth
    expectations
    demographics
    taxation
32. intercept

Section 2: Investment

1. Investment
2. autonomous (independent)
3. Planned
4. lower
5. Rate of return
6. rises
7. falls
8. rise
9. the interest rate
   profit expectations
   technological change
   the cost of capital goods
   the rate of capacity utilization

Section 3: Government Spending

1. second
2. autonomous (independent)

Section 4: Net Exports

1. Net exports
2. surplus
3. autonomous (independent)
4. foreign incomes
   tastes
   government trade restrictions
   exchange rates
5. fall
6. greater
7. marginal propensity to import (MPI)
8. fall
9. lower
10. foreign and domestic income
    tastes
    government trade restrictions
    exchange rates

Section 5: The Aggregate Expenditures Function

1. Aggregate expenditures (AE)
2. disposable income; national income; net national product
3. increase; decrease
4. smaller
5. consumption; net exports

6.

Y	C	I	G	X	AE
$1,000	$1,000	$30	$70	$ 100	$1,200
2,000	1,900	30	70	0	2,000
3,000	2,800	30	70	−100	2,800
4,000	3,700	30	70	−200	3,600
5,000	4,600	30	70	−300	4,400
6,000	5,500	30	70	−400	5,200

   a. MPC = change in consumption/change in disposable income
        = $900/$1,000 = .9

   b. MPS = 1 − MPC = 1 − .9 = .1

   c. MPI = change in imports/change in income
        = $100/$1,000 = −.1

Thinking About and Applying Aggregate Expenditures

I. Aggregate Expenditures and Its Determinants

Component	Effect on Component	Effect on Aggregate Expenditures
1. Investment	Decrease	Decrease
2. Net exports	Increase	Increase
3. Government spending	Increase	Increase
4. Net exports	Increase	Increase
5. Consumption	Increase	Increase
6. Investment	Decrease	Decrease
7. Consumption	Decrease	Decrease
8. Investment	Increase	Increase

II. Determinants of Saving

1. taxation
2. taxation
3. expectations about future incomes
4. demographics

APPENDIX TO CHAPTER 9
An Algebraic Model of Aggregate Expenditures

SUMMARY

Each of the components of aggregate expenditures can be represented by an equation:

$$\text{Consumption:} \quad C = C^a + c\, Yd$$

where C^a is autonomous consumption and c is the MPC.

$$\text{Net exports:} \quad EX^a - (IM^a + im\, Yd)$$

where EX^a is autonomous exports, IM^a is autonomous imports, and im is the MPI.

Since investment and government spending are autonomous of income, they are represented by constants: I^a and G^a.

Since $AE = C + I + G + X$, then

$$AE = (C^a + c\, Yd) + I^a + G^a + (EX^a - IM^a - im\, Yd)$$

Gathering like terms, we have

$$AE = C^a + I^a + G^a + EX^a - IM^a + (c - im)Yd$$

PRACTICE QUESTIONS AND PROBLEMS

1. Consider the consumption function $C = \$45 + .8Yd$. Autonomous consumption is _____ and the MPC is _____ .
   a. $45; .8
   b. $30; .9
   c. $.8; 45
   d. $45, .2
   e. None of the above are correct.

2. Consider the consumption function $C = \$500 + .75Yd$. If disposable income equals $24,000, consumption equals _____ and saving equals _____ .
   a. $18,000; $500
   b. $18,000; $6,000
   c. $18,500; $6,000
   d. $18,500; $5,500
   e. $31,333; $7,333

3. Consider the net exports function $15 - .15Yd$. What is the marginal propensity to import?
   a. 15
   b. −15
   c. .15
   d. −.15
   e. 0

4. Consider the following:
   $C = 50 + .90Y$
   $I = 40$
   $G = 60$
   $X = 50 - .10Y$

   Construct the equation for aggregate expenditures.

   _____

   _____

   _____

   _____

   Plot the consumption and aggregate expenditures functions on the graph below. Note that the slope of aggregate expenditures is flatter than the slope of the consumption function.

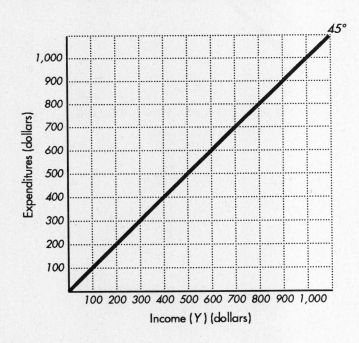

ANSWERS

1. a
2. d
3. c
4. $AE = C + I + G + X$
   $= (\$50 + .90Y) + 40 + 60 + (\$50 - .10Y)$
   $= \$200 + .80Y$

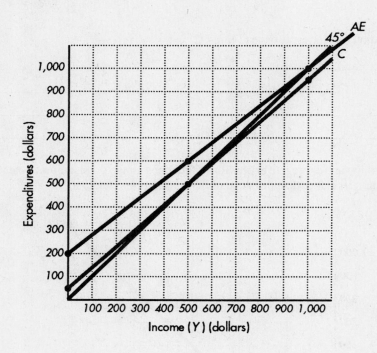

CHAPTER 10
Income and Expenditures:
Foundations of Aggregate Demand

1. How do aggregate expenditures affect income?

   Saying that aggregate expenditures exceed income is the same as saying that planned expenditures exceed current output. If people are planning to buy more output than is currently being produced, the goods must come from somewhere. Producers replace their stocks from inventories, and inventories fall. Since producers like to see a certain level of inventory, when inventories fall, producers increase production. Increased production leads to increased income.

   If aggregate expenditures are less than income, it means that people are planning to buy fewer goods and services than are currently being produced. Since not all goods and services will be sold, inventories will pile up. When producers see inventories building up, they decrease production, and incomes fall.

2. What does equilibrium mean in macroeconomics?

   When aggregate expenditures are equal to income, people are planning to buy all that is currently being produced. Inventories stay at the level at which producers like to see them, so there is no need to increase or decrease production. Equilibrium is reached.

   Another way to determine macroeconomic equilibrium is to find where *leakages* from the income stream equal *injections* into the income stream. If injections are greater than leakages, aggregate expenditures are greater than income. Inventories will fall, production will increase, and the increase in production leads to higher national income. If leakages are greater than injections, people are not planning to buy all the output that is produced. Inventories build up, production decreases, and national income falls.

3. What are the leakages from and injections to spending?

   Leakages reduce autonomous expenditures. *Saving* is a leakage from the income stream. The more households save, the less they spend. Less household spending means less consumption, and consumption is one of the components of aggregate demand. *Taxes* transfer income away from households, forcing them to consume less, and are another leakage from the income stream. *Imports* reduce spending on domestic goods and services, and constitute the third leakage from the income stream.

   Injections into the income stream parallel the leakages. The saving of households is used by businesses for investment, which increases aggregate expenditures. The taxes collected by the government finance government spending, another component of aggregate expenditures. Besides U.S. spending on foreign goods, there is also foreign spending on U.S. goods. Exports also increase aggregate expenditures.

4. Why does equilibrium income change by a multiple of a change in autonomous expenditures?

The basic reason is that the change in expenditures becomes income for someone, who spends part of it and saves part of it. The part that the person spends becomes income to someone else, who saves part and spends part, and so on. To see how this works, let's assume that businesses decide to increase investment by $50 this year. Assume that the MPC is .75 and that this is a closed economy: exports and imports are both equal to zero. During the first round, the increase in investment is income to someone, so income increases by $50. The initial increase in income of $50 induces an increase in consumption of $37.50 (.75 × $50) and an increase in saving of $12.50 (.25 × $50). The $37.50 spent on domestic goods and services becomes income to someone else, who spends $28.13 (.75 × $37.50) and saves $9.37 (.25 × $37.50). The spiral continues, and the increases to income get smaller and smaller. In this example, all the increases in income sum to $200: four times the original increase in autonomous spending.

Round	Increase in National Income	Increase in Consumption	Increase in Saving
1—Increase in *I* of $50	$50	$37.5 = .75($50)	$12.5
2	$37.5	$28.125 = .75($37.5)	$9.375
3	$28.125	$21.09375	$7.03125
4	$21.09375	$15.820312	$5.273438
.	.	.	.
.	.	.	.
.	.	.	.
Total	$200	$150	$50

5. What is the multiplier?

The **multiplier** measures the change in income produced by a change in autonomous expenditures, and is equal to 1/(MPS + MPI).

6. What is the relationship between the GNP gap and the recessionary gap?

The GNP gap is the difference between equilibrium GNP and potential GNP. It tells us the change in income needed to get to potential GNP. The **recessionary gap** tells us the change in autonomous expenditures that is necessary to close the GNP gap.

7. How does international trade affect the size of the multiplier?

The simple multiplier understates the true multiplier because it does not take into account the foreign repercussions of domestic spending. If Americans spend money on foreign goods, foreign incomes increase. The increase in foreign incomes increases U.S. exports, but the change in exports is not picked up by the simple multiplier.

KEY TERMS

multiplier
recessionary gap

QUICK CHECK QUIZ

Section 1: Equilibrium Income and Expenditures

1. Actual expenditures always equal
    a. planned income.
    b. planned output.
    c. consumption.
    d. income and output.
    e. planned expenditures.

2. When aggregate expenditures exceed national income, inventories (rise, fall), production (increases, decreases), and national income (increases, decreases).
    a. rise; increases; increases
    b. rise; increases; decreases
    c. rise; decreases; increases
    d. fall; increases; increases
    e. fall; increases; decreases

3. The equilibrium level of income is that point at which
    a. aggregate expenditures equal national income.
    b. national income equals output.
    c. unplanned spending equals aggregate expenditures.
    d. the aggregate expenditures curve lies above the 45-degree line.
    e. the aggregate expenditures curve lies below the 45-degree line.

4. Which of the following are NOT leakages from the income stream?
    a. saving
    b. investment
    c. taxes
    d. imports
    e. saving and taxes

5. For equilibrium to occur,
    a. investment must equal saving.
    b. government spending must equal taxes.
    c. exports must equal imports.
    d. leakages must equal injections.
    e. all of the above must occur.

6. When leakages exceed injections, planned spending is (less than, greater than) current income, so production and national income (rise, fall).
    a. less than; rise
    b. less than; fall
    c. greater than; rise
    d. greater than; fall
    e. There is no relationship between planned spending and the equality of leakages and injections.

Section 2: Changes in Equilibrium Income and Expenditures

1. Assume that the MPC is .85 and the MPI is .10. What is the multiplier?
   a. 1.1764705
   b. 10
   c. 1.0526315
   d. 1.3333333
   e. 4.0

2. Suppose the MPC = .9 and the MPI = .15. If government spending decreased by $25, national income would _____ by _____ .
   a. increase; $100
   b. decrease; $100
   c. increase; $25
   d. decrease; $25
   e. decrease; $23.81

3. The equation for the recessionary gap is
   a. potential GNP + real GNP.
   b. real GNP – actual GNP.
   c. GNP gap/multiplier.
   d. multiplier/GNP gap.
   e. potential GNP/multiplier.

4. Suppose the potential GNP is $400 and the economy is at equilibrium at $350. The MPC = .8 and the MPI = .05. The GNP gap is $_____ , the multiplier is _____ , and the recessionary gap is $_____ .
   a. 50; 4; 12.50
   b. 12.50; 4; 50
   c. 50; 1.18; 42.50
   d. 42.58; 1.18; 50
   e. 50; .7692307; 65

5. Which of the following statements is true?
   a. The simple multiplier understates the actual multiplier in a closed economy.
   b. The simple multiplier overstates the actual multiplier in a closed economy.
   c. The simple multiplier understates the true multiplier because it does not take into account the foreign repercussions of domestic spending.
   d. The simple multiplier overstates the true multiplier because it does not take into account the foreign repercussions of domestic spending.
   e. The multiplier effect is lower with foreign repercussions than without.

6. The U.S. spending multiplier for Germany is .2. If U.S. investment decreases by $40, German equivalent national income will _____ by _____ .
   a. increase; $40
   b. decrease; $40
   c. increase; $8
   d. decrease; $8
   e. decrease; $200

Section 3: The Keynesian Model Reviewed

1. A drawback of the Keynesian model is that it
   a. assumes that shortages of goods and services will be met by rising prices.
   b. assumes that surpluses of goods and services will be met by rising prices.
   c. assumes that shortages of goods and services will be met by rising prices and increased production.
   d. assumes that shortages of goods and services will be met by rising prices and decreased production.
   e. is a fixed-price model.

PRACTICE QUESTIONS AND PROBLEMS

Section 1: Equilibrium Income and Expenditures

1. In macroeconomics, _____ is the level of income and expenditures that the economy tends to move toward and remain at until autonomous spending changes.

2. The aggregate expenditures function represents _____ expenditures at different levels of income.

3. _____ expenditures always equal income and output because they reflect changes in inventories.

4. When planned spending on goods and services _____ the current value of output, the production of goods and services and national income increase.

5. When aggregate expenditures are less than income, inventories _____ (become depleted, accumulate), production _____ (increases, decreases), and income _____ (rises, falls).

6. The equilibrium level of income is at the point where _____ equal _____.

7. Leakages _____ autonomous aggregate expenditures.

8. The three types of leakages from the domestic income stream are _____, _____, and _____.

9. The three types of injections of spending into the income stream are _____, _____, and _____.

10. For equilibrium to occur, total leakages must equal total _____.

11. When leakages exceed injections, national income _____ (rises, falls).

Section 2: Changes in Equilibrium Income and Expenditures

1. Consumption changes by the _____ multiplied by the change in income.

2. Imports change by the marginal propensity to import multiplied by the _____.

3. The percentage of a change in income that is spent domestically is equal to _____ (use abbreviations).

4. The multiplier is equal to _____ (use abbreviations).

5. The greater the leakages, the _____ (greater, smaller) the multiplier.

6. An economy that does not trade with the rest of the world is called a _____ economy.

7. According to the Keynesian view, equilibrium _____ (does, does not) necessarily occur at potential GNP.

8. The _____ is how much GNP needs to change to yield equilibrium at potential GNP. It is the _____ (horizontal, vertical) distance between equilibrium income and potential income.

9. The _____ is the change in spending necessary for equilibrium income to rise to potential GNP. It is the _____ (horizontal, vertical) distance between the aggregate expenditures curve and the 45-degree line at the potential income level.

10. The simple multiplier (1/[MPS + MPI]) _____ (overstates, understates) the true multiplier effects of increases in autonomous spending because of the foreign repercussions of domestic spending.

11. U.S. spending increases have a _____ (larger, smaller) effect on foreign income than foreign spending increases have on U.S. income.

12. The _____ measures the change in income produced by a change in autonomous spending.

Section 3: The Keynesian Model Reviewed

1. A drawback of the Keynesian model is that it assumes that the supply of goods and services in the economy always adjusts to aggregate expenditures. It is a _____ model.

2. Shortages of goods and services may be met by increased production or by _____ .

THINKING ABOUT AND APPLYING INCOME AND EXPENDITURES: FOUNDATIONS OF AGGREGATE DEMAND

I. Aggregate Expenditures = National Income Approach

1. Complete the table below and answer the following questions.

Y	C	I	G	E	AE	Unplanned Change in Inventories	Change in National Income
$ 0	$ 40	$20	$30	$30	$_____	$_____	_____
160	136	20	30	14	_____	_____	_____
180	148	20	30	12	_____	_____	_____
200	160	20	30	10	_____	_____	_____
220	172	20	30	8	_____	_____	_____
240	184	20	30	6	_____	_____	_____
260	196	20	30	4	_____	_____	_____
280	208	20	30	2	_____	_____	_____
300	220	20	30	0	_____	_____	_____
320	232	20	30	–2	_____	_____	_____

a. The equilibrium level of income is _____.

b. The MPC is _____, and the MPS is _____.

c. The MPI is _____.

d. The multiplier is _____.

e. If the potential GNP is $300, the GNP gap is _____, and the recessionary gap

is _____.

f.   Plot aggregate expenditures on the graph below. Show the GNP gap and the recessionary gap.

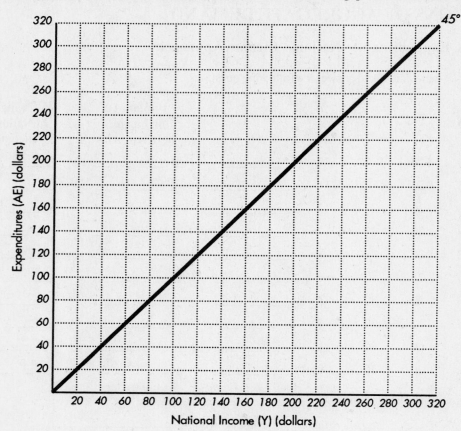

2. Use the graph below to answer the following questions. Assume that this is a closed economy and that government spending is $15 and investment is $5. Plot aggregate expenditures.

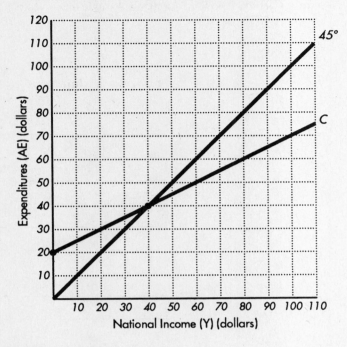

a. The equilibrium level of income is _____.

b. The MPC is _____, and the MPS is _____.

c. The multiplier is _____.

d. If the potential GNP is $100, the GNP gap is _____, and the recessionary gap

 is _____.

II. Leakages = Injections Approach

1. Complete the table below and answer the following questions. Assume that investment equals $10, government spending is $20, and exports are $20.

Y	S	T	IM	Leakages	Injections	Change in National Income
$ 0	$–20	$0	$15	$_____	$_____	_____
100	–5	0	25	_____	_____	_____
120	–2	0	27	_____	_____	_____
140	1	0	29	_____	_____	_____
160	4	0	31	_____	_____	_____
180	7	0	33	_____	_____	_____
200	10	0	35	_____	_____	_____
220	13	0	37	_____	_____	_____
240	16	0	39	_____	_____	_____
260	19	0	41	_____	_____	_____

a. The equilibrium level of income is _____.

b. The MPS is _____, and the MPC is _____.

c. The MPI is _____.

d. The multiplier is _____.

e. If the potential GNP is $300, the GNP gap is _____, and the recessionary gap

is _____.

2. Use the graph below to answer the following questions. Assume a closed economy with investment = $10, government spending = $20, and taxes = 0. Plot leakages and injections.

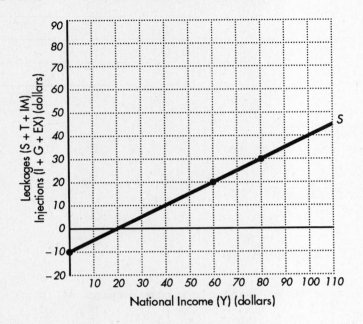

a. What is the MPS? _____ the MPC? _____

b. What is the multiplier? _____

c. What is the equilibrium level of income? _____

III. Menem's Economic Policies

The "Economically Speaking" article in the text describes Carlos Saúl Menem's attempts to revive the Argentine economy by getting rid of government budget deficits. The text analyzed the effects of the reduction in government spending. Now let's look at the government's seizure of bank deposits. These deposits were converted into forced ten-year loans to the government at low interest rates. In effect, the government took income away from the depositors, imposing a "quasi-tax." Use the graph below to predict the effect of the government's actions on national income. Label your new aggregate expenditures curve AE_2.

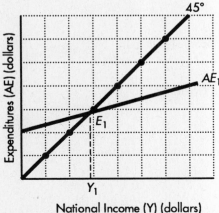

What happened to equilibrium income?

_____

_____

_____

_____

ANSWERS

Quick Check Quiz

Section 1: Equilibrium Income and Expenditures

1. d; 2. d; 3. a; 4. b; 5. d; 6. b
   If you missed any of these questions, you should go back and review pages 244–250 in Chapter 10.

Section 2: Changes in Equilibrium Income and Expenditures

1. e; 2. b; 3. c; 4. a; 5. c; 6. d
   If you missed any of these questions, you should go back and review pages 250–261 in Chapter 10.

Section 3: The Keynesian Model Reviewed

1. e
   If you missed this question, you should go back and review page 262 in Chapter 10.

Practice Questions and Problems

Section 1: Equilibrium Income and Expenditures

1. equilibrium
2. planned
3. Actual
4. exceeds
5. accumulate; decreases; falls
6. aggregate expenditures; national income (or output)
7. reduce
8. saving; taxes; imports
9. investment; government spending; exports
10. injections
11. falls

Section 2: Changes in Equilibrium Income and Expenditures

1. marginal propensity to consume (MPC)
2. change in income

3. MPC – MPI
4. 1/(MPS + MPI)
5. smaller
6. closed
7. does not
8. GNP gap; horizontal
9. recessionary gap; vertical
10. understates
11. larger
12. multiplier

Section 3: The Keynesian Model Reviewed

1. fixed-price
2. rising prices

Thinking About and Applying Income and Expenditures: Foundations of Aggregate Demand

I. Aggregate Expenditures = National Income Approach

1.

Y	C	I	G	E	AE	Unplanned Change in Inventories	Change in National Income
$ 0	$ 40	$20	$30	$30	$120	$–120	Increase
160	136	20	30	14	200	–40	Increase
180	148	20	30	12	210	–30	Increase
200	160	20	30	10	220	–20	Increase
220	172	20	30	8	230	–10	Increase
240	184	20	30	6	240	0	No change
260	196	20	30	4	250	10	Decrease
280	208	20	30	2	260	20	Decrease
300	220	20	30	0	270	30	Decrease
320	232	20	30	–2	280	40	Decrease

a. $240
b. MPC = change in consumption/change in income
$= \$12/\$20 = .6$
MPS = 1 – MPC = 1 – .6 = .4
c. MPI = change in imports/change in income = 2/20 = .1
(Since exports are autonomous, the change in net exports equals the change in imports.)
d. Multiplier = 1 /(MPS + MPI) = 1/(.4 + .1) = 1/.5 = 2
e. GNP gap = potential GNP – national income
$= \$300 – \$240 = \$60$
Recessionary gap = GNP gap/multiplier = $60/2 = $30

f.

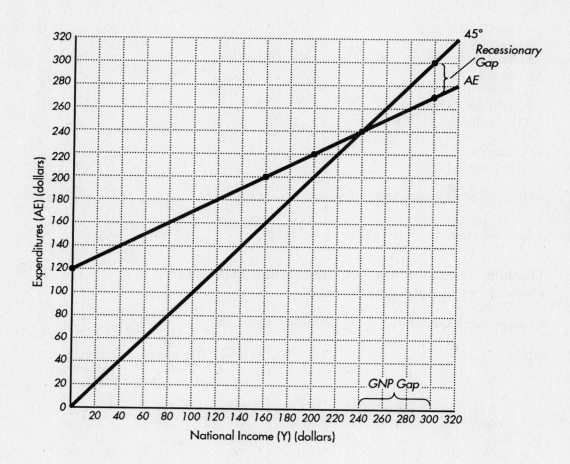

2.

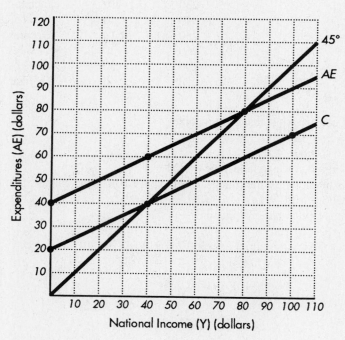

a. $80
b. .5; .5
c. 2
d. $20; $10

II. Leakages = Injections Approach

1.

Y	S	T	IM	Leakages	Injections	Change in National Income
$ 0	$–20	$0	$15	$–5	$50	Increase
100	–5	0	25	20	50	Increase
120	–2	0	27	25	50	Increase
140	1	0	29	30	50	Increase
160	4	0	31	35	50	Increase
180	7	0	33	40	50	Increase
200	10	0	35	45	50	Increase
220	13	0	37	50	50	No change
240	16	0	39	55	50	Decrease
260	19	0	41	60	50	Decrease

a. $220
b. MPS = change in saving/change in income
    = $15/$100 = .15
   MPC = 1 – MPS = 1 – .15 = .85
c. MPI = change in imports/change in income = $10/$100 = .1
d. Multiplier = 1/(MPS + MPI) = 1/(.15 + .1) = 1/.25 = 4
e. GNP gap = potential GNP – national income
            = $300 – $220 = $80
   Recessionary gap = GNP gap/multiplier = $80/4 = $20

2.

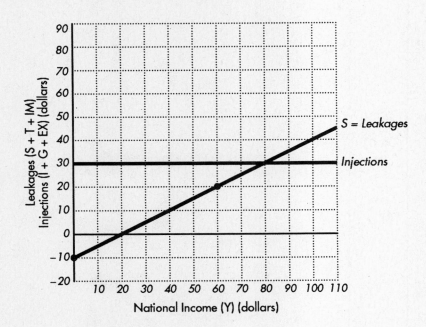

a. 1/2; 1/2
b. 2
c. $80

III. Menem's Economic Policies

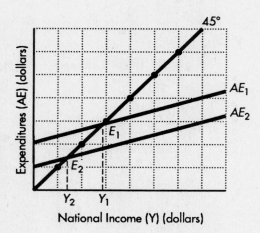

The forced loans had an effect similar to the effect of higher taxes: they reduced consumption. The reduction in autonomous consumption reduced aggregate expenditures, and equilibrium income declined.

APPENDIX TO CHAPTER 10
An Algebraic Model of Income and Expenditures Equilibrium

SUMMARY

In Chapter 9, we learned that each of the components of aggregate expenditures can be represented by an equation. In that chapter we combined the equations to get an equation for aggregate expenditures:

$$AE = C^a + I^a + G^a + EX^a - IM^a + (c - im)Yd$$

Since we know that aggregate expenditures must be equal to national income at macroeconomic equilibrium, we find equilibrium by setting

$$Y = AE$$

$$Y = C^a + I^a + G^a + EX^a - IM^a + (c - im)Yd$$

$$Y = 1/(1 - [c - im]) \times (C^a + I^a + G^a + EX^a - IM^a)$$

The first term on the right-hand side is the multiplier; the second term is autonomous expenditures.

PRACTICE QUESTIONS AND PROBLEMS

1. Given:

$$C = \$50 + .90Y$$
$$I = \$40$$
$$G = \$60$$
$$X = \$50 - .10Y$$

a. The equilibrium level of income is _____ .
b. The multiplier is _____ .
c. If potential GNP is $1,250, the GNP gap is _____ , and the recessionary gap is _____ .

2. Given:

$$C = \$100 + .8Y$$
$$I = \$50$$
$$G = \$60$$
$$X = \$70 - .15Y$$

a. The equilibrium level of income is _____ .
b. The multiplier is _____ .
c. If potential GNP is $1,000, the GNP gap is _____ , and the recessionary gap is _____ .

ANSWERS

1. a. $Y = C + I + G + X$
         $Y = (\$50 + .90Y) + \$40 + \$60 + (\$50 - .10Y)$
         $Y = \$200 + .80Y$
      $.20Y = \$200$
         $Y = \$1,000$
    b. Multiplier $= 1/(MPS + MPI) = 1/(.1 + .1) = 1/.2 = 5$
    c. GNP gap = potential GNP − actual GNP = $\$1,250 - \$1,000$
                $= \$250$
       Recessionary gap = GNP gap/multiplier = $\$250/5 = \$50$

2. a. $Y = C + I + G + X$
         $Y = (\$100 + .8Y) + \$50 + \$60 + (\$70 - .15Y)$
         $Y = \$280 + .65Y$
      $.35Y = \$280$
         $Y = \$800$
    b. Multiplier $= 1/(MPS + MPI)$
                $= 1/(.2 + .15) = 1/.35 = 2.8571428$
    c. GNP gap = potential GNP − actual GNP
                $= \$1,000 - \$800 = \$200$
       Recessionary gap = GNP gap/multiplier
                        $= \$200/2.8571428$
                        $= \$70$

CHAPTER 11
Macroeconomic Equilibrium: Aggregate Demand and Supply

1. Why does the aggregate expenditures curve shift with changes in the price level?

    There are three reasons why the aggregate expenditures curve shifts with changes in price: the **wealth effect,** the **interest rate effect,** and the **international trade effect.**

    When prices increase, the value of money falls. People and businesses feel less wealthy, so consumption and investment decrease. Since consumption and investment are components of total spending, the aggregate expenditures curve shifts.

    When the price level rises, people and businesses need more money for transactions. To acquire money, they sell bonds, which drives the prices of bonds down. Interest rates therefore rise, which causes investment to fall. Since investment is a component of total spending, this interest rate effect causes aggregate expenditures to shift.

    The international trade effect has to do with the effect of domestic prices on exports and imports. If domestic prices rise, domestic goods become expensive for foreigners. Exports drop, and since net exports are a component of total spending, the aggregate expenditures curve shifts.

2. What is the aggregate demand curve?

    The **aggregate demand curve** shows the equilibrium level of income at different price levels. It is derived from the aggregate expenditures curve. Its downward slope is a result of the wealth effect, the interest rate effect, and the international trade effect.

3. What causes the aggregate demand curve to shift?

    The aggregate demand curve will shift if expectations, foreign incomes, foreign prices, or government policy changes.

4. What is the aggregate supply curve?

    The **aggregate supply curve** shows the quantity of national output (or income) produced at different price levels. It has an upward slope because higher prices, ceteris paribus, mean higher profits, which induce producers to offer more output for sale.

5. What causes the aggregate supply curve to shift?

    The aggregate supply curve shifts if resource prices, technology, or expectations change.

6. Why does the short-run aggregate supply curve become steeper as national income increases?

As the level of national income increases, more and more sectors of the economy approach capacity. In order to lure resources from other uses, firms must offer higher and higher resource payments. Prices must rise higher and higher to induce increases in output. Finally, no more output can be produced and existing output must be "rationed" to those who are willing to pay the highest prices.

7. Why is the long-run aggregate supply curve vertical?

The **long-run aggregate supply curve** is vertical because in the long run there is no relationship between changes in the price level and changes in output. The economy has made all of its adjustments, and no further output can be produced with existing resources and technology. In particular, higher prices cannot induce more output.

8. What determines the equilibrium price level and national income?

The equilibrium price level and national income are determined by the intersection of aggregate demand and aggregate supply.

KEY TERMS

wealth effect
interest rate effect
international trade effect

aggregate demand curve
aggregate supply curve
Keynesian region

long-run aggregate supply curve
(LRAS)

QUICK CHECK QUIZ

Section 1: Aggregate Demand

1. Which of the following is a reason for the aggregate expenditures curve to shift with changes in the level of prices?
   a. the substitution effect
   b. the income effect
   c. the interest rate effect
   d. the expectations effect
   e. the foreign price level effect

2. When prices increase, people and businesses need _____ money. They _____ bonds, causing interest rates to _____ and aggregate expenditures to _____ .
   a. more; buy; fall; rise
   b. more; sell; fall; rise
   c. more; buy; rise; fall
   d. more; sell; rise; fall
   e. less; buy; fall; rise

3. When the price level falls, domestic goods become _____ for foreigners. Net exports _____ , and aggregate expenditures _____ . This is called the _____ effect.
   a. cheaper; rise; rise; international trade
   b. cheaper; fall; fall; international trade
   c. cheaper; rise; fall; international trade
   d. more expensive; fall; fall; international trade
   e. cheaper; rise; rise; wealth effect

4. When the price level falls, the value of household and business assets _____ . Households and firms spend _____ , and aggregate expenditures _____ . This is called the _____ effect.
   a. increases; more; rise; income
   b. increases; more; rise; wealth
   c. decreases; less; fall; income
   d. decreases; less; fall; wealth
   e. decreases; more; rise; wealth

5. A higher price level _____ autonomous consumption, autonomous investment, and net exports, causing aggregate expenditures to _____ . The aggregate expenditures curve would shift from AE_1 to _____ on the graph below.

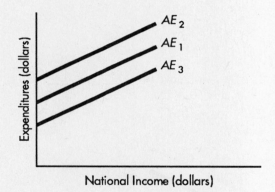

   a. increases; rise; AE_2
   b. increases; rise; AE_3
   c. increases; fall; AE_3
   d. decreases; fall, AE_2
   e. decreases; fall; AE_3

6. Which of the following do/does NOT cause aggregate demand to have a negative slope?
   a. wealth effect
   b. substitution effect
   c. income and substitution effects
   d. international trade effect
   e. interest rate effect

7. Which of the following do NOT cause aggregate demand to shift?
   a. changes in expectations
   b. changes in the price level
   c. changes in foreign incomes
   d. changes in foreign prices
   e. changes in government policy

Section 2: Aggregate Supply

1. The aggregate supply curve illustrates a _____ relationship between the quantity of national output and different price levels. This relationship is explained by the effect of _____ .
   a. negative; changing prices on profits
   b. positive; changing prices on profits
   c. negative; relative price changes
   d. positive; negative price changes
   e. positive; changes in interest rates

2. Which of the following will cause aggregate supply to shift?
   a. changes in the domestic price level
   b. changes in national income
   c. changes in foreign incomes
   d. changes in resource prices
   e. changes in national output

3. If a change in technology reduces costs, we move from _____ to _____ on the graph below.

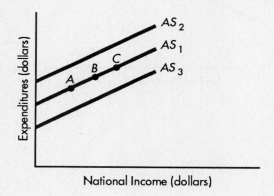

   a. point A; point B
   b. point B; point C
   c. point A; point C
   d. AS_1; AS_2
   e. AS_1; AS_3

4. The short-run aggregate supply curve reflects excess capacity in
   a. the Keynesian region.
   b. both the Keynesian region and the intermediate range.
   c. the Keynesian region, the intermediate range, and the vertical region.
   d. the intermediate region.
   e. the vertical region.

5. The long-run aggregate supply curve is
   a. upward sloping because of the effect of higher prices on profits.
   b. horizontal, reflecting excess capacity in all parts of the economy.
   c. upward sloping, reflecting excess capacity in some parts of the economy.
   d. horizontal because there is no relationship between the price level and national income in the long run.
   e. vertical because there is no relationship between the price level and national income in the long run.

6. Which of the following statements is false?
   a. The long-run aggregate supply curve can shift to the right if new technologies are developed.
   b. The long-run aggregate supply curve can shift to the left if the quality of the factors of production decreases.
   c. The long-run aggregate supply curve is fixed at potential output and cannot shift.
   d. In the Keynesian region of the short-run aggregate supply curve, the price level does not change.
   e. The intermediate range of the short-run aggregate supply curve has a positive slope.

Section 3: Aggregate Demand and Supply Equilibrium

1. If aggregate demand increases and price and income both increase,
   a. the economy must be in the Keynesian region of the short-run aggregate supply curve.
   b. the economy must be in the intermediate region of the short-run aggregate supply curve.
   c. the economy must be in the vertical region of the short-run aggregate supply curve.
   d. the economy must be in either the Keynesian region or the intermediate region of the short-run aggregate supply curve.
   e. the economy must be in either the vertical region or the intermediate region of the short-run aggregate supply curve.

2. If aggregate demand decreases and income decreases but price does not change,
   a. the economy must be in the Keynesian region of the short-run aggregate supply curve.
   b. the economy must be in the intermediate region of the short-run aggregate supply curve.
   c. the economy must be in the vertical region of the short-run aggregate supply curve.
   d. the economy must be in either the Keynesian region or the intermediate region of the short-run aggregate supply curve.
   e. the economy must be in either the vertical region or the intermediate region of the short-run aggregate supply curve.

3. If aggregate demand increases and price increases but income does not change,
   a. the economy must be in the Keynesian region of the short-run aggregate supply curve.
   b. the economy must be in the intermediate region of the short-run aggregate supply curve.
   c. the economy must be in the vertical region of the short-run aggregate supply curve.
   d. the economy must be in either the Keynesian region or the intermediate region of the short-run aggregate supply curve.
   e. the economy must be in either the vertical region or the intermediate region of the short-run aggregate supply curve.

4. Which of the following statements is true?
   a. In the long run, the short-run aggregate demand curve shifts so that changes in aggregate supply determine the price level, not the equilibrium level of income.
   b. In the long run, the short-run aggregate demand curve shifts so that changes in aggregate supply determine the equilibrium level of income, not the price level.
   c. In the long run, the equilibrium level of output never changes.
   d. In the long run, there is a positive relationship between the level of prices and the level of output.
   e. In the long run, the short-run aggregate supply curve shifts so that changes in aggregate demand determine the price level, not the equilibrium level of income.

PRACTICE QUESTIONS AND PROBLEMS

Section 1: Aggregate Demand

1. List the two limitations of the Keynesian approach to equilibrium discussed in the "Preview."

   _____

   _____

2. List the three reasons why the aggregate expenditures curve shifts with changes in the price level.

   _____

   _____

   _____

3. As the level of prices increases, the purchasing power of money _____ (increases, decreases) and the real value of assets _____ (increases, decreases). The _____ effect, or real-balance effect, predicts that the real value of aggregate expenditures will _____ (rise, fall).

4. When prices increase, people _____ (buy, sell) bonds to get money. Bond prices _____ (increase, decrease), and interest rates _____ (rise, fall). The _____ effect suggests that aggregate expenditures will _____ (rise, fall).

5. If domestic prices rise while foreign prices and foreign exchange rates remain constant, domestic goods will become _____ (less expensive, more expensive) for foreigners. Net exports will _____ (rise, fall), causing aggregate expenditures to _____ (rise, fall).

6. When the price level falls, aggregate expenditures _____ (rise, fall).

7. The _____ shows how the equilibrium level of expenditures changes as the price level changes.

8. The aggregate demand curve slopes _____ .

9. Use the aggregate expenditures curves below to derive and plot the aggregate demand curve. Be sure to label your axes.

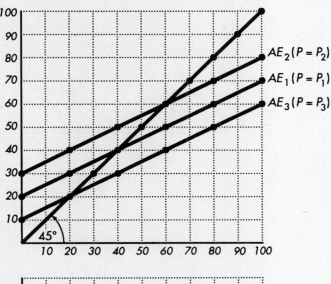

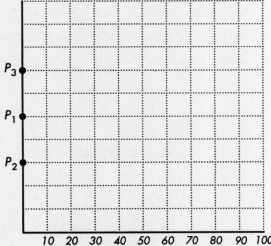

10. List the three nonprice determinants of aggregate demand.

_____

_____

_____

11. Positive expectations about the economy increase _____ and

_____ , which in turn _____ (increases, decreases) aggregate demand.

12. Higher foreign incomes cause _____ to rise, causing _____

(a movement along the aggregate demand curve, a shift in aggregate demand to the right).

13. If foreign prices fall, foreign goods become _____ (less expensive, more expensive), which causes _____ (a movement along the aggregate demand curve, a shift to the left of the aggregate demand curve).

14. A fall in the domestic price level causes _____ (a movement along the aggregate demand curve, a shift in aggregate demand to the left).

Section 2: Aggregate Supply

1. The _____ shows the quantity of national output (or income) produced at different price levels.

2. The slope of the short-run aggregate supply curve is _____ because of the effect of changing prices on _____ .

3. If the prices of output increase while all other prices remain unchanged, business profits will _____ (increase, decrease), and producers will produce _____ (more, less) output.

4. The _____ is the period of time when costs are variable.

5. The _____ is the period of time when all production costs remain constant.

6. List the three nonprice determinants of short-run aggregate supply.

   _____

   _____

   _____

7. When the prices of resources fall, the short-run aggregate supply curve shifts to the

   _____ .

8. Which resource prices impact the aggregate supply curve?

   _____

   _____

   _____

   _____

9. If a change in technology increases productivity, the aggregate supply curve will shift to the

   _____ .

10. Anticipated higher prices cause aggregate supply to shift to the _____ .

11. The _____ region is the horizontal part of the short-run aggregate supply curve.

12. The horizontal region of the short-run aggregate supply curve is the product of

    _____ or _____ .

13. The _____ range of the short-run aggregate supply curve is upward sloping, re-flecting the fact that some sectors of the economy are approaching capacity.

14. Where the capacity output is reached, the short-run aggregate supply curve is a

_____ line.

15. Draw a short-run aggregate supply curve on the graph below. Label your axes and the three regions.

16. The _____ curve is a vertical line at the potential level of national income.

Section 3: Aggregate Demand and Supply Equilibrium

1. The short-run equilibrium level of income on the graph below is _____ .

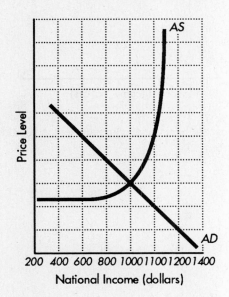

2. In the long run, there _____ (is, is not) a relationship between the level of prices and the level of output.

3. In the short run, changes in aggregate demand determine the level of prices and income. In the long run, changes in aggregate demand determine only the _____ .

4. Assume that the following are short-run situations.
   a. On the graph below, show how an increase in aggregate demand could produce a higher output with no change in prices.

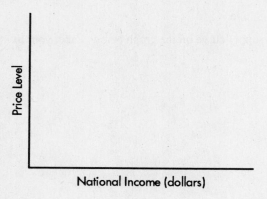

   b. On the graph below, show a decrease in aggregate demand that produces a lower price level and lower national income.

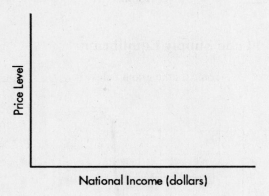

   c. On the graph below, show how an increase in aggregate demand could result in higher prices at the same level of national income.

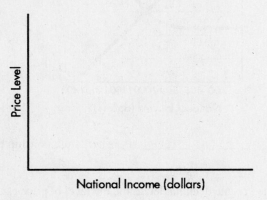

THINKING ABOUT AND APPLYING MACROECONOMIC EQUILIBRIUM: AGGREGATE DEMAND AND SUPPLY

I.   A Long-Run Analysis of the Effects of a Slump in Productivity

The "Economically Speaking" article in your text analyzes the short-run implications of an increase in productivity. The article points out why the recent decrease in productivity growth is alarming and also discusses the effects of productivity growth on short-run aggregate demand and supply.

   Now let's take a different perspective. Suppose that the growth of productivity in the United States not only slows, but actually decreases. This could result from declines in basic skills that some educators believe are surfacing in the nation's high schools. What will happen to the equilibrium price level and national income in the long run? Use the graph below to analyze this problem. Be sure to label your axes.

Quick Check Quiz

Section 1: Aggregate Demand

1. c; 2. d; 3. a; 4. b; 5. e; 6. c; 7. b
   If you missed any of these questions, you should go back and review pages 270–277 in Chapter 11.

Section 2: Aggregate Supply

1. b; 2. d; 3. e; 4. b; 5. e; 6. c
   If you missed any of these questions, you should go back and review pages 277–283 in Chapter 11.

Section 3: Aggregate Demand and Supply Equilibrium

1. b; 2. a; 3. c; 4. e
   If you missed any of these questions, you should go back and review pages 283–286 in Chapter 11.

Practice Questions and Problems

Section 1: Aggregate Demand

1.   It assumes that the level of prices is fixed.
     It fails to assign an active role to the supply side of the economy.

2. wealth effect
   interest rate effect
   international trade effect
3. decreases; decreases; wealth; fall
4. sell; decrease; rise; interest rate; fall
5. more expensive; fall; fall
6. rise
7. aggregate demand curve
8. downward

9.

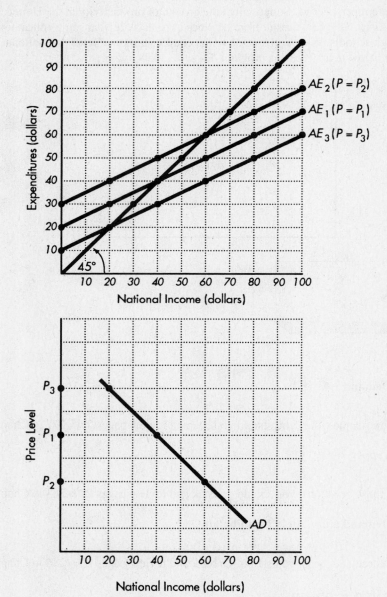

10. expectations
    foreign income and price levels
    government policy

11. consumption; investment; increases
12. net exports; a shift in aggregate demand to the right
13. less expensive; a shift to the left of the aggregate demand curve
14. a movement along the aggregate demand curve

Section 2: Aggregate Supply

1. aggregate supply curve
2. positive; profits
3. increase; more
4. long run
5. short run
6. resource prices
   technology
   expectations
7. right
8. Only those changes in resource prices that raise the costs of production in the economy as a whole shift aggregate supply.
9. right
10. left
11. Keynesian
12. unemployment; excess capacity
13. intermediate
14. vertical

15.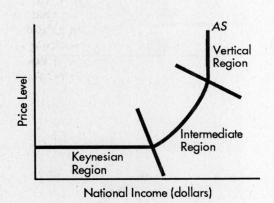

16. long-run aggregate supply

Section 3: Aggregate Demand and Supply Equilibrium

1. $1,000
2. is not
3. price level
4. a. You need to draw your aggregate demand curves so that the shifts are confined to the Keynesian (horizontal) region of the short-run aggregate supply curve.

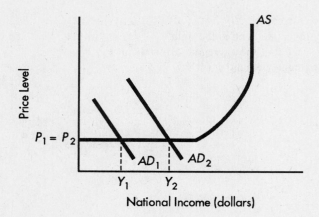

b. You need to draw your aggregate demand curves so that the shifts are confined to the intermediate (upward-sloping) region of the short-run aggregate supply curve.

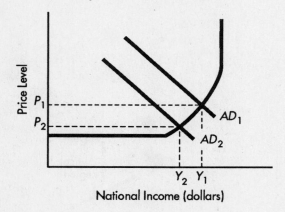

c. You need to draw your aggregate demand curves so that the shifts are confined to the vertical region of the short-run aggregate supply curve.

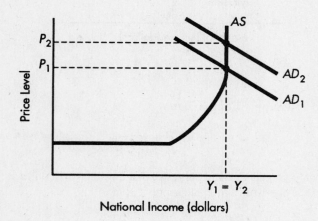

Thinking About and Applying Macroeconomic Equilibrium: Aggregate Demand and Supply

I.   A Long-Run Analysis of the Effects of a Slump in Productivity

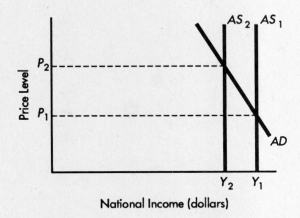

A decrease in productivity causes the long-run aggregate supply curve to shift to the left. If aggregate demand does not change, equilibrium national income (output) will be lower and the price level will be higher—a very sorry prospect indeed.

CHAPTER 12
Fiscal Policy

1. How can fiscal policy eliminate a recessionary gap?

   Fiscal policy can eliminate a recessionary gap by increasing government spending (which directly increases aggregate demand) or by decreasing taxes (which increases consumption). The changes in government spending and taxes have a multiplied effect on income.

2. What happens to equilibrium national income when government spending and taxes both increase by the same amount?

   The **balanced-budget multiplier** is 1, which means that an increase in government spending that is financed by an equal increase in taxes will increase equilibrium income by the amount of the change in government spending. This statement assumes that the economy is operating in the Keynesian region of the short-run aggregate supply curve. If the economy is not in this range, the increase in equilibrium income will be less than the increase in government spending.

3. How has U.S. fiscal policy changed over time?

   Government spending has increased from 3 percent of the GNP before the Great Depression to approximately 23 percent of the GNP. The Employment Act of 1946 made the federal government responsible for creating and maintaining low inflation and low unemployment.

4. What are the effects of budget deficits?

   Budget deficits can be harmful to the economy. If the deficit is financed by tax increases, the opportunity cost of not working decreases, so output may fall. If the deficit is financed by borrowing, interest rates may be driven up, and private domestic investment may be crowded out. The higher interest rates make U.S. financial instruments attractive to foreigners, and the resulting increase in the demand for dollars may cause the dollar to appreciate. The appreciation of the dollar decreases net exports.

5. How does fiscal policy differ across countries?

   Industrial countries spend more of their budgets on social programs than do developing countries, and they depend more on direct taxes and less on indirect taxes as sources of revenue.

KEY TERMS

spending multiplier
tax multiplier
balanced-budget multiplier
crowding out
discretionary fiscal policy

automatic stabilizers
progressive tax
transfer payment
value-added tax (VAT)

QUICK CHECK QUIZ

Section 1: Fiscal Policy and Aggregate Expenditures

Use the table below to answer questions 1 through 10.

Y	C	I	G	X	Aggregate Expenditures
$ 0	$ 80	$30	$40	$50	$200
100	155	30	40	35	260
200	230	30	40	20	320
300	305	30	40	5	380
400	380	30	40	−10	440
500	455	30	40	−25	500
600	530	30	40	−40	560
700	605	30	40	−55	620

1. The equilibrium level of income is
   a. $300.
   b. $400.
   c. $500.
   d. $600.
   e. $700.

2. If potential income is $600, the GNP gap is
   a. $100.
   b. $40.
   c. $50.
   d. $30.
   e. $200.

3. The marginal propensity to consume is
   a. .15.
   b. .75.
   c. .85.
   d. .25.
   e. 2.5.

4. The marginal propensity to save is
   a. .15.
   b. .75.
   c. .85.
   d. .25.
   e. 2.5.

5. The marginal propensity to import is
   a. .15.
   b. .75.
   c. .85.
   d. .25.
   e. 2.5.

6. The spending multiplier is
   a. .15.
   b. .75.
   c. .85.
   d. .25.
   e. 2.5.

7. The recessionary gap is
   a. $100.
   b. $30.
   c. $50.
   d. $40.
   e. $200.

8. The tax multiplier is
   a. −.15.
   b. −.75.
   c. −.85.
   d. −1.5.
   e. −2.5.

9. In order to close the recessionary gap, the government could increase government spending by _____ or decrease taxes by _____ .
   a. $66.67; $40
   b. $66.67; $66.67
   c. $40; $66.67
   d. $40; $40
   e. $100; $40

10. If government spending and taxes both increased by $50, equilibrium income would increase by
    a. $125.
    b. $50.
    c. $33.33.
    d. $200.
    e. $100.

11. Which of the following statements is true?
    a. If the price level rises as national income rises, the multiplier effects of any given change in aggregate expenditures are larger than they would be if the price level remained constant.
    b. Spending and tax multipliers overestimate the change in expenditures needed to close a recessionary gap.
    c. If aggregate supply shifts in response to an increase in government spending financed by an increase in taxes, the effects of government spending may be enhanced.
    d. David Ricardo stated that the effects of a deficit financed by an increase in taxes are different than the effects of a deficit financed by borrowing.
    e. The spending multiplier overestimates the expansionary effect of an increase in government spending unless the economy is in the Keynesian region of short-run aggregate supply.

Section 2: Fiscal Policy in the United States

1. Discretionary fiscal policy refers to
   a. government spending at the discretion of the president.
   b. government spending at the discretion of the Congress.
   c. elements of fiscal policy that automatically change in value as national income changes.
   d. government spending at the discretion of the president and the Congress.
   e. changes in government spending and taxation aimed at achieving a policy goal.

2. Which of the following is NOT a harmful effect of government deficits?
   a. lower private investment as a result of crowding out
   b. lower net exports as a result of the appreciation of the dollar
   c. increased investment caused by foreign savings placed in U.S. bonds
   d. an increase in saving caused by anticipated future increases in taxes
   e. an increase in imports

3. Which of the following is NOT an example of an automatic stabilizer?
   a. unemployment insurance
   b. lump-sum taxes
   c. progressive taxes
   d. food stamps
   e. welfare benefits

4. The following tax table represents a _____ tax schedule.

Income	Tax Payment
$100	$ 45
200	80
300	105
400	120

   a. regressive
   b. progressive
   c. proportional
   d. lump-sum
   e. constant rate

5. Which of the following is NOT an expected result of government budget deficits?
   a. increases in saving
   b. increases in imports
   c. decreases in investment
   d. increases in consumption
   e. decreases in exports

Section 3: Fiscal Policy in Different Countries

1. Which of the following statements is false?
   a. Historically, government spending has played an increasingly larger role over time in industrial countries.
   b. Government plays a larger role in investment spending in developing countries.
   c. Developed countries rely more on their governments to provide the infrastructure of the economy than do developing countries.
   d. State-owned enterprises account for a larger percentage of economic activity in developing countries than in developed countries.
   e. Industrial nations spend a larger percentage of their budgets on social programs than do developing countries.

2. Which of the following statements is true?
   a. Developing countries rely more heavily on direct taxes than do developed countries.
   b. Developing countries rely more heavily on indirect taxes than do developed countries.
   c. Developing countries rely more heavily on personal income taxes than do developed countries.
   d. Developing countries rely more heavily on Social Security taxes than do developed countries.
   e. Developed countries rely more heavily on import and export taxes than do developing countries.

PRACTICE QUESTIONS AND PROBLEMS

Section 1: Fiscal Policy and Aggregate Expenditures

1. Fiscal policy is changing _____ and _____ .

2. The _____ gave the federal government the responsibility for creating and maintaining low inflation and unemployment.

3. Use the table below to answer the following questions.

Y	C	I	G	X	AE
0	$ 30	$20	$ 30	$ 40	$120
$100	110	20	30	30	190
200	190	20	30	20	260
300	270	20	30	10	330
400	350	20	30	0	400
500	430	20	30	−10	470
600	510	20	30	−20	540
700	590	20	30	−30	610

a. The equilibrium level of income is _____ .

b. Suppose the potential GNP is $600. The GNP gap is _____ .

c. The recessionary gap is _____ .

d. The multiplier is _____ .

e. Plot aggregate expenditures on the graph below. Show the GNP gap and the recessionary gap.

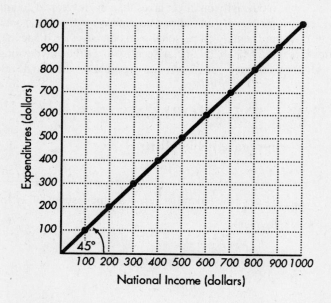

f. Government spending needs to change by _____ to close the recessionary gap and achieve potential GNP.

g. On the graph above, draw the new aggregate expenditures curve that would result from the increase in government spending. Label your new curve AE_2.

4. The spending multiplier is _____ (formula).

5. The tax multiplier is _____ (formula).

6. The tax multiplier is always a _____ (positive, negative) number.

7. Go back to the table in problem 3 to answer the following questions.

   a. The marginal propensity to consume (MPC) is _____.

   b. The marginal propensity to save (MPS) is _____.

   c. The marginal propensity to import (MPI) is _____.

   d. The tax multiplier is _____.

   e. For the data in problem 3, taxes must _____ (rise, fall) by

      _____ to close the recessionary gap.

8. If government spending increases by the same amount as taxes, the effect is _____

   (expansionary, contractionary).

9. The balanced-budget multiplier is _____.

10. If government spending and taxes both increase by $100, equilibrium income will

    _____ (increase, decrease) by _____.

11. An increase in government spending or a decrease in taxes causes the aggregate demand curve to shift to

    the _____.

12. When prices go up, the multiplier effect of an increase in spending is _____ (en-

    hanced, reduced). The spending and tax multipliers _____ (understate, overstate)

    the effect of a change in aggregate expenditures.

13. List the three ways government spending may be financed.

    _____

    _____

    _____

14. An increase in taxes can shift aggregate supply to the _____.

15. The graph below shows equilibrium at Y_1 and P_1. Show the effect of government spending financed by
    taxes if the aggregate supply curve *is* affected by the change in taxes.

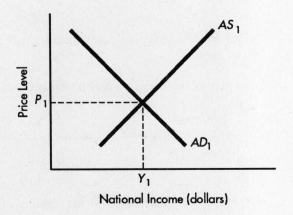

16. A government borrows funds by _____ (buying bonds from, selling bonds to) the public.

17. _____ refers to the notion that the effects on the economy are the same whether the government finances its spending through tax increases or through borrowing.

18. Ricardian equivalence assumes that aggregate demand will decrease as a result of government spending financed by borrowing because people will increase _____ to pay for future taxes.

19. An increase in government spending that reduces private spending is called _____ .

20. Crowding out may occur if government borrowing drives up _____ .

Section 2: Fiscal Policy in the United States

1. Fiscal policy in the United States is a product of the budget process, which involves the _____ and _____ branches of government.

2. As part of the budget process, federal agencies submit their budgets to the _____ (OMB), which reviews and modifies each agency's requests and consolidates all of the proposals into a single budget.

3. The _____ (CBO) reports to Congress on the validity of the economic assumptions made in the president's budget.

4. The federal budget is determined as much by _____ as by economics.

5. The _____ Act (1985) limits federal deficits and requires cuts in spending when the OMB and CBO determine that deficit targets are being exceeded.

6. List the two kinds of fiscal policy.

   _____

   _____

7. _____ refers to changes in government spending and taxation aimed at achieving a policy goal.

8. _____ are elements of fiscal policy that automatically change in value as national income changes.

9. Historically, except in times of war, the federal government deficit increased the most during _____ .

10. Government deficits can harm the economy by dampening _____ and _____ .

11. As income falls, automatic stabilizers _____ spending.

12. _____ are taxes that are a flat dollar amount regardless of income.

13. With _____ taxes, as income rises, so does the rate of taxation.

14. With _____ taxes, the tax rate falls as income rises.

15. With _____ taxes, the tax rate is constant as income rises.

16. Look at the tax payment schedules below. Which is progressive? _____

    Regressive? _____ Proportional? _____

Income	A Tax Payment	B Tax Payment	C Tax Payment
$100	$10	$ 50	$ 10
200	20	80	30
300	30	90	60
400	40	100	100

17. _____ taxes are an example of an automatic stabilizer.

18. A _____ is a payment to one person that is funded by taxing others.

19. In the 1980s, federal spending has been about _____ percent of the GNP.

Section 3: Fiscal Policy in Different Countries

1. Government plays a bigger role in investment spending in the _____ (developing, industrial) countries. Give two reasons why this should be so.

   _____

   _____

2. Low-income countries _____ (do, do not) spend a greater percentage of their budgets on social programs as compared with industrialized countries.

3. The relative cost of an education is _____ (higher, lower) in developing countries than it is in industrial countries.

4. _____ taxes are taxes on individuals and firms.

5. _____ taxes are taxes on goods and services.

6. _____ taxes are hard to collect in developing countries because so much of household production is for personal consumption.

7. In general, developing countries rely more heavily on _____ (direct, indirect) taxes than do developed countries.

8. VAT stands for _____, an indirect tax imposed on each sale at each stage of production.

THINKING ABOUT AND APPLYING FISCAL POLICY

I. More on the Deficit

The "Economically Speaking" article in your text discusses the harmful effects of budget deficits and the various political considerations involved in getting rid of them. Since a budget deficit results from government spending that is greater than tax revenues, reducing the deficit implies reducing government spending, increasing taxes, or both. But, to quote Publius Syrus, "There are some remedies worse than the disease" (Maxim 301). The article suggests that the economy might be thrown into a recession if spending cuts and tax increases are adopted.

1. Consider the graph below, where the economy is at equilibrium at P_1 and Y_1. Show what will happen if spending cuts and tax increases are implemented.

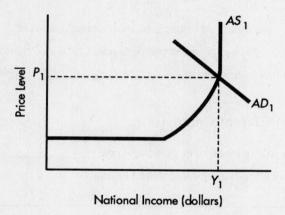

What will happen to equilibrium income and price level?

_____

_____

_____

_____

2. Now consider an economy operating in the vertical region of the aggregate supply curve. Can you draw a curve that illustrates tax increases and spending cuts but does *not* throw the economy into a recession?

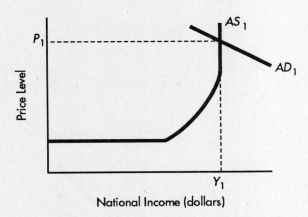

_____

_____

_____

_____

ANSWERS

Quick Check Quiz

Section 1: Fiscal Policy and Aggregate Expenditures

1. c; 2. a; 3. b; 4. d; 5. a; 6. e; 7. d; 8. d; 9. c; 10. b; 11. e
   If you missed any of these questions, you should go back and review pages 294–305 in Chapter 12.

Section 2: Fiscal Policy in the United States

1. e; 2. c; 3. b; 4. a; 5. d
   If you missed any of these questions, you should go back and review pages 305–313 in Chapter 12.

Section 3: Fiscal Policy in Different Countries

1. c; 2. b
   If you missed either of these questions, you should go back and review pages 313–318 in Chapter 12.

Practice Questions and Problems

Section 1: Fiscal Policy and Aggregate Expenditures

1. taxation; government spending
2. Employment Act of 1946
3. a. $400 (where income equals aggregate expenditures)
   b. $200 (GNP gap = potential income − equilibrium income = $600 − $400 = $200)
   c. $60 (At an income of $600, aggregate expenditures are $540. The recessionary gap = income − aggregate expenditures.)
   d. Multiplier = GNP gap/recessionary gap
      = $200/$60 = 3 1/3

   e.

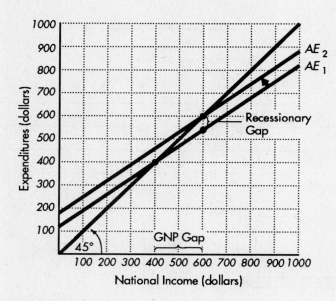

   f. $60 (the amount of the recessionary gap)
   g. See the graph for answer e.
4. 1/(MPS + MPI)
5. −(MPC − MPI) × 1/(MPS + MPI)
6. negative
7. a. MPC = change in consumption/change in income
      = $80/$100 = .8
   b. MPS = 1 − MPC = 1 − .8 = .2
   c. MPI = change in net exports/change in income
      = $10/$100 = .1
   d. Tax multiplier = −(MPC − MPI) × 1/(MPS + MPI)
      = −(.8 − .1) × 1/(.2 + .1) = −2 1/3
   e. Change in taxes needed to close recessionary gap = GNP gap/tax multiplier = $200/−2 1/3
      = −$85.71 (approximately)

      Taxes must fall by $85.71.
8. expansionary
9. 1
10. increase; $100
11. right

12. reduced; overstate
13. taxes
    change in government debt (borrowing)
    change in the stock of government-issued money
14. left

15.

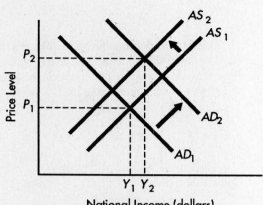

16. selling bonds to
17. Ricardian equivalence
18. saving
19. crowding out
20. interest rates

Section 2: Fiscal Policy in the United States

1. legislative; executive
2. Office of Management and Budget
3. Congressional Budget Office
4. politics
5. Gramm-Rudman-Hollings
6. discretionary fiscal policy
   automatic stabilizers
7. Discretionary fiscal policy
8. Automatic stabilizers
9. recessions
10. investment; net exports
11. increase
12. Lump-sum taxes
13. progressive
14. regressive
15. proportional
16. *C; B; A*
    To determine what kind of tax it is, we must first calculate the tax *rate* at each level of income.

Income	A Tax Payment	A Tax Rate	B Tax Payment	B Tax Rate	C Tax Payment	C Tax Rate
$100	$10	.10	$ 50	.50	$ 10	.10
200	20	.10	80	.40	30	.15
300	30	.10	90	.30	60	.20
400	40	.10	100	.25	100	.25

Since A's tax *rate* is constant at .10, A is a proportional tax schedule. B's tax *rate* decreases with income, so B is a regressive tax. C's tax *rate* increases with income, so C is a progressive tax schedule.

Note: If you just look at the *dollar* amount of taxes paid, all three schedules look "progressive" because the dollar amount of tax payments increases as income increases. But we classify these taxes according to how the tax *rate* changes as income increases.

17. Progressive
18. transfer payment
19. 23

Section 3: Fiscal Policy in Different Countries

1. developing
    State-owned enterprises account for a larger percentage of economic activity in developing countries as compared with industrial countries. Also, developing countries rely on their governments, as opposed to private investment, to build their infrastructure.
2. do not
3. higher
4. Direct
5. Indirect
6. Personal income
7. indirect
8. value-added tax

Thinking About and Applying Fiscal Policy

I. More on the Deficit

1.

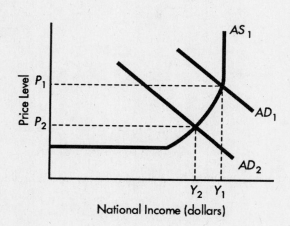

Government spending cuts and tax increases both decrease aggregate demand. If the economy is operating in the Keynesian or intermediate regions, decreasing aggregate demand will decrease national income. If the economy is in the intermediate range, the price level will decline. If it is in the Keynesian region, there will be no change in the price level. These are the dire results that the economic analysts fear.

2.

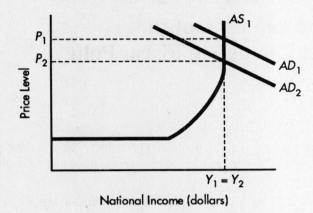

If the economy is operating in the vertical region of short-run aggregate supply (above), a decrease in aggregate demand may bring only a decrease in the price level with no decrease in national income.

APPENDIX TO CHAPTER 12
An Algebraic Examination of the Balanced-Budget Change in Fiscal Policy

SUMMARY

The spending multiplier is 1/(MPS + MPI). The tax multiplier is –(MPC – MPI) × 1/(MPS + MPI). If we have equal changes in taxes and government spending, the multiplier equals the spending multiplier plus the taxation multiplier:

$$\{1/(MPS + MPI)\} + \{-(MPC - MPI) \times 1/(MPS + MPI)\}$$

$$or$$

$$\{1 - (MPC - MPI)\} \times 1/(MPS + MPI)$$

Simplifying, we have

$$(1 - MPC + MPI) \times \{1/(MPS + MPI)\}$$

Since MPS = 1 – MPC, we can substitute:

$$(MPS + MPI) \times \{1/(MPS + MPI)\}, \text{ which equals 1.}$$

PRACTICE QUESTIONS AND PROBLEMS

Given:

$$C = 50 + .90Y$$

$$I = 40$$

$$G = 60$$

$$X = 50 - .10Y$$

Verify that the balanced budget multiplier equals 1.

ANSWERS

The MPC = .9, so the MPS = .1.
The MPI = .1.
The spending multiplier is 1/(MPS + MPI) = 1/(.1 + .1) = 1/.2 = 5.
The taxation multiplier is –(MPC – MPI) × 1/(MPS + MPI)
= –(.9 – .1) × 1/(.1 + .1) = –.8/.2 = – 4.
Adding the two multipliers together, we get 5 + – 4 = 1.

CHAPTER 13
Money and Banking

1. What is money?

   Money is anything that is generally acceptable to sellers in exchange for goods and services. Money serves as a medium of exchange, a unit of account, a store of value, and a standard of deferred payment.

2. How is the U.S. money supply defined?

   There are three definitions of the U.S. money supply. The narrowest definition, the **M1 money supply**, consists of currency, travelers' checks, demand deposits, and other checkable deposits. M2 adds overnight repurchase agreements, overnight Eurodollar deposits, money market deposit accounts, savings and small-denomination time deposits, and individual money market fund balances. M3 equals M2 plus large time deposits, term repurchase agreements, term Eurodollar deposits, and institution-only money market mutual fund balances.

3. How do countries pay for international transactions?

   Countries use the foreign exchange market to convert national currencies to pay for trade. They also use **international reserve assets**, like gold, or **international reserve currencies**, like the dollar.

4. Why are banks considered intermediaries?

   Banks act as middlemen between savers and borrowers. They accept deposits from savers and use those deposits to make loans to borrowers.

5. How does international banking differ from domestic banking?

   Domestic banking is heavily regulated, whereas international banking is not. Because they are not restricted by regulations, international banks can usually offer depositors and borrowers better terms than can domestic banks.

6. How do banks create money?

   Banks create money by making loans up to the amount of their excess reserves. The banking system can increase the money supply by the **deposit expansion multiplier** times the **excess reserves** in the system.

KEY TERMS

money
liquid asset
currency substitution
credit
M1 money supply
transactions account
international reserve asset
international reserve currency
European currency unit (ECU)

composite currency
special drawing right (SDR)
Federal Deposit Insurance Corporation (FDIC)
Eurocurrency market (offshore banking)
international banking facility (IBF)
fractional reserve banking system
required reserves
excess reserves
deposit expansion multiplier

QUICK CHECK QUIZ

Section 1: What Is Money?

1. Which of the following is NOT one of the functions of money?
   a. a medium of exchange
   b. a unit of account
   c. a resource for production
   d. a store of value
   e. a standard of deferred payment

2. A $34 price tag on a sweater is an example of money functioning as a
   a. medium of exchange.
   b. unit of account.
   c. resource for production.
   d. store of value.
   e. standard of deferred payment.

3. For money to function as a store of value, it is most important that it have which of the following properties?
   a. durability
   b. divisibility
   c. portability
   d. ability to be easily identified as genuine
   e. optimal scarcity

4. Which of the following is NOT a component of the M1 money supply?
   a. demand deposits
   b. other checkable deposits
   c. currency
   d. money market deposit accounts
   e. travelers' checks

5. Which of the following is NOT a transactions account?
   a. negotiable order of withdrawal
   b. credit union share draft account
   c. savings account
   d. automated transfer system account
   e. demand deposit at a commercial bank

6. Currency represents ____ percent of the M1 money supply.
   a. 1
   b. 28
   c. 35
   d. 36
   e. 10

7. Which of the following accounts are offered by savings and loans?
   a. negotiable orders of withdrawal
   b. credit union share draft accounts
   c. savings accounts
   d. automated transfer system accounts
   e. demand deposits at commercial banks

8. Demand deposits and other checkable deposits together make up ____ percent of the M1 money supply.
   a. 1
   b. 28
   c. 35
   d. 36
   e. 71

9. Which of the following is NOT a component of the M2 money supply?
   a. individual money market mutual fund balances
   b. overnight Eurodollar deposits
   c. overnight RPs
   d. savings deposits
   e. large time deposits

10. Which of the following is NOT a component of the M3 money supply?
    a. term Eurodollar deposits
    b. value of stocks and bonds
    c. term RPs
    d. institution-only money market mutual fund balances
    e. M2

11. The European currency unit is an average of the values of seven individual European currencies. Which of the following is NOT one of the seven currencies?
    a. the U.K. pound
    b. the Spanish peseta
    c. the Luxembourg franc
    d. the Swedish krone
    e. the Greek drachma

12. The special drawing right is an average of the values of currencies of five major industrial countries. Which of the following is NOT one of the five?
    a. the United States
    b. the United Kingdom
    c. France
    d. Spain
    e. Japan

Section 2: Banking

1. Which of the following statements is false?
   a. The 1980 Depository Institutions Deregulation and Monetary Control Act was intended to stimulate competition among financial intermediaries.
   b. The 1980 Depository Institutions Deregulation and Monetary Control Act narrowed the distinctions between commercial banks and thrifts.
   c. The 1980 Depository Institutions Deregulation and Monetary Control Act narrowed the distinctions between state banks and national banks.
   d. The 1980 Depository Institutions Deregulation and Monetary Control Act created the Federal Deposit Insurance Corporation.
   e. The 1980 Depository Institutions Deregulation and Monetary Control Act permitted thrift institutions to offer many of the same services as commercial banks.

2. Which of the following statements is true?
   a. The laws regulating international banks typically are very restrictive, whereas domestic banks go relatively unregulated.
   b. Offshore banking, called the Euromarket, refers to international banking transactions among the seven Western European industrial powers.
   c. Offshore banks are typically able to offer a higher return on deposits and a lower rate on loans than domestic banks.
   d. International banking is dominated by the United States and the United Kingdom.
   e. U.S. banks that participate in international banking on U.S. soil are subject to the same regulations as domestic banks.

3. Which of the following statements is false?
   a. The FDIC does not permit banks to fail, for fear of causing a bank panic.
   b. Many states permit entry to banks located out of state.
   c. A Eurodollar is a dollar-denominated deposit outside the U.S. banking industry.
   d. International banking is riskier than domestic banking.
   e. International banking facilities are not physical entities.

Section 3: Banks and the Money Supply

1. Deposits at the Third National Bank are $200,000, and the reserve requirement is 10 percent. Cash reserves equal $50,000. Required reserves equal
   a. $40,000.
   b. $20,000.
   c. $50,000.
   d. $30,000.
   e. $10,000.

2. Deposits at the ABC Bank are $600,000, and the reserve requirement is 20 percent. Cash reserves equal $160,000. Excess reserves equal
   a. $120,000.
   b. $160,000.
   c. $32,000.
   d. $40,000.
   e. $128,000.

3. Deposits at the XYZ Bank are $400,000, and the reserve requirement is 20 percent. Cash reserves equal $6,000. The deposit expansion multiplier is
   a. .20.
   b. .80.
   c. 5.
   d. 1.25.
   e. 1.

4. The deposit expansion multiplier will be larger the
   a. smaller the reserve requirement.
   b. greater the currency drain.
   c. greater the percentage of excess reserves held by banks.
   d. larger the bank.
   e. greater the value of the assets held by the bank.

5. The Golden State Bank has cash reserves of $110,000, deposits of $200,000, and loans of $90,000. The reserve requirement is 5 percent. This bank can make additional loans up to the amount of _____
   a. $4,500.
   b. $10,000.
   c. $5,500.
   d. $100,000.
   e. $190,000.

6. Suppose that excess reserves in the Stranda National Bank are $15,000 and the reserve requirement is 4 percent. The maximum amount that the money supply can be increased is
   a. $60,000.
   b. $600.
   c. $375,000.
   d. $15,000.
   e. $72,000.

7. Banks increase the money supply by
   a. cashing checks.
   b. making loans.
   c. providing currency.
   d. printing money.
   e. printing money and coining currency.

8. A bank has $200,000 in deposits and $10,000 in cash. The reserve requirement is 4 percent. The bank's required reserves are _____ , and its excess reserves are _____ .
    a. $400; $199,600
    b. $199,600; $400
    c. $8,000; $192,000
    d. $2,000; $8,000
    e. $8,000; $2,000

PRACTICE QUESTIONS AND PROBLEMS

Section 1: What Is Money?

1. _____ is anything that is generally acceptable to sellers in exchange for goods and services.

2. A _____ asset is an asset that can easily be exchanged for goods and services.

3. List the four functions of money.

    _____

    _____

    _____

    _____

4. _____ is the direct exchange of goods and services for other goods and services.

5. The use of money as a medium of exchange lowers _____ costs.

6. Money eliminates the need for a _____ , which is necessary for barter to work.

7. For money to be an effective medium of exchange, it must be _____ and

    _____ .

8. The use of money as a unit of account lowers _____ costs.

9. For money to be an effective store of value, it must be _____ .

10. _____ is the use of foreign money as a substitute for domestic money when the domestic money has a high rate of inflation.

11. _____ is available savings that are lent to borrowers to spend.

12. List the four components of the M1 money supply.

    _____

    _____

    _____

    _____

13. A checking account at a bank or other financial institution that can be drawn on to make payments is called a _____ account.

14. Currency represented _____ percent of the M1 money supply in 1989.

15. The U.S. dollar is backed by _____. This type of monetary system is called a _____ monetary system.

16. Money that has an intrinsic value is called _____ money.

17. _____ is the tendency to hoard currency as its commodity value increases.

18. Travelers' checks accounted for _____ percent of the M1 money supply in 1989.

19. _____ pay no interest and must be paid immediately on the demand of the depositor.

20. _____ are checking accounts at financial institutions that pay interest and give the depositor check-writing privileges.

21. _____ (NOW) accounts are interest-bearing checking accounts offered by savings and loan institutions.

22. _____ (ATS) accounts are accounts at commercial banks that combine an interest-bearing savings account with a non-interest-bearing checking account.

23. Credit unions offer their members interest-bearing checking accounts called _____ .

24. _____ are nonprofit savings and loan institutions.

25. Demand and other checkable deposits made up _____ percent of the M1 money supply in 1989.

26. List the seven components of the M2 money supply.

    _____

    _____

    _____

    _____

    _____

    _____

    _____

27. An _____ is an agreement between a bank and a customer under which the customer buys U.S. government securities from the bank one day and sells them back to the bank the next day.

28. Overnight deposits denominated in dollars but held outside the U.S. domestic bank market are called _____ deposits.

29. Accounts at commercial banks and savings and loans that require a minimum balance and that place limits on the number of transactions permitted per month are called _____ accounts.

30. _____ deposits are deposits at banks and savings and loans that earn interest but offer no check-writing privileges.

31. Small-denomination time deposits are also called _____ .

32. _____ combine the deposits of many individuals and invest them in government Treasury bills and other short-term securities.

33. List the five components of the M3 money supply.

    _____

    _____

    _____

    _____

    _____

34. Sales contracts between developed countries are usually invoiced in the national currency of the _____ , whereas sales between a developed and a developing country are usually invoiced in the currency of the _____ .

35. An asset used to settle debts between governments is called an _____ asset.

36. Currencies that are held to settle debts between governments are called _____ currencies.

37. The _____ is a unit of account used by the industrial nations of Western Europe to settle debts between them.

38. A _____ currency is a unit of account whose value is an average of the values of certain national currencies.

39. The value of the _____ is an average of the values of the U.S. dollar, the French franc, the German mark, the Japanese yen, and the U.K. pound.

Section 2: Banking

1. Thrift institutions include _____ , _____ , and _____ .

2. _____ banks are banks chartered by the federal government, whereas _____ banks are chartered under state law.

3. A bank is allowed to operate in only one location in a _____ banking state.

4. The _____ is a federal agency that insures deposits in commercial banks so that depositors do not lose their deposits when a bank fails.

5. The international deposit and loan market is often called the _____ or _____ .

6. Typically, domestic banks are subject to _____ regulations, whereas offshore banks are subject to _____ regulation.

7. _____ (Domestic/Offshore) banks are usually able to offer better terms to their customers.

8. Eurodollar transactions are _____ (more risky/less risky) than domestic transactions in the United States because of the lack of regulation and deposit insurance.

9. International banking is dominated by _____ and _____ banks.

10. _____ are permitted to take part in international banking activities on U.S. soil.

11. The _____ (1980) eliminated many of the differences between commercial banks and thrift institutions, and between state banks and national banks.

Section 3: Banks and the Money Supply

1. In a _____ banking system, banks keep less than 100 percent of their deposits on reserve.

2. A financial statement that records a firm's assets and liabilities is called a _____ .

3. _____ are what the firm owns, and _____ are what the firm owes.

4. In the United States, reserve requirements are set by the _____ .

5. _____ reserves are the cash reserves a bank must keep on hand or on deposit with the Fed.

6. _____ reserves are total reserves minus required reserves.

7. A bank is _____ when it has zero excess reserves.

8. The deposit expansion multiplier equals _____ (formula).

9. The deposit expansion multiplier tells us the _____ (maximum, minimum) change in total deposits when a new deposit is made.

10. If people withdraw deposits from banks, _____ occurs and the deposit expansion multiplier will be less than the reciprocal of the reserve requirement.

11. Any single bank can only lend up to the amount of its _____ .

12. Banks increase the money supply by _____ .

13. McDougall Bank and Trust has vault cash in the amount of $300,000, loans of $900,000, and deposits of $1,200,000.
    a. Prepare a balance sheet for this bank.

    _____

    _____

    _____

    _____

b. If the bank maintains a reserve requirement of 5 percent, what is the largest loan it can make?

_____

c. What is the maximum amount the money supply can be increased by the banking system due to McDougall Bank and Trust's new loan? _____

14. The State Bank of Oswald has cash reserves of $5,000, loans of $495,000, and deposits of $500,000. The bank maintains a reserve requirement of 1 percent.
   a. Calculate this bank's excess reserves.

   _____

   b. The bank receives a new deposit of $100,000. What is the largest loan the bank can make?

   _____

   c. What is the maximum amount the money supply can be increased as a result of the State Bank of Oswald's new loan? _____

THINKING ABOUT AND APPLYING MONEY AND BANKING

I. The Coming Mess in Deposit Insurance

The "Economically Speaking" article in your text discusses the problems that the Resolution Trust Corp. is having trying to clean up the savings and loan mess. At one point, the commentary mentions that S&Ls had an incentive to make risky loans because they stood to gain if the loans were repaid and the FSLIC would absorb the losses if the loans were not repaid. A similar situation exists with respect to deposit insurance.

As it currently stands, all financial institutions pay a flat rate for deposit insurance, no matter what kind of assets they hold. What are the incentives for banks to act in an inappropriate manner?

_____

_____

_____

_____

ANSWERS

Quick Check Quiz

Section 1: What Is Money?

1. c; 2. b; 3. a; 4. d; 5. c; 6. b; 7. a; 8. e; 9. e; 10. b; 11. d; 12. d
   If you missed any of these questions, you should go back and review pages 326–335 in Chapter 13.

Section 2: Banking

1. d; 2. c; 3. a

    If you missed any of these questions, you should go back and review pages 335–344 in Chapter 13.

Section 3: Banks and the Money Supply

1. b; 2. d; 3. c; 4. a; 5. d; 6. c; 7. b; 8. e

    If you missed any of these questions, you should go back and review pages 344–348 in Chapter 13.

Practice Questions and Problems

Section 1: What Is Money?

1. Money
2. liquid
3. medium of exchange
   unit of account
   store of value
   standard of deferred payment
4. Barter
5. transactions
6. double coincidence of wants
7. portable; divisible
8. information
9. durable
10. Currency substitution
11. Credit
12. currency
    travelers' checks
    demand deposits
    other checkable deposits (OCDs)
13. transactions
14. 28
15. the confidence of the public; fiduciary
16. commodity
17. Gresham's Law
18. 1
19. Demand deposits
20. Other checkable deposits (OCDs)
21. Negotiable order of withdrawal
22. Automated transfer system
23. share drafts
24. Mutual savings banks
25. 71
26. M1
    overnight repurchase agreements (RPs)
    overnight Eurodollar deposits
    money market deposit accounts
    savings deposits
    small-denomination time deposits (certificates of deposit, or CDs)
    individual money market mutual fund balances

27. overnight repurchase agreement
28. overnight Eurodollar
29. money market deposit
30. Savings
31. certificates of deposit
32. Individual money market mutual fund balances
33. M2
    large time deposits
    term RPs
    term Eurodollar deposits
    institution-only money market mutual fund balances
34. exporter; developed country
35. international reserve
36. international reserve
37. European currency unit (ECU)
38. composite
39. special drawing right (SDR)

Section 2: Banking

1. savings and loans; mutual savings banks; credit unions
2. National; state
3. unit
4. Federal Deposit Insurance Corporation (FDIC)
5. Eurocurrency market; offshore banking
6. restrictive; little or no
7. Offshore
8. more risky
9. Japanese; U.S.
10. International Banking Facilities (IBFs)
11. Depository Institutions Deregulation and Monetary Control Act

Section 3: Banks and the Money Supply

1. fractional reserve
2. balance sheet
3. Assets; liabilities
4. Federal Reserve Board
5. Required
6. Excess
7. loaned up
8. 1/reserve requirement
9. maximum
10. currency drain
11. excess reserves
12. making loans

13. a.

Assets		Liabilities	
Cash	$ 300,000	Deposits	$1,200,000
Loans	900,000		
Total	1,200,000	Total	1,200,000

b. $240,000

Required reserves = .05($1,200,000) = $60,000. Excess reserves = total reserves − required reserves = $300,000 − $60,000 = $240,000. Since a bank can make loans up to the amount of its excess reserves, this bank can loan out $240,000.

c. $4,800,000

The deposit expansion multiplier = 1/reserve requirement = 1/.05 = 20. Change in the money supply = deposit expansion multiplier × excess reserves = 20($240,000) = $4,800,000.

14. a. Required reserves = .01($500,000) = $5,000. Excess reserves = $5,000 − $5,000 = 0.

b. Cash = $105,000. Deposits = $600,000. Required reserves = .01($600,000) = $6,000. Excess reserves = $105,000 − $6,000 = $99,000.

c. Deposit expansion multiplier = 1/.01 = 100. Maximum amount of money that can be created = deposit expansion multiplier × excess reserves = 100($99,000) = $9,900,000.

Thinking About and Applying Money and Banking

I. The Coming Mess in Deposit Insurance

The situation would be similar to life insurance companies charging a 110-year-old cancer patient the same rate as a 20-year-old athlete. The risks are not the same. Charging a flat rate for deposit insurance encourages banks to take risks because they pay the same rate whether they take a risk or not. The FDIC is considering proposals to classify assets according to the degree of riskiness and to charge higher premiums for riskier assets. But it is very difficult to assess riskiness before the fact.

CHAPTER 14
Monetary Policy

1. What are the determinants of the demand for money?

There are three aspects to the demand for money. Consumers and firms demand money in order to conduct transactions (the **transactions demand for money**), to take care of emergencies (the **precautionary demand for money**), and to be able to take advantage of a fall in the price of an asset that they want (the **speculative demand for money**).

The amount of money held depends on the interest rate and nominal income. Increases in nominal income generate a greater volume of transactions, so more money is needed. The demand for money is therefore positively related to nominal income. The interest rate is the opportunity cost of holding money. A higher interest rate means that it costs more to hold money, so less money will be held. The demand for money is negatively related to the interest rate.

2. How does monetary policy affect the equilibrium level of national income?

Monetary policy refers to controlling the money supply. An increase in the money supply decreases interest rates, which increases consumption and investment. The increases in consumption and investment increase aggregate demand, which increases the equilibrium level of national income. A decrease in the money supply increases interest rates, which decreases consumption and investment. The decreases in consumption and investment decrease aggregate demand, which decreases the equilibrium level of income. So increases in the money supply are expansionary, whereas decreases in the money supply are contractionary.

3. What does the Federal Reserve do?

The Federal Reserve is the central bank of the United States. As such, the Fed accepts deposits from and makes loans to financial institutions, acts as a banker for the federal government, supervises the banking system, and controls the money supply.

4. How is monetary policy set?

The **Federal Open Market Committee (FOMC)** is the policy-making body of the Federal Reserve. It consists of the seven-member Federal Reserve Board and five of the twelve Federal Reserve Bank presidents, who serve on a rotating basis. The FOMC issues directives to the Federal Reserve Bank of New York, which implements its directives.

5. What are the tools of monetary policy?

The tools of monetary policy are the reserve requirement, the **discount rate**, and **open market operations.** The reserve requirement is the percentage of deposits that financial institutions must keep on hand or at the Fed. The higher the reserve requirement, the smaller the deposits banks can create, and the smaller the money supply. The discount rate is the rate at which the Fed lends to financial institutions. The higher the discount rate, the smaller the money supply. Open market operations are the buying and selling of bonds to change the money supply. The Fed buys bonds if it wants to increase the money supply and sells bonds to decrease the money supply. Open market operations are the Fed's most important tool.

6. What role do central banks play in the foreign exchange market?

Central banks may intervene in the foreign exchange market to stabilize or change exchange rates. For example, the Fed might buy francs to bolster the price of the franc if U.S. goods and services became too expensive for the French.

KEY TERMS

transactions demand for money
precautionary demand for money
speculative demand for money
Federal Open Market Committee (FOMC)
intermediate target
equation of exchange
velocity of money
quantity theory of money

FOMC directive
legal reserves
federal funds rate
discount rate
open market operations
foreign exchange market intervention
sterilization

QUICK CHECK QUIZ

Section 1: Monetary Policy and Equilibrium Income

1. A student who cashes a check at the student union in order to go shopping is an example of the
   a. transactions demand for money.
   b. speculative demand for money.
   c. precautionary demand for money.
   d. income effect.
   e. substitution effect.

2. An increase in the interest rate will cause
   a. an increase in the demand for money.
   b. an increase in the quantity demanded of money.
   c. a decrease in the demand for money.
   d. a decrease in the quantity demanded of money.
   e. an increase in the supply of money.

3. A decrease in nominal income will cause
   a. an increase in the demand for money.
   b. an increase in the quantity demanded of money.
   c. a decrease in the demand for money.
   d. a decrease in the quantity demanded of money.
   e. a decrease in the supply of money.

4. The supply of money is
   a. a positive function of interest rates.
   b. a negative function of interest rates.
   c. a positive function of income.
   d. a negative function of income.
   e. independent of income and interest rates.

5. A bond selling for $998 pays $54.89 in interest annually. The current interest rate is
   a. .18.
   b. .055.
   c. .82.
   d. .945.
   e. .125.

6. If the interest rate is above the equilibrium rate, there is an excess _____ of money. People will _____ bonds, and the interest rate will _____ .
   a. demand; sell; rise
   b. demand; sell; drop
   c. demand; buy; drop
   d. supply; buy; drop
   e. supply; sell; rise

7. If the Fed wants to increase equilibrium income, it should _____ the supply of money, which will _____ interest rates. The change in interest rates will _____ consumption and investment, causing aggregate demand to _____ .
   a. decrease; increase; decrease; decrease
   b. decrease; decrease; increase; increase
   c. increase; decrease; increase; increase
   d. increase; increase; decrease; decrease
   e. increase; increase; increase; increase

8. Consider the graph below. The demand for money is Md_1, and the supply of money is Ms_1. The equilibrium interest rate is i_1, and the equilibrium quantity of money is M_1. If income decreases,

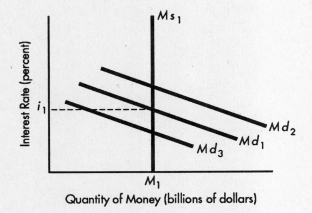

a. the demand for money shifts to Md_2, and the interest rate and equilibrium quantity rise.
b. the demand for money shifts to Md_2, and the interest rate rises.
c. the demand for money shifts to Md_3, and the interest rate and equilibrium quantity fall.
d. the demand for money shifts to Md_3, and the interest rate falls.
e. the supply of money shifts to the left, the interest rate rises, and the equilibrium quantity of money falls.

9. A bond sells for $990 and has a yield of 8.5 percent. The bond must be paying _____ in interest annually.
   a. $84.15
   b. $8415
   c. $8.415
   d. $116.47
   e. $1,164.71

Section 2: The Federal Reserve System

1. Which of the following is NOT a function of the Fed?
   a. accepting deposits from banks
   b. making loans to banks
   c. controlling taxes
   d. acting as a banker for the federal government
   e. controlling the money supply

2. The _____ is/are the policy-making entity of the Fed.
   a. Federal Reserve chairman
   b. Federal Reserve Board
   c. 12 Federal Reserve district banks
   d. 12 Federal Reserve Bank presidents
   e. FOMC

3. The Fed's most important function is
   a. providing services to the banking community.
   b. controlling the money supply.
   c. supervising the banking community.
   d. clearing checks.
   e. holding bank reserves.

Section 3: Implementing Monetary Policy

1. The ultimate goal of monetary policy is
   a. economic growth with stable prices.
   b. stable exchange rates.
   c. stable interest rates.
   d. a low federal funds rate.
   e. steady growth in bank reserves.

2. According to the equation of exchange,
   a. if the money supply increases and velocity is constant, real GNP must rise.
   b. if the money supply increases and velocity is constant, nominal GNP must rise.
   c. an increase in the money supply causes an increase in the price level.
   d. an increase in the money supply causes an increase in real GNP and higher prices.
   e. if the money supply increases, nominal GNP must rise.

3. To increase the money supply, the Fed would
   a. increase the reserve requirement and the discount rate, and sell bonds.
   b. increase the reserve requirement and the discount rate, and buy bonds.
   c. decrease the reserve requirement and the discount rate, and sell bonds.
   d. decrease the reserve requirement and the discount rate, and buy bonds.
   e. increase the reserve requirement, decrease the discount rate, and buy bonds.

4. Consider the First National Bank of Rozzelle. The bank has deposits of $600,000, loans of $500,000, vault cash of $30,000, and deposits at the Fed of $70,000. The reserve requirement is 4 percent. The bank's legal reserves are _____ , and excess reserves are _____ . The deposit expansion multiplier is _____ , and the banking system could create a maximum of _____ in new money.
   a. $30,000; $6,000; 25; $150,000
   b. $30,000; $26,000; 25; $650,000
   c. $100,000; $96,000; 25; $2,400,000
   d. $100,000; $76,000; 4; $304,000
   e. $100,000; $76,000; 25; $1,900,000

5. If the Fed wants to decrease the money supply, it can
   a. buy bonds.
   b. sell bonds.
   c. lower the reserve requirement.
   d. lower the federal funds rate.
   e. lower the discount rate.

6. Suppose that the U.K. pound is currently equivalent to $1.818 and that the Fed wants the dollar to depreciate versus the pound. The Fed will most likely
   a. buy dollars.
   b. buy pounds.
   c. sell dollars.
   d. sell pounds.
   e. ask the U.K. central bank to buy pounds.

7. If the Fed intervened in the foreign currency market to buy another currency, the domestic money supply would _____ , and the Fed might _____ bonds to offset its foreign currency operations. This process is called _____ .
   a. decrease; buy; sterilization
   b. decrease; sell; sterilization
   c. increase; sell; sterilization
   d. increase; buy; sterilization
   e. increase; sell; depreciation

PRACTICE QUESTIONS AND PROBLEMS

Section 1: Monetary Policy and Equilibrium Income

1. The _____ demand for money is a demand to hold money in order to spend it on goods and services.

2. The _____ demand for money is a demand to hold money to take care of emergencies.

3. The _____ demand for money is created by uncertainty about the value of other assets.

4. The demand for money depends on _____ and _____ .

5. There is a(n) _____ relationship between the interest rate and the quantity of money demanded.

6. The greater nominal income, the _____ (greater, smaller) the demand for money.

7. The _____ sets the money supply.

8. The supply of money _____ (does, does not) depend on interest rates and nominal income.

9. The formula for the current interest rate is _____ .

10. A bond pays $200 a year in interest and sells for $2,500. The current interest rate is

    _____ .

11. As bond prices increase, the current interest rate _____ .

12. A decrease in the money supply causes interest rates to _____ (rise, fall), which causes consumption and investment to _____ (rise, fall). The changes in consumption and investment cause aggregate demand to _____ (increase, decrease), which causes equilibrium income to _____ (rise, fall). Use the graphs below to illustrate the sequence of events following a decrease in the money supply.

13. Norm and Debbie keep 1.5 months income in a NOW account for emergencies. This is an example of the _____ demand for money.

14. A young couple cashes in a bond to buy a crib and changing table to prepare for the birth of their first child. This is an example of the _____ demand for money.

15. If nominal income increases, the demand for money _____ (does not change, shifts to the right).

16. You read in *The Wall Street Journal* that the bond markets rallied yesterday (bond prices increased). Interest rates must have _____ (increased, decreased).

17. A bond sells for $975 and pays $68.25 in interest annually. The current rate of interest is _____. If the bond market plummets (demand falls), the price of this bond will _____ (rise, fall) and the interest rate will _____ (rise, fall).

Section 2: The Federal Reserve System

1. The Federal Reserve System was intended to be a _____ (centralized, decentralized) system.

2. There are _____ Federal Reserve districts, each with its own Federal Reserve bank.

3. Monetary policy is largely set by the _____.

4. The chairman of the Federal Reserve Board of Governors is appointed by the _____ and serves a _____ -year term. Governors serve _____ -year terms.

5. Each of the Fed's 12 district banks has a _____ -member board of directors.

6. The _____ is the official policy-making body of the Federal Reserve System. It consists of the Board of Governors plus _____ of the Federal Reserve bank presidents.

7. List the six main functions of the Fed.

_____

_____

_____

_____

_____

_____

8. The most important function of the Fed is _____ .

9. The Federal Reserve is the _____ bank of the United States.

10. The _____ has been called the second most powerful person in the United States.

Section 3: Implementing Monetary Policy

1. The goal of monetary policy is _____ with _____ .

2. An _____ is an objective used to achieve some ultimate policy goal.

3. $MV = PY$ is the _____ .

4. The _____ of money is the average number of times each dollar is spent on final goods and services in a year.

5. The _____ states that if the money supply increases and the velocity of money is constant, nominal GNP must rise.

6. In the late 1970s and early 1980s, the M1 velocity of money _____ (fluctuated erratically, remained relatively stable).

7. The Fed monitors _____ , _____ , and _____ and considers them in setting policy.

8. The Federal Reserve Bank of _____ implements monetary policy for the Fed.

9. An _____ is instructions issued by the FOMC to the Federal Reserve Bank in New York to implement monetary policy.

10. List the three tools the Fed uses to change reserves.

   _____

   _____

   _____

11. Large banks must hold a _____ (greater, smaller) percentage of deposits in reserve than do small banks.

12. _____ deposits are time deposits held by business firms.

13. Legal reserves consist of _____ and _____ .

14. The Fed can reduce the money-creating potential of the banking system by _____ (raising, lowering) the reserve requirement.

15. The _____ rate is the rate of interest the Fed charges banks. In other countries, this rate is called the _____ rate.

16. Banks borrow from other banks in the _____ market.

17. If the Fed wants to increase the money supply, it _____ (raises, lowers) the discount rate.

18. _____ are the buying and selling of government bonds by the Fed and are the Fed's major monetary policy tool.

19. To increase the money supply, the Fed _____ (buys, sells) bonds.

20. _____ indicate how the money supply should react to a change in the short-run target.

21. The Fed has been using _____ as its short-run operating target since the fall of 1979.

22. _____ is the buying and selling of foreign exchange by a central bank in order to move exchange rates up or down.

23. If the Fed wants the dollar to appreciate against the yen, it will buy _____ (dollars, yen).

24. _____ is the use of open market operations to offset the effects of a foreign exchange market intervention on the domestic money supply.

25. If the Fed wishes to support a foreign currency, it _____ (increases, decreases) the domestic money supply, unless offsetting operations are undertaken.

26. List the four other factors that the Fed considers in its FOMC directives.

   _____

   _____

   _____

   _____

27. The Bank of McDonald has the following balance sheet:

Assets		Liabilities	
Vault cash	$ 20,000	Deposits	$ 400,000
Deposits in the Fed	30,000		
Loans	350,000		

   If this bank's reserve requirement is 5 percent,

   a. legal reserves are _____ .

   b. required reserves are _____ .

   c. excess reserves are _____ .

   d. the deposit expansion multiplier is _____ .

   e. this bank can create _____ of additional deposits.

   f. the banking system could create a maximum of _____ .

THINKING ABOUT AND APPLYING MONETARY POLICY

I. More on Foreign Exchange Market Intervention

If the Fed feels that the price of the dollar in terms of U.K. pounds is unacceptably high, it may choose to intervene directly in the foreign exchange markets. To bolster the pound, the Fed will _____ (buy, sell) pounds. In the process, the domestic money supply will _____ (increase, decrease).

In the absence of any sterilization actions by the Fed, domestic interest rates will _____ (increase, decrease) as a result of the change in the money supply. The change in domestic interest rates will _____ (increase, decrease) the demand for U.S. securities. The dollar will _____ (appreciate, depreciate) in value. The effect of the change in the money supply _____ (reinforced, opposed) the Fed's actions in the foreign exchange market.

II. More on the P* Theory

Suppose that the Federal Reserve is concerned that the underlying level of inflation in the economy is too high. If the inflation rate is over 5 percent, the Fed will pursue a restrictive monetary policy.

The information available to the Fed is this year's money supply, which is $2,788.1645 billion, and potential GNP, which the Fed believes is $4,189.0903 billion. Use the P* theory to calculate the underlying level of inflation in the economy. What are your assumptions? Should the Fed clamp down on the money supply?

_____

_____

_____

_____

ANSWERS

Quick Check Quiz

Section 1: Monetary Policy and Equilibrium Income

1. a; 2. d; 3. c; 4. e; 5. b; 6. d; 7. c; 8. d; 9. a
   If you missed any of these questions, you should go back and review pages 354–360 in Chapter 14.

Section 2: The Federal Reserve System

1. c; 2. e; 3. b
   If you missed any of these questions, you should go back and review pages 360–364 in Chapter 14.

Section 3: Implementing Monetary Policy

1. a; 2. b (Answer a is false, and the others are true only if certain assumptions are made. For c to be true, velocity must be constant and the economy must be at full employment, so that Y cannot rise. For d to be true, velocity must be constant and there must be some unemployment in the economy. Answer e may be true if velocity is constant.); 3. d; 4. e (LR = vault cash + deposits at the Fed = $30,000 + $70,000 = $100,000. $RR = rD$ = .04[$600,000] = $24,000. $ER = LR − RR$ = $100,000 − $24,000 = $76,000. The deposit expansion multiplier = 1/r = 1/.04 = 25. The change in the money supply = l/r[ER] = 25[$76,000] = $1,900,000.); 5. b; 6. b (The Fed can keep this up indefinitely, since it can create dollars to buy pounds. It does not need the help of the U.K. central bank to depreciate the dollar.); 7. c

   If you missed any of these questions, you should go back and review pages 365–378 in Chapter 14.

Practice Questions and Problems

Section 1: Monetary Policy and Equilibrium Income

1. transactions
2. precautionary
3. speculative
4. nominal income; interest rates
5. inverse
6. greater
7. Federal Reserve
8. does not
9. annual interest payment/bond price
10. .08 (annual interest payment/bond price = $200/$2,500 = .08)
11. decreases
12. rise; fall; decrease; fall

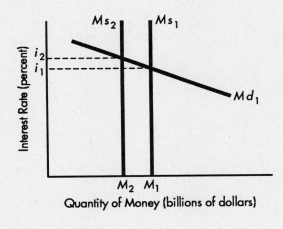
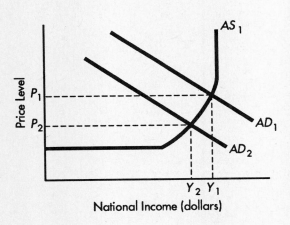

13. precautionary
14. transactions
15. shifts to the right
16. decreased
17. .07 (annual interest payment/bond price = $68.25/$975 = .07); fall; rise

Section 2: The Federal Reserve System

1. decentralized
2. 12
3. Board of Governors
4. president; four; fourteen
5. nine
6. Federal Open Market Committee (FOMC); five
7. provides currency
   holds reserves
   clears checks
   supervises commercial banks
   acts as a banker for the federal government
   controls the money supply
8. controlling the money supply
9. central
10. Fed chairperson

Section 3: Implementing Monetary Policy

1. economic growth; stable prices
2. intermediate target
3. equation of exchange
4. velocity
5. quantity theory of money
6. fluctuated erratically
7. commodity prices; interest rates; foreign exchange rates
8. New York
9. FOMC directive
10. reserve requirement
    discount rate
    open market operations
11. greater
12. Nonpersonal time
13. vault cash; deposits in the Fed
14. raising
15. discount; bank
16. federal funds
17. lowers
18. Open market operations
19. buys
20. Short-run operating targets
21. bank reserves
22. Foreign exchange market intervention
23. dollars
24. Sterilization
25. increases
26. federal funds rate
    the growth of real GNP
    the rate of inflation
    foreign exchange rate of the dollar

27. a. $50,000 ($LR$ = vault cash + deposits in the Fed = $20,000 + $30,000)
     b. $20,000 ($RR = rD$ = .05[$400,000])
     c. $30,000 ($ER = LR - RR$ = $50,000 - $20,000)
     d. 20 ($1/r$ = 1/.05)
     e. $30,000 (the amount of ER)
     f. $600,000 (change in money supply = deposit expansion multiplier × excess reserves = 20[$30,000])

Thinking About and Applying Monetary Policy

I.   More on Foreign Exchange Market Intervention

buy; increase; decrease; decrease; depreciate; reinforced

II.   More on the P* Theory

From the "Economically Speaking" article in your text,

$$P* = \text{(money supply} \times \text{velocity)/potential GNP}$$

The article suggests that velocity is constant and equal to 1.6527. Substituting in, we have

$$P* = (2{,}788.1645 \text{ billion} \times 1.6527)/4{,}189.0903 \text{ billion} = 1.10$$

We have assumed that velocity will continue to be 1.6527. Since the rate of underlying inflation is greater than 5 percent, the Fed should pursue a more restrictive monetary policy.

CHAPTER 15

Macroeconomic Policy: Trade-offs, Expectations, Credibility, and Sources of Business Cycles

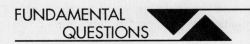

FUNDAMENTAL QUESTIONS

1. What is the Phillips curve?

   The **Phillips curve** is a graph showing the relationship between the inflation rate and the rate of unemployment. In the short run, the Phillips curve has a downward slope, indicating a possible trade-off between inflation and unemployment. In the long run, the Phillips curve is vertical, indicating that no such trade-off is possible.

2. Why does the Phillips curve vary from the short to the long run?

   The short-run shape of the Phillips curve is caused by shifts in aggregate demand while aggregate supply stays constant. In the long run, adaptations are made and the aggregate supply curve shifts.

3. What is the relationship between unexpected inflation and the unemployment rate?

   Unexpected inflation can decrease unemployment in three ways. If workers have constant **reservation wages** and constant expectations about inflation, an unexpected increase in inflation raises nominal wages without raising real wages. Workers do not realize that inflation has increased, so they accept smaller real wages and unemployment decreases.

   When aggregate demand is greater than expected, inventories fall and prices on remaining goods in stock are higher. Businesses hire new workers to increase production to offset the falling inventories.

   If wage contracts exist, employers must adjust employment to changing conditions. If revenues fall, employers must reduce costs, either by lowering wages or by getting rid of workers. If a wage contract precludes lowering wages, a decrease in inflation will result in unemployment.

4. How are macroeconomic expectations formed?

   Adaptive expectations are expectations based on past experience. People expect things to be as they were before, and they take nothing else into account. **Rational expectations** are formed using all available information, including, but not limited to, past events.

5. What makes government policies credible?

   A government's policies are credible only if they are not **time inconsistent**. People will refuse to believe the announcements of a government that changes its policies when conditions change.

6. How are business cycles related to political elections?

Some economists believe in the existence of a political business cycle, in which the incumbent administration stimulates the economy just before the election. After the election, unemployment and inflation rise. There is no conclusive evidence of political business cycles in the United States.

7. How do real shocks to the economy affect business cycles?

Real **shocks** are changes in real economic variables, such as the weather, technology, and so forth. These shocks are to be distinguished from discretionary fiscal and monetary policies.

8. How is inflationary monetary policy related to government fiscal policy?

The government must finance its spending through taxes, borrowing, or changes in the money supply. If the government cannot or will not borrow and deficits continue, monetary policy must be inflationary.

KEY TERMS

Phillips curve
reservation wage
adaptive expectation
rational expectation

time inconsistent
shock
monetary reform

QUICK CHECK QUIZ

Section 1: The Phillips Curve

1. According to the short-run Phillips curve,
   a. inflation is inversely related to unemployment.
   b. inflation is positively related to unemployment.
   c. inflation is not related to unemployment.
   d. high inflation necessarily requires high unemployment.
   e. low inflation and low unemployment can occur at the same time.

2. The long-run Phillips curve
   a. is downward sloping, illustrating the possibility of trading off higher inflation for lower unemployment.
   b. is upward sloping, indicating that high unemployment is associated with rising prices.
   c. is horizontal, indicating that no trade-off is possible between unemployment and inflation in the long run.
   d. is vertical, indicating no relationship between inflation and unemployment in the long run.
   e. is horizontal, indicating an infinite number of trade-offs between inflation and unemployment.

3. Which of the following statements is false?
   a. In the long run, as the economy adjusts to an increase in aggregate demand, there is a period in which national income falls and the price level rises.
   b. The trade-off between unemployment and inflation worsened from the 1960s through the 1970s.
   c. A decrease in aggregate supply is reflected in a movement along the Phillips curve.
   d. The long-run Phillips curve is a vertical line at the natural rate of unemployment.
   e. The trade-off between unemployment and inflation disappears in the long run.

Section 2: The Role of Expectations

1. Unexpected inflation can affect the unemployment rate through
   a. the income effect.
   b. the substitution effect.
   c. the wealth effect.
   d. wage contracts.
   e. the interest rate effect.

2. Which of the following could NOT cause a movement along the Phillips curve?
   a. a change in inflation that is not expected by workers
   b. an unexpected increase in inflation that causes inventories to decline
   c. wage contracts that did not correctly anticipate the inflation rate
   d. an anticipated rise in nominal wages
   e. All of the above cause movements along the short-run Phillips curve.

3. Which of the following is an example of rational rather than adaptive expectations?
   a. The crowd expects a 95 percent free-throw shooter to hit the free throw to win the state basketball championship.
   b. A professor has been 10 minutes late to class three times in a row. Students come to the fourth class 10 minutes late.
   c. The fans of a pro football team that had four wins, ten losses, and one tie last year find another team to root for this year.
   d. Stockholders of a firm that had losses three years in a row sell off their stocks.
   e. A company with a poor earnings record over the past five years finds itself swamped by investors when word of its new superproduct leaks out.

Section 3: Credibility and Time Inconsistency

1. The central bank announces a low-monetary-growth policy. If the goal of the central bank is to keep unemployment as low as possible, it will follow a
   a. low-money-growth policy if a low-wage contract is signed.
   b. high-money-growth policy if a low-wage contract is signed.
   c. low-money-growth policy if a high-wage contract is signed.
   d. high-money-growth policy if a high-wage contract is signed.
   e. high-money-growth policy no matter which labor contract is signed.

2. Which of the following statements is false?
   a. The Federal Reserve has a credibility problem because of time inconsistency.
   b. The Fed is required to follow the plans it announces to Congress in conformance with the Full Employment and Balanced Growth Act (1978).
   c. If the public does not believe the Fed, the Fed's policies may not have their intended effect.
   d. The Fed's policies could gain credibility if Congress were to pass a law requiring the Fed to increase the money supply at a fixed rate.
   e. If the Fed abandoned the goal of reducing unemployment below the natural rate, the problem of inflation would disappear.

Section 4: Sources of Business Cycles

1. Which of the following statements is true?
   a. Economists have clear evidence that political business cycles occur in the United States.
   b. The effort to exploit the short-run Phillips curve for political gain would shift the Phillips curve in a manner consistent with recent data.
   c. The end result of the political business cycle is that the economy returns to its original equilibrium price level and output after the election.
   d. Real business cycles are caused by discretionary monetary policy.
   e. Real business cycles are caused by discretionary fiscal policy.

2. Which of the following would NOT be a cause of a real business cycle?
   a. a decrease in government borrowing
   b. a drought in the Midwest
   c. oil prices skyrocketing as a result of an accident on the world's largest offshore oil rig
   d. a labor strike that cripples the steel industry
   e. an improvement in the technology for solar energy that yields a lightweight solar battery that can be used to power cars for long trips

Section 5: The Link Between Monetary and Fiscal Policies

1. The government budget constraint
   a. always holds true.
   b. demonstrates that there is no link between fiscal and monetary policy.
   c. demonstrates that an expansionary fiscal policy implies a contractionary monetary policy.
   d. shows that the change in the money supply equals government spending minus borrowing.
   e. demonstrates that monetary reform will always halt inflation.

2. Which of the following is false?
   a. In most developed countries, monetary and fiscal policies are conducted by separate independent agencies.
   b. Fiscal policy can impose an inflationary burden on monetary policy.
   c. In typical developing countries, monetary and fiscal policies are controlled by the same central authority.
   d. Using money to finance deficits has produced severe deflation in many countries.
   e. Monetary control is not possible until fiscal policy is under control.

PRACTICE QUESTIONS AND PROBLEMS

Section 1: The Phillips Curve

1. The _____ illustrates the inverse relationship between inflation and the unemployment rate.

2. The Phillips curve trade-off between inflation and unemployment _____ (does, does not) persist over the long run.

3. Over the long run, the Phillips curve is _____ .

4. Plot the following unemployment and inflation data on the graph below. Be sure to label your axes.

	Inflation Rate	**Unemployment Rate**
1974	14.6	5.6
1975	13.5	8.5
1976	9.3	7.7
1977	11	7.1
1978	13.9	6.1

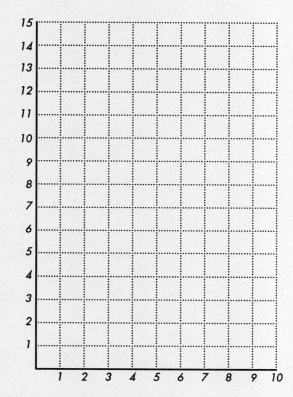

Does your graph imply the existence of a short-run Phillips curve during this period? _____

5. The downward slope of the short-run Phillips curve is caused by shifts in _____ ,

with _____ remaining constant.

Section 2: The Role of Expectations

1. A _____ is the minimum wage that an unemployed worker is willing to accept.

2. List the two assumptions underlying the short-run Phillips curve.

_____

_____

3. The _____ wage is the number of dollars earned; the _____

wage is the purchasing power of those dollars.

4. If people's expectations about inflation do not change, the short-run effect of disinflation is rising

_____ .

5. The short-run trade-off between inflation and unemployment comes from _____

inflation.

6. Unexpected inflation can affect the employment rate in the following three ways.

_____

_____

_____

7. As economic conditions change, firms with expiring wage contracts can adjust

_____ to those conditions; firms with existing contracts must adjust

_____ to those conditions.

8. _____ expectations are expectations that are determined by what has happened in

the recent past.

9. _____ expectations are based on all available relevant information.

10. Your economics professor bases her first exam solely on material from the textbook. Before the second

exam, she announces that this exam will be based primarily on lecture material. If you only study the text-

book, you are acting on the basis of _____ expectations.

11. When the inflation rate is unexpectedly high, unemployment _____ .

12. If wages were always flexible, unexpected changes in aggregate demand would be met by

_____ adjustments rather than by _____ adjustments.

Section 3: Credibility and Time Inconsistency

1. _____ gives the Fed a credibility problem.

2. If the public does not believe the low-money-growth plans of the central bank, high-wage contracts will

always be signed and the central bank will always have to follow a _____-

money-growth policy to maintain the natural rate of unemployment.

3. The central bank could eliminate the problem of _____ if it eliminated the goal of

reducing unemployment below its natural rate.

4. List two ways to establish the credibility of the Fed.

_____

_____

5. A plan is _____ when it changes over time in response to changing conditions.

Section 4: Sources of Business Cycles

1. The _____ refers to macroeconomic policy used to promote the re-election of incumbent politicians.

2. The _____ refers to a business cycle that is not related to discretionary policy actions.

3. The political business cycle argument suggests that incumbent administrations follow _____ macroeconomic policies just before an election.

4. Economists _____ (do, do not) agree on whether a political business cycle exists in the United States.

5. A _____ is an unexpected change in a variable.

6. A _____ is an expansion and contraction of the economy caused by a change in the weather, technology, or other real factors.

Section 5: The Link Between Monetary and Fiscal Policies

1. Write the equation for the government budget restraint.

   _____

2. A _____ is a new monetary policy that includes the introduction of a new monetary unit.

3. The only way to reduce the amount of money being created is to reduce the _____ minus _____ .

THINKING ABOUT AND APPLYING MACROECONOMIC POLICY: TRADE-OFFS, EXPECTATIONS, CREDIBILITY, AND SOURCES OF BUSINESS CYCLES

I. The Link Between Fiscal and Monetary Policy in Brazil

The "Economically Speaking" article in your text describes President Fernando Collor de Mello's attempt to end the hyperinflation in Brazil. Experts agree that a great deal will depend on Mr. Collor's ability to reduce the government deficit.

   The items below are key elements in Mr. Collor's plan. Use the modified government budget constraint equation

$$\Delta M = (G - T) - B$$

to explain how each of these policies will help to end Brazil's hyperinflation.

1. cutting government payrolls
2. privatization of two-thirds of Brazil's state companies

3. raising taxes
4. cracking down on tax cheats
5. freezing savings and money market funds
6. wage and price controls
7. privatization certificates

ANSWERS

Quick Check Quiz

Section 1: The Phillips Curve

1. a; 2. d; 3. c
   If you missed any of these questions, you should go back and review pages 384–389 in Chapter 15.

Section 2: The Role of Expectations

1. d; 2. d (Only unanticipated inflation makes the inflation-unemployment trade-off possible.); 3. e
   If you missed any of these questions, you should go back and review pages 389–396 in Chapter 15.

Section 3: Credibility and Time Inconsistency

1. e; 2. b
   If you missed either of these questions, you should go back and review pages 396–400 in Chapter 15.

Section 4: Sources of Business Cycles

1. b; 2. a
   If you missed either of these questions, you should go back and review pages 400–404 in Chapter 15.

Section 5: The Link Between Monetary and Fiscal Policies

1. a; 2. d
   If you missed either of these questions, you should go back and review pages 404–407 in Chapter 15.

Practice Questions and Problems

Section 1: The Phillips Curve

1. Phillips curve
2. does not
3. vertical

4.

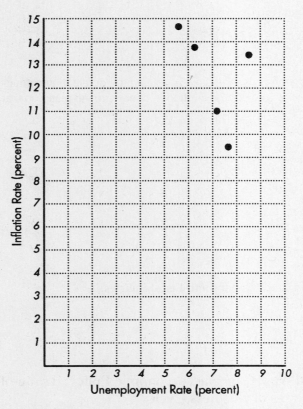

Since the curve does slope down, there is evidence of a short-run Phillips curve trade-off between inflation and unemployment.

5. aggregate demand; aggregate supply (Note that aggregate supply does shift in the long run.)

Section 2: The Role of Expectations

1. reservation wage
2. constant expected rate of inflation
   constant reservation wage
3. nominal; real
4. unemployment
5. unexpected
6. wage expectations
   inventory fluctuations
   wage contracts
7. wages; employment
8. Adaptive
9. Rational
10. adaptive
11. decreases
12. wage; employment

Section 3: Credibility and Time Inconsistency

1. Time inconsistency
2. high
3. inflation
4. Pass a law requiring the Fed to maintain a certain growth rate in the money supply. Create incentives for Fed policymakers to follow through with low-money-growth plans, so that the Fed establishes a reputation for consistency.
5. time inconsistent

Section 4: Sources of Business Cycles

1. political business cycle
2. real business cycle
3. expansionary
4. do not
5. shock
6. real business cycle

Section 5: The Link Between Monetary and Fiscal Policies

1. $G = T + B + \Delta M$
2. monetary reform
3. fiscal deficit; borrowing

Thinking About and Applying Macroeconomic Policy: Trade-offs, Expectations, Credibility, and Sources of Business Cycles

I. The Link Between Fiscal Policy and Monetary Policy in Brazil

1. Cutting government payrolls directly reduces the G in the equation. All other things being equal, a smaller G implies a smaller ΔM.
2. The privatization of Brazil's state-owned companies will have the same effect as raising T, since selling these companies will bring in revenue for the government. Mr. Collor also expects to reduce G, since some of the companies were not well run while in the government's hands. Decreases in G and increases in T reduce ΔM.
3. Raising taxes directly increases T, which reduces the deficit and decreases ΔM.
4. Cracking down on tax cheats directly increases T.
5. Freezing savings and money market funds directly affects the money supply—M in the equation.
6. Wage and price controls are temporary measures to control inflation and will not work in the long run. They do not directly enter into the government budget constraint equation.
7. Forcing banks and insurance companies to buy privatization certificates is a way to spur the selling off of government-owned companies, and it enters into the budget constraint equation in the same way as item 2.

Most of these measures amount to reducing the government deficit. Hence the comment by the congressman that Mr. Collor will either do away with the deficit or the deficit will do away with Mr. Collor.

CHAPTER 16
Macroeconomic Viewpoints:
New Keynesian, Monetarist, and New Classical

FUNDAMENTAL
QUESTIONS

1. What do Keynesian economists believe today?

   Keynesians believe the following:
   Wages and prices are not flexible in the short run.
   The economy is not always in equilibrium.
   The government must take an active role in the economy to stabilize aggregate demand.
   The private sector, especially investment, is an important source of shifts in aggregate demand.
   The aggregate supply curve is not horizontal, but slopes upward as national income approaches its potential level.

2. What role do monetarists believe the government should play in the economy?

   Monetarists believe that the economy is inherently stable and that government intervention in the economy makes business cycles worse. They therefore favor minimal government intervention in the economy.

3. What is new classical economics?

   New classical economists emphasize rational expectations and believe that the economy tends toward equilibrium. They also believe that fiscal and monetary policy can only change the equilibrium level of real national income if the changes are unexpected. Any predictable policy simply affects prices.

4. How do new theories of economics develop over time?

   New economic theories develop in response to new economic situations or perceived failings in old theories. Thus Keynesian theory evolved to explain the Great Depression, and monetarist and new classical economics evolved to explain the problem of simultaneous unemployment and inflation.

KEY TERMS

Keynesian economics   classical economics
monetarist economics   new classical economics

223

QUICK CHECK QUIZ

Section 1: Keynesian Economics

1. Which of the following is NOT common to Keynesian and new Keynesian economists?
   a. the belief that wages and prices are not flexible in the short run
   b. the belief that the aggregate supply curve is a horizontal line
   c. the belief that monetary policy should be used to manage aggregate demand
   d. the belief that fiscal policy should be used to stabilize aggregate demand
   e. the belief that disequilibrium occurs in the labor market

2. Keynesians
   a. believe that the price system efficiently allocates resources.
   b. believe that monetary policy operates with long and variable lags.
   c. emphasize rational expectations.
   d. believe that the government needs to take an active role in managing aggregate demand.
   e. believe that only unexpected changes in the money supply affect real national income.

Section 2: Monetarist Economics

1. Monetarists believe that
   a. fiscal policy is an effective way to manage aggregate demand.
   b. the government should use only monetary policy to achieve its goals of low inflation and economic growth.
   c. government intervention should be kept to a minimum.
   d. the government should change monetary and fiscal policies to suit current conditions.
   e. government policies have an effect on real output only if the changes are unanticipated.

2. Monetarists
   a. have great faith that the market system allocates resources efficiently.
   b. believe that government intervention accentuates business cycles.
   c. believe that the government should follow a fixed rule for monetary growth.
   d. believe that government intervention in the economy is ineffective because of long and variable lags.
   e. All of these statements are true.

3. The effect lag
   a. is the time it takes for the effects of a policy to work their way through the economy once the policy is implemented.
   b. is the time it takes for policymakers to realize there is a problem.
   c. is the time it takes for policymakers to formulate a policy once they recognize there is a problem.
   d. is the time from when policymakers realize there is a problem until the effects of the policy work their way through the economy.
   e. is the time from when policymakers formulate a policy until the effects of the policy work their way through the economy.

Section 3: New Classical Economics

1. New classical economists agree with Keynesians that
    a. wages and prices are flexible.
    b. the aggregate supply curve is vertical.
    c. markets are always in equilibrium.
    d. any predictable macroeconomic policy has an effect only on prices.
    e. monetary and fiscal policies can achieve a low, stable rate of inflation.

2. New classical economics and classical economics both
    a. emphasize rational expectations.
    b. assume perfect information.
    c. assume a horizontal aggregate supply curve.
    d. believe that wages and prices are flexible.
    e. believe that formal rules should govern economic policy making.

3. Monetarists and new classical economists agree that
    a. only unexpected changes in prices have effects on real national income.
    b. wages and prices are not flexible in the short run.
    c. any predictable macroeconomic policy has an effect only on prices.
    d. attempts by the government to manage aggregate demand make business cycles worse.
    e. the government should not try to affect the equilibrium level of real output.

Section 4: Comparison and Influence

1. Which of the following favor an active role for government in promoting low inflation and economic growth?
    a. only Keynesians
    b. only monetarists
    c. only new classical economists
    d. monetarists and new classical economists
    e. monetarists and Keynesians

2. Which of the following believe that wages and prices are flexible in the short run?
    a. only Keynesians
    b. only monetarists
    c. only new classical economists
    d. monetarists and new classical economists
    e. monetarists and Keynesians

3. Which of the following emphasize rational expectations?
    a. only Keynesians
    b. only monetarists
    c. only new classical economists
    d. monetarists and new classical economists
    e. monetarists and Keynesians

4. Which group's theory(ies) developed as a response to the problem of unemployment and inflation at the same time?
   a. only Keynesian theory
   b. only monetarist theory
   c. only new classical economist theory
   d. monetarist and new classical economist theories
   e. monetarist and Keynesian theories

5. Which of the following believe that the economy tends toward equilibrium?
   a. only Keynesians
   b. only monetarists
   c. only new classical economists
   d. monetarists and new classical economists
   e. monetarists and Keynesians

6. Which of the following favor fixed rules for money growth?
   a. only Keynesians
   b. only monetarists
   c. only new classical economists
   d. monetarists and new classical economists
   e. monetarists and Keynesians

7. Which of the following believe that monetary and fiscal policies are effective only if people cannot anticipate the changes?
   a. only Keynesians
   b. only monetarists
   c. only new classical economists
   d. monetarists and new classical economists
   e. monetarists and Keynesians

PRACTICE QUESTIONS AND PROBLEMS

Section 1: Keynesian Economics

1. _____ economics focuses on the role government plays in stabilizing the economy by managing aggregate demand.

2. New Keynesians _____ (do, do not) believe that wages and prices are not flexible in the short run.

3. New Keynesians believe that the economy _____ (is, is not) always in equilibrium.

4. New Keynesian economists _____ (do, do not) believe that the government must play an active role in stabilizing the economy.

Section 2: Monetarist Economics

1. _____ is the leading monetarist economist.

2. Monetarists believe that changes in the money supply directly affect _____ and
   _____ .

3. Monetarists believe that fiscal and monetary policies have only _____ effects on
   real national income.

4. Monetarists believe that, in the long run, a change in the money supply will affect only the
   _____ .

5. Monetarists believe that the economy _____ (does, does not) tend toward
   equilibrium.

6. Monetarists _____ (do, do not) believe that the government needs to play an active
   role in stabilizing the economy.

7. Between 1957 and 1989, the inflation rate seemed to follow changes in the growth rate of the money supply with a lag of _____ or _____ years.

8. _____ lag is the time it takes policymakers to realize that a problem exists.

9. _____ lag is the time it takes policymakers to formulate an appropriate policy once
   they realize that a problem exists.

10. The _____ lag is the time it takes for the effects of the policy to work through the
    economy.

11. Monetarists believe that government attempts at achieving full employment and low inflation make the
    economy _____ .

12. Instead of discretionary fiscal and monetary policy, monetarists advocate fiscal and monetary
    _____ .

13. Monetarists emphasize the role of the _____ in determining equilibrium income
    and prices.

14. Monetarists believe that government intervention makes the economy worse because of the existence of
    long and variable _____ .

Section 3: New Classical Economics

1. Classical economists believed that the aggregate supply curve was _____ and that
   changes in aggregate demand affected only the _____ level, not the level of
   _____ .

2. Classical economists believed that prices and wages _____ (were, were not) perfectly flexible.

3. New classical economists believe that wages and prices _____ (are, are not) flexible.

4. New classical economists emphasize _____ expectations. Classical economists assumed _____ information.

5. It is much easier for policymakers to make unexpected changes in policy if expectations are formed _____ rather than _____ .

6. New classical economists believe that the economy _____ (does, does not) tend toward equilibrium.

7. New classical economists believe that during recessions low real wages cause workers to substitute _____ activities for work.

8. New classical economists believe that changes in fiscal and monetary policy can affect the equilibrium level of income only if those changes are _____ .

9. New classical economists believe that any predictable policy simply affects _____ .

10. New classical economists believe that the goal of monetary and fiscal policies should be a low, stable rate of _____ .

Section 4: Comparison and Influence

1. Macroeconomic theories develop in response to _____ in existing theories.

2. Only _____ economics supports an active role for government; the other two theories suggest that government should not intervene.

3. _____ and _____ economists believe that the economy tends toward equilibrium.

THINKING ABOUT AND APPLYING MACROECONOMIC VIEWPOINTS: NEW KEYNESIAN, MONETARIST, AND NEW CLASSICAL

I.   The Roots of "Fresh Water" Economists

The "Economically Speaking" article in your text discusses the "fresh water" economists, so named for the origins of this group at universities along the shores of the Great Lakes. Like other economic theories, the theory of this group incorporates parts of economic theories that came before it. For each tenet of "fresh water" economic thought, place a K if the tenet has Keynesian roots, an M if it has monetarist roots, and an N if it has new classical roots. A tenet may have more than one letter next to it.

1. The government should not tinker with (or fine-tune) the economy. _____

2. Consumers, workers, business executives, and investors anticipate changes in the economy faster than the government and can adjust to them better on their own. _____

3. People anticipate the effects of changes in government policy and sometimes blunt the government's objectives in devising ways to accommodate the changes. _____

4. Recessions are not a problem, and the government can't do anything about them anyway.

   _____

5. Tax cuts have no effect on consumption. _____

6. Fresh water economists are rational expectationalists. _____

7. There is a lag before Congress recognizes that there is a problem and acts, and another lag before the acts have effects. _____

8. Government intervention could accentuate the business cycle. _____

9. Free markets work. _____

ANSWERS

Quick Check Quiz

Section 1: Keynesian Economics

1. b; 2. d
   If you missed either of these questions, you should go back and review pages 414–415 in Chapter 16.

Section 2: Monetarist Economics

1. c; 2. e; 3. a
   If you missed any of these questions, you should go back and review pages 416–419 in Chapter 16.

Section 3: New Classical Economics

1. e; 2. d; 3. e
   If you missed any of these questions, you should go back and review pages 419–423 in Chapter 16.

Section 4: Comparison and Influence

1. a; 2. d; 3. c; 4. d; 5. d; 6. b; 7. c
   If you missed any of these questions, you should go back and review pages 423–424 in Chapter 16.

Practice Questions and Problems

Section 1: Keynesian Economics

1. Keynesian
2. do
3. is not
4. do

Section 2: Monetarist Economics

1. Milton Friedman
2. consumption; investment
3. short-term
4. price level
5. does
6. do not
7. one; two
8. Recognition
9. Reaction
10. effect
11. worse
12. rules
13. money supply
14. lags

Section 3: New Classical Economics

1. vertical; price; output
2. were
3. are
4. rational; perfect
5. adaptively; rationally
6. does
7. nonlabor
8. unexpected
9. prices
10. inflation

Section 4: Comparison and Influence

1. shortcomings
2. Keynesian
3. Monetarists; new classical

Thinking About and Applying Macroeconomic Viewpoints: New Keynesian, Monetarist, and New Classical

I.   The Roots of "Fresh Water" Economists

1. M, N
2. N
3. N
4. M, N
5. M, N
6. N
7. N, M
8. M
9. M, N

CHAPTER 17
Macroeconomic Links Between Countries

1. How does change in the exchange rate affect the price of goods traded between countries?

Changes in exchange rates change the prices people must pay for imported products. When the domestic currency depreciates (decreases in value) against another currency, foreign goods become more expensive for domestic buyers and domestic goods become less expensive for foreign buyers. When the domestic currency appreciates (increases in value) against another currency, foreign goods become less expensive for domestic buyers and domestic goods become more expensive for foreign buyers.

A few examples will help make this clearer. Let's say that yesterday the U.S. dollar exchange rate for the Japanese yen was $1 = 200Y. Today, the exchange rate changed to $1 = 300Y. The dollar has appreciated relative to the yen, since a dollar will buy more yen than before. A Japanese VCR that costs 60,000Y in Japan sold for $300 yesterday (60,000Y/200Y per $) but only costs $200 today (60,000Y/300Y per $): foreign goods become less expensive to domestic buyers when a currency appreciates. On the other hand, a bushel of wheat that sells for $3 in the United States cost buyers in Japan 600Y yesterday ($3 × 200Y per $) but costs them 900Y today ($3 × 300Y per $): domestic goods become more expensive to foreign buyers when a currency appreciates.

Let's say that yesterday the U.S. dollar exchange rate for the German mark was $1 = 3DM. Today, the exchange rate changed to $1 = 2DM. The dollar has depreciated relative to the mark, since a dollar will buy fewer marks than before. A German BMW that costs 60,000DM in Germany sold for $20,000 yesterday (60,000DM/3DM per $) but costs $30,000 today (60,000DM/2DM per $): foreign goods become more expensive to domestic buyers when a currency depreciates. On the other hand, a bushel of wheat that sells for $3 in the United States costs buyers in Germany 9DM yesterday ($3 × 3DM per $), but only costs them 6DM today ($3 × 2DM per $): domestic goods become less expensive to foreign buyers when a currency depreciates.

2. Why don't similar goods sell for the same price all over the world?

Before we answer this question, let's look at why we would expect similar goods to sell at the same price. Let's suppose that gold sells for $350 per ounce in Philadelphia and for $400 per ounce in New York today. You (and many other people) could make a profit through **arbitrage** by buying gold in Philadelphia, driving to New York, and selling the gold there. But if you and others do this, the demand for gold in Philadelphia will increase, pushing the price of gold above $350, while in New York the supply of gold will increase, pulling the price of gold below $400. Arbitrage moves the prices of gold in Philadelphia and New York toward the same price; arbitrage will continue until gold has the same price in both cities.

In world markets, we would expect the same sort of process to work: arbitrage should make the cost of a good the same in all countries. If gold costs $400 per ounce in the United States, and the exchange rate between U.S. dollars and French francs is $1 = FF5, gold should cost FF2,000 ($400 × FF5 per $) in France. If gold doesn't cost FF2,000, then there are opportunities for arbitrage, which will eventually bring the price of gold to the same value in both New York and Paris. When monies have the same purchasing power in different markets, there is **purchasing power parity (PPP)**.

In reality, prices around the world frequently differ from purchasing power parity. A McDonald's Big Mac may cost $2.20 in New York but cost the equivalent of $3.15 in Paris. Deviations from PPP occur for the following reasons:

a. Goods are not identical in different countries. Although McDonald's tries hard to make Big Macs identical around the world, the atmosphere of eating on 7th Avenue in New York isn't the same as on the Champs Elysees.

b. Information is costly. A Parisian would have to make an international phone call to find out the price of a Big Mac today in New York.

c. Shipping costs affect prices. The cost of mailing a Big Mac from New York to Paris is more than the price difference.

d. Tariffs and other restrictions on trade affect prices. If the French government has a tax on imported hamburgers, the cost to the Parisian will be higher.

3. What is the relationship between inflation and changes in the exchange rate?

Exchange rates tend to change with differences in inflation rates between countries. Starting with purchasing power parity, if prices in the United States go up 10 percent faster than they do in France, the dollar must depreciate by 10 percent to restore PPP.

4. What is the domestic currency return from a foreign bond?

In addition to buying and selling goods between countries, the world economy also trades financial instruments like stocks and bonds. To be able to decide whether buying a U.S. bond or buying a Japanese bond is the better choice, you need to calculate the domestic currency return on the Japanese bond to find how much the interest paid in yen is expected to be worth in dollars in the future; you already know the return in dollars for the U.S. bond, since it pays interest in dollars. The domestic currency return on the Japanese bond is the interest rate paid by the bond plus the percentage change in the exchange rate. For example, if the Japanese bond pays 4 percent interest and the exchange rate between the dollar and the yen stays constant, the domestic currency return is still 4 percent. If instead the yen is expected to appreciate by 3 percent per year, buying the Japanese bond gives you a 7 percent return: the 4 percent interest plus the 3 percent increase in the value of the yen.

5. What is the relationship between domestic and foreign interest rates and changes in the exchange rate?

We have already looked at the idea of purchasing power parity and how arbitrage can bring prices of internationally traded goods into line. The same idea can be applied to international financial investments. **Interest rate parity (IRP)** occurs when the domestic currency return is the same for investments in different countries. When interest rate parity does not hold, arbitrageurs can make a profit by buying financial assets in one country and simultaneously selling similar assets in another country. In the process, exchange rates will change to make domestic currency returns move toward equality.

6. Why don't similar financial assets yield the same return all over the world?

The reasons why interest rate parity doesn't always hold are similar to some of the reasons why purchasing power parity doesn't always hold: financial assets are not identical in different countries (some investments are riskier than others and a **risk premium** must be paid), there are government controls on trade (similar to other restrictions on trade), and there are differences in tax structures (similar in effects to tariffs).

7. How does fiscal policy affect exchange rates?

   Fiscal policy affects exchange rates through its effects on interest rates. When the U.S. government increases borrowing to finance a larger deficit, U.S. interest rates rise relative to foreign interest rates. Investments in U.S. bonds become more attractive to foreigners, who increase their demand for dollars to buy U.S. bonds. The increased demand for dollars causes the dollar to appreciate. The dollar appreciation in turn reduces U.S. exports (they've become more expensive to foreigners) and increases U.S. imports (they've become cheaper for U.S. buyers). If the government decreases borrowing, all the changes go in the opposite direction.

8. How does monetary policy affect exchange rates?

   Monetary policy also affects exchange rates through interest rates. If the money supply is increased to finance a larger deficit, nominal interest rates will rise in the United States because of increased inflation caused by the increase in the money supply. To maintain PPP, the dollar must depreciate to counteract the increased inflation. IRP will also be maintained, since the depreciation of the dollar will counterbalance the increased inflation rate and higher nominal interest rates. If both PPP and IRP are maintained, U.S. monetary policy will not affect the amounts of U.S. imports and exports.

9. What can countries gain by coordinating their macroeconomic policies?

   We have seen that the macroeconomic policies followed by one nation can affect other nations through changes in exchange rates and changes in imports and exports. By coordinating their macroeconomic policies, countries have a better chance of attaining their policy goals, have greater access to economic information, and can achieve better outcomes than they could by acting on their own.

KEY TERMS

arbitrage
open economy
purchasing power parity (PPP)

interest rate parity (IRP)
capital control
risk premium

QUICK CHECK QUIZ

Section 1: Prices and Exchange Rates

1. When one currency increases in value relative to other currencies, we say that the currency has
   a. depreciated.
   b. appreciated.
   c. diminished.
   d. expanded.
   e. been redevalued.

2. When one currency decreases in value relative to other currencies, we say that the currency has
   a. depreciated.
   b. appreciated.
   c. diminished.
   d. expanded.
   e. been revalued.

3. If the exchange rate between U.S. dollars and French francs changes from $.15 = FF1 to $.20 = FF1, the French franc has
   a. depreciated.
   b. appreciated.
   c. diminished.
   d. expanded.
   e. been redevalued.

4. If the exchange rate between U.S. dollars and French francs changes from $.15 = FF1 to $.20 = FF1, the U.S. dollar has
   a. depreciated.
   b. appreciated.
   c. diminished.
   d. expanded.
   e. been derevalued.

5. Arbitrage is
   a. simultaneously buying different goods in the same market.
   b. the condition that exists when average wages buy the same market basket of goods in different countries.
   c. simultaneously buying in a market where the price is low and selling in a market where the price is high to profit from the price differential.
   d. the condition under which monies have the same purchasing power in different markets.
   e. the settlement of disputes concerning foreign exchange by outside mediators.

6. Purchasing power parity (PPP) is
   a. simultaneously buying different goods in the same market.
   b. the condition that exists when average wages buy the same market basket of goods in different countries.
   c. simultaneously buying in a market where the price is low and selling in a market where the price is high to profit from the price differential.
   d. the condition under which monies have the same purchasing power in different markets.
   e. the settlement of disputes concerning foreign exchange by outside mediators.

7. Which of the following is NOT a reason why purchasing power parity (PPP) may not exist?
   a. different wages in different countries
   b. costly information
   c. goods that are not identical in different countries
   d. tariffs and legal restrictions on international trade
   e. shipping costs

Section 2: Interest Rates and Exchange Rates

1. When deciding whether to buy a bond denominated in a foreign currency or a domestic bond, the buyer must take into account
   a. only the interest rate on the domestic bond.
   b. only the interest rate on the foreign bond.
   c. only the interest rates on both domestic and foreign bonds.
   d. the interest rates on the foreign and domestic bonds, and the expected changes in the exchange rate.
   e. the interest rates on the foreign and domestic bonds, and the current exchange rate.

2. Interest rate parity exists when the domestic interest rate equals the
   a. foreign interest rate.
   b. exchange rate.
   c. expected change in the exchange rate.
   d. foreign interest rate plus the expected change in the exchange rate.
   e. expected change in the foreign bond price.

3. When foreign-issued assets are subject to political risks, buyers must be paid
   a. in their own domestic currency.
   b. in another country's currency.
   c. a risk premium.
   d. below-market interest rates.
   e. interest rates based only on IRP.

Section 3: Policy Effects

1. An increase in U.S. government borrowing will
   a. increase real rates in the United States and cause the dollar to depreciate.
   b. increase real interest rates in the United States and cause the dollar to appreciate.
   c. decrease real interest rates in the United States and cause the dollar to depreciate.
   d. decrease real interest rates in the United States and cause the dollar to appreciate.
   e. leave real interest rates and the value of the dollar unchanged.

2. A decrease in U.S. government borrowing will
   a. increase real interest rates in the United States and cause the dollar to depreciate.
   b. increase real interest rates in the United States and cause the dollar to appreciate.
   c. decrease real interest rates in the United States and cause the dollar to depreciate.
   d. decrease real interest rates in the United States and cause the dollar to appreciate.
   e. leave real interest rates and the value of the dollar unchanged.

3. An increase in the U.S. money supply growth rate will
   a. increase real interest rates in the United States and cause the dollar to appreciate.
   b. increase nominal interest rates in the United States and cause the dollar to appreciate.
   c. affect exchange rates but not affect international trade if PPP holds.
   d. affect international trade but not affect exchange rates if PPP holds.
   e. affect neither international trade nor exchange rates if PPP holds.

4. Which of the following is NOT true when the money supply growth rate changes and both PPP and IRP hold?
   a. The expected change in the exchange rate equals the interest rate differential between domestic and foreign bonds.
   b. The expected change in the exchange rate equals the expected inflation differential between domestic and foreign countries.
   c. The interest rate differential between domestic and foreign bonds equals the expected inflation differential between domestic and foreign countries.
   d. All of the above are true when PPP and IRP hold.

Section 4: International Policy Coordination

1. Which of the following is NOT a reason why countries would benefit from coordinating their macroeconomic policies?
    a. Coordination could make reaching the goals of macroeconomic policy easier.
    b. Nations have access to more information.
    c. Coordination could help nations attain goals they couldn't reach on their own.
    d. Policymakers in most countries now agree on economic theories and appropriate policies.
    e. Overall economic performance would improve.

PRACTICE QUESTIONS AND PROBLEMS

Section 1: Prices and Exchange Rates

1. An economy that trades goods and financial assets with the rest of the world is

    _____ .

2. We say that a currency has appreciated when its value _____ (increases, decreases)

    relative to other currencies; we say that a currency has depreciated when its value

    _____ (increases, decreases) relative to other currencies.

3. Yesterday the exchange rate between the U.S. dollar and the British pound was £1 = $1.50. Today the exchange rate between the U.S. dollar and the British pound is £1 = $2.00.

    a. Yesterday the exchange rate was $1 = _____ .

    b. Today the exchange rate is $1 = _____ .

    c. The pound has _____ (appreciated, depreciated) relative to the dollar.

    d. The dollar has _____ (appreciated, depreciated) relative to the pound.

    e. A British Rolls-Royce costs £150,000. Yesterday the Rolls-Royce would have cost an American

        _____ ; today the Rolls-Royce costs _____ . The dollar

        has _____ (appreciated, depreciated) relative to the pound, making the

        Rolls-Royce _____ (more, less) expensive to Americans.

    f. An American Boeing airliner costs $60 million. Yesterday the Boeing would have cost a British airline

        _____ ; today the Boeing costs _____ . The dollar has

        _____ (appreciated, depreciated) relative to the pound, making the Boeing

        _____ (more, less) expensive to the British airline.

4. When the domestic currency depreciates, domestic goods become _____ expensive

    to foreign buyers and foreign goods become _____ expensive to domestic buyers.

5. When the domestic currency appreciates, domestic goods become _____ expensive

    to foreign buyers and foreign goods become _____ expensive to domestic buyers.

6. Let's say that the exchange rate between dollars and pounds is $1.50 = £1 and that an ounce of gold sells for £300 in London.

   a. What must the price of gold in New York be for purchasing power parity to hold? _____

   b. If gold sells for $400 in New York and £300 in London, would you buy gold in New York or in London to make a profit from arbitrage? _____

   c. If the inflation rate in the United States is 10 percent this year and there is no inflation in Britain, what will the exchange rate be in a year if purchasing power parity is maintained? _____

7. Let's say that the exchange rate between dollars and German marks is $.50 = DM1 and that an ounce of gold sells for $300 in New York.

   a. What must the price of gold in Berlin, Germany, be for purchasing power parity to hold? _____

   b. If gold sells for $400 in New York and DM400 in Berlin, would you buy gold in New York or Berlin to make a profit from arbitrage? _____

   c. If the inflation rate in the United States is 20 percent this year and there is no inflation in Germany, what will the exchange rate be in a year if purchasing power parity is maintained? _____

Section 2: Interest Rates and Exchange Rates

1. The domestic currency return from a foreign bond equals the foreign _____ plus the percentage change in the _____. Differences in inflation rates are one reason why the _____ may change.

2. When similar financial assets from different countries have the same interest rate when measured in the same currency, we have _____.

3. When the domestic interest rate equals the foreign interest rate plus the expected change in the exchange rate, we have _____.

4. List three factors that may create deviations from interest rate parity.

   _____

   _____

   _____

5. Let's say that the interest rate on U.S. government bonds is 10 percent, and the interest rate on similar bonds issued by the French government is 15 percent. Interest rate parity holds between the United States and France.

a. What do people expect to happen to the exchange rate between the U.S. dollar and the French franc?

_____

_____

_____

_____

b. Do people expect the dollar to appreciate or depreciate? Why?

_____

_____

_____

_____

c. If the expected change in the exchange rate is caused only by differences in the expected exchange rate, do people expect inflation to be higher in the United States or in France?

_____

_____

_____

_____

6. If interest rate parity holds and people expect higher inflation in Italy than in Germany, will interest rates be higher in Italy or in Germany? Why?

_____

_____

_____

_____

Section 3: Policy Effects

1. An increase in government spending financed by increased borrowing tends to _____ (raise, lower) real interest rates in the United States, causing the dollar to _____ (appreciate, depreciate).

2. A decrease in government spending leading to decreased borrowing tends to _____ (raise, lower) real interest rates in the United States, causing the dollar to _____ (appreciate, depreciate).

3. When the dollar appreciates, people in other countries will tend to buy _____ (more, fewer) U.S. products and people in the United States will _____ (increase, decrease) their purchases of imported goods.

4. If your objective as a government policymaker is to increase U.S. net exports (exports minus imports), will increasing or decreasing government borrowing be more likely to help? Explain why.

   _____

   _____

   _____

   _____

5. An increase in the growth rate of the money supply will _____ (increase, decrease) the expected inflation differential between domestic and foreign countries.

6. If PPP and IRP both hold, then the change in the expected inflation differential will equal both the expected change in the _____ rate and the _____ rate differential between domestic and foreign bonds.

Section 4: International Policy Coordination

1. Two organizations promoting economic coordination and communication are the IMF and the OECD. What do these acronyms stand for?

   IMF: _____

   OECD: _____

2. List the countries that are members of the Group of 7 (or G7).

   _____   _____

   _____   _____

   _____   _____

   _____

3. List three ways that countries can coordinate their economic policies.

   _____

   _____

   _____

4. List three obstacles to increased coordination of macroeconomic policies.

   _____

   _____

   _____

THINKING ABOUT AND APPLYING MACROECONOMIC LINKS BETWEEN COUNTRIES

I. The Hamburger Standard

The "Economically Speaking" section in this chapter looks at the prices of Big Macs in different countries relative to the exchange rates for those countries, and it compares those prices with the U.S. price of a Big Mac (the average price for New York, Chicago, San Francisco, and Atlanta) to look at whether purchasing power parity (PPP) holds. Although such comparisons are fun to do, comparing the prices of one product may not tell us much, since PPP is really based on the overall price level in different countries.

1. Figure 1 in the text shows the prices of various goods in New York City, Kansas City, and six major cities in other countries. The price of a Big Mac in Kansas City is much lower than the price in New York. Think about what inputs go into making a Big Mac (labor, real estate for the store, hamburger meat, rolls), and explain why the price of a Big Mac is higher in New York, a very large city, than in Kansas City, a much smaller city.

   _____

   _____

   _____

   _____

2. Use your reasons to explain why a Big Mac might have different prices in different countries.

   _____

   _____

   _____

   _____

3. Using information from the table in the "Economically Speaking" section, calculate the equivalent price in U.S. dollars of a Big Mac in Australia and in Canada. Compare these prices with the prices of a Big Mac in New York and Kansas City, shown in Figure 1, and determine whether the U.S. dollar is overvalued or undervalued relative to the Australian dollar and the Canadian dollar.

   U.S. dollar price of Big Mac in Australia: _____

   Is the U.S. dollar overvalued or undervalued in Australia? _____

   U.S. dollar price of Big Mac in Canada: _____

   Is the U.S. dollar overvalued or undervalued in Canada? _____

```
ANSWERS
```

Quick Check Quiz

Section 1: Prices and Exchange Rates

1. b; 2. a; 3. b; 4. a

If you answered c, d, or e to any of these questions, review Section 1.a in the text before going on: you need to become familiar with the terminology of foreign exchange.

If you answered a when the right answer was b, or b when the right answer was a, you know the correct terms but have the directions reversed; that's easy to do with foreign exchange problems. Go back through the examples in Sections 1 and 1.a in the text, go through the examples in the answers to Fundamental Questions 1 and 2 above, and then try the questions again.

5. c; 6. d; 7. a

If you missed any of questions 5 through 7, you should go back and review pages 431–438 in Chapter 17.

Section 2: Interest Rates and Exchange Rates

1. d; 2. d; 3. c

If you missed any of these questions, you should go back and review pages 438–442 in Chapter 17.

Section 3: Policy Effects

1. b; 2. c; 3. c; 4. d

If you missed any of these questions, you should go back and review pages 442–447 in Chapter 17.

Section 4: International Policy Coordination

1. d

If you missed this question, you should go back and review pages 447–451 in Chapter 17.

Practice Questions and Problems

Section 1: Prices and Exchange Rates

1. open
2. increases; decreases
3. a. £.67
   b. £.50
   c. appreciated (A pound buys *more* dollars than before.)
   d. depreciated (A dollar buys *fewer* pounds than before.)
   e. $225,000; $300,000; depreciated; more
      If the Rolls-Royce costs £150,000 and each pound cost an American $1.50 yesterday, the cost of the Rolls-Royce in dollars is £150,000 × $1.50 per pound = $225,000. If the Rolls-Royce costs £150,000 and each pound cost an American $2.00 today, the cost of the Rolls-Royce in dollars is £150,000 × $2.00 per pound = $300,000.
   f. £40 million; £30 million; depreciated; less
      If the Boeing airliner costs $60 million and the exchange rate was $1.50 per pound yesterday, the cost of the Boeing in pounds is $60 million/$1.50 per pound = £40 million. If the Boeing airliner costs $60

million and the exchange rate is $2.00 per pound today, the cost of the Boeing in pounds is $60 million/$2.00 per pound = £30 million.

4. less; more
5. more; less
6. a. $450

   This is just the dollar value of £300 (£300 × $1.50 per pound).

   b. New York

   The price in dollars of gold is $400 in New York and $450 in London (answer a). For arbitrage to work, you must buy in the lower-price market and sell in the higher-price market.

   c. $1.65 = £1

   The number of dollars needed to buy a pound will increase by 10 percent of the old exchange rate ($1.50 + [$1.50 × 10 percent]).

7. a. DM600

   b. Berlin

   DM400 is equivalent to $200 (DM400 × $.50 per DM), so gold is cheaper in Berlin.

   c. $.60 =DM1

   The number of dollars needed to buy a DM will increase by 20 percent of the old exchange rate ($.50 + [$.50 × 20 percent]).

Section 2: Interest Rates and Exchange Rates

1. interest rate; exchange rate; exchange rate
2. interest rate parity
3. interest rate parity
4. government controls
   political risk
   different tax structures
5. a. Since IRP holds even though the present interest rates are different, there must be an expected change in the exchange rate between dollars and francs.

   b. People expect the dollar to appreciate relative to the franc: that's why people are willing to buy bonds denominated in dollars even though the interest rate is lower.

   c. Inflation is expected to be 5 percent higher in France than in the United States. The higher interest rate in France compensates people for the expected decrease in the value of the franc.
6. Interest rates will be higher in Italy to compensate for the decrease in the value of the Italian lira caused by inflation.

Section 3: Policy Effects

1. raise; appreciate
   More demand for borrowing increases interest rates; higher interest rates increase the demand for the dollar, raising the exchange rate.
2. lower; depreciate
   The same logic as above applies here, but in the opposite direction.
3. fewer; increase
4. Decreasing government borrowing would be expected to lower interest rates in the United States, causing a dollar depreciation and increased exports and lower imports.
5. increase
   Higher money growth usually leads to higher inflation.
6. exchange; interest

Section 4: International Policy Coordination

1. IMF: International Monetary Fund
   OECD: Organization for Economic Cooperation and Development
2. Canada   France
   Germany   Italy
   Japan   United Kingdom
   United States
3. setting joint goals
   exchanging information
   forming and executing policy cooperatively
4. disagreements over goals
   disagreements over current economic conditions
   disagreements over macroeconomic theory

Thinking About and Applying Macroeconomic Links Between Countries

I. The Hamburger Standard

1. Labor and real estate are both likely to be more expensive in larger cities than in smaller cities on average. Kansas City is much closer to the major beef- and wheat-producing regions of the United States, so shipping costs for beef and roll flour would be lower. Other factors, such as taxes, would also tend to make the costs of running a McDonald's lower in Kansas City, resulting in a lower price for Big Macs.
2. Different countries have different amounts of competition for real estate use, as well as different prices for real estate. Different countries also have different costs for producing other inputs.
3. in Australia: $1.77
   in Canada: $1.89
      The U.S. dollar price of Big Macs in Australia is the price of a Big Mac in Australian dollars (A$2.30) divided by the exchange rate (A$1.32 = US$1.00); for Canada, it's C$2.19 divided by 1.16. The price of a Big Mac in New York is $2.19, higher than the prices in Australia and Canada; the price of a Big Mac is $1.45 in Kansas City, lower than the prices in Australia and Canada. We can't really tell much about the relative value of the U.S. dollar compared with the Australian and Canadian dollars, since we have conflicting evidence from Big Macs. We need a much wider variety of goods for the comparison to make sense.

CHAPTER 18
Economic Growth

1. What is economic growth?

    Economists define **economic growth** as an increase in real national income, usually measured in terms of the percentage increase in gross national product (GNP) or gross domestic product (GDP). An alternative way of defining economic growth, one that more clearly shows growth's effects on individual people, is to look at growth as the percentage increase in the **per capita real national income**: to look at changes in real national income per person in the economy. After all, if real national income increases 5 percent at the same time population increases 5 percent, real national income may be higher, but the people in the economy are no better off than before: the increase in output is only enough to keep everyone at the same level as before. In this case, per capita real national income would show no growth.

    Although growth in per capita real national income shows us how much is available to consume per person, it does not tell us everything about people's standards of living; we also need to look at income distribution and the quality of life. If all of the increase in output goes to a small proportion of the people within a country, most people's standard of living will be unchanged. If economic growth is accompanied by large decreases in environmental quality (more pollution, less wilderness, and so forth), many people may feel that their quality of life has decreased rather than increased.

2. How are economic growth rates determined?

    Economic growth means a shift rightward of the aggregate supply curve, increasing the potential output of the economy. A country's economic growth rate is determined by the factors that determine the aggregate supply curve: the amount of productive resources available and technology. The faster the growth of productive resources and technological advancement, the higher a country's growth rate will be.

3. What is productivity?

    Productivity is one way to look at the impact of advances in **technology** on economic growth. Productivity is the ratio of output produced to the amount of input used. Improvements in technology mean that productivity increases as we find new and better ways to use inputs to produce output. More specifically, **total factor productivity (TFP)** is a nation's output divided by its stock of labor and capital. Economic growth is the sum of the growth rate of total factor productivity and the growth rate of available resources.

4. Why has U.S. productivity changed?

The growth rate of total factor productivity (TFP) in the United States has decreased over the last several decades. Between 1948 and 1965, TFP grew at an average annual rate of about 2 percent. From 1965 to 1973, TFP only grew at about 1 percent, and from 1973 to 1987 the growth in TFP was only .2 percent. Several changes in the U.S. economy help account for this drop, including a drop in the quality of the U.S. labor force; a drop-off in technological innovation, as shown by the decrease in the number of **patents** issued to U.S. firms; increases in energy prices; and the shift from manufacturing to service industries.

KEY TERMS

economic growth
rule of 72
per capita real national income

technology
total factor productivity (TFP)
patent

QUICK CHECK QUIZ

Section 1: Defining Economic Growth

1. Economic growth is defined as an increase in
   a. nominal national income.
   b. real national income.
   c. real national inputs.
   d. nominal national inputs.
   e. real government expenditures.

2. Economic growth is usually measured as the
   a. absolute increase in GNP or GDP.
   b. nominal increase in GNP or GDP.
   c. percentage increase in GNP or GDP.
   d. marginal increase in GNP or GDP.
   e. total increase in GNP or GDP.

3. For a country with a constant rate of growth, the time required for real national income to double can be found by using the rule of
   a. net interest.
   b. 100.
   c. 10.
   d. 72.
   e. total interest.

4. Per capita real national income is real national income divided by
   a. nominal national income.
   b. real GNP.
   c. 72.
   d. government expenditures.
   e. population.

Section 2: The Determinants of Growth

1. In terms of the aggregate demand–aggregate supply model, economic growth is shown as a/an
   a. rightward shift in the aggregate demand curve.
   b. rightward shift in the aggregate supply curve.
   c. leftward shift in the aggregate demand curve.
   d. leftward shift in the aggregate supply curve.
   e. upward shift in both aggregate demand and aggregate supply.

2. An abundance of natural resources
   a. is always necessary for economic growth.
   b. is necessary for economic growth only in capitalist countries.
   c. is necessary for economic growth only in developing countries.
   d. has no effect on economic growth.
   e. can contribute to economic growth but is not necessary for growth.

3. Growth in a country's capital stock is tied to
   a. increases in the amounts of natural resources available.
   b. current and future saving.
   c. improvements in technology.
   d. increases in the amount of labor available.
   e. decreases in the labor force participation ratio.

4. Which of the following is NOT one of the determinants of economic growth?
   a. the size and quality of the labor force
   b. the amount of capital goods available
   c. technology
   d. natural resources
   e. the shape of the aggregate demand curve

Section 3: Productivity

1. Total factor productivity is the ratio of
   a. a firm's marginal revenue to its marginal cost.
   b. a firm's total revenues to its total costs.
   c. a nation's total income divided by its total output.
   d. a nation's output to its stock of labor and capital.
   e. a nation's labor supply to its capital stock.

2. Economic growth is the sum of
   a. total factor productivity and resources.
   b. total factor productivity and marginal factor productivity.
   c. growth in total factor productivity and growth in resources.
   d. national income and national output.
   e. GNP and GDP.

3. From 1948 through 1987, total factor productivity in the United States
   a. increased at a constant rate.
   b. decreased at a constant rate.
   c. increased, but at a slower and slower rate.
   d. increased, but at a faster and faster rate.
   e. decreased, but at an uneven rate.

4. Which of the following is NOT one of the reasons why U.S. labor quality may have fallen in recent years?
   a. reduced quality of education
   b. increased numbers of inexperienced workers in the work force as the baby boomers entered the work force
   c. increased numbers of inexperienced workers in the work force as more women and immigrants entered the work force
   d. changes in attitudes toward work
   e. increases in the number of days lost to illness

PRACTICE QUESTIONS AND PROBLEMS

Section 1: Defining Economic Growth

1. Economic growth is an increase in _____, usually measured as a percentage

   change in _____ or _____ .

2. Small differences in rates of growth are magnified over time because growth is _____ .

3. In 1987, the real GNP of the country of Lalaland was 200 million lals; in 1988, the real GNP was 210 million lals. What was the growth rate in Lalaland in 1988?
   a. 10 million
   b. 10 percent
   c. 5 percent
   d. 4.76 percent
   e. .05 percent

4. The income of the town of Kennebunkport has been growing by 3 percent per year. If this growth continues into the future, how long will it take until the town's income has doubled?
   a. about 33 years
   b. about 24 years
   c. about 2 years
   d. about 3 years
   e. about 216 years

5. Per capita real national income is _____ divided by _____ .

6. The table below shows the GDP and population in 1985 and 1986 in Aaaland and Zeeland (all figures are in millions).

	1985		1986	
Country	Real GDP	Population	Real GDP	Population
Aaaland	20,000	25	20,600	25
Zeeland	40,000	40	42,000	41

a. Calculate the growth rates in GDP and in GDP per capita for the two countries.

Aaaland: GDP growth rate: _____

GDP per capita growth rate: _____

Zeeland: GDP growth rate: _____

GDP per capita growth rate: _____

b. Which country is growing faster? Explain.

_____

_____

7. Looking at growth rates in GNP or GDP per capita does not give you a complete picture of the standard of living in different countries. What important factors are not included in the GNP or GDP per capita figures?

_____

_____

Section 2: The Determinants of Growth

1. Economic growth shifts the aggregate _____ (demand, supply) curve to the

_____ (right, left).

2. The long-run growth of the economy rests on growth in productive resources such as

_____ , _____ , and _____ and on

advances in _____ .

3. The size of a country's labor force is determined by the _____ and the

_____ of the population in the labor force.

4. Growth in a country's capital stock depends on current and future _____ .

5. Technology is ways of combining _____ to produce _____ .

6. What are two factors that cause developing countries to lag behind in the development and implementation of new technology?

_____

_____

Section 3: Productivity

1. Productivity is the ratio of _____ to the amount of _____ .

2. _____ is the nation's income (or output) divided by its stock of labor and capital.

3. In the United States, labor receives about 70 percent of national income and capital receives about 30 percent. If total factor productivity increases by 1 percent, labor increases by 1 percent, and capital increases by 3 percent, by what percentage will national income increase? _____

4. A _____ is a legal document that gives an inventor the legal rights to an invention.

5. List four factors that may help explain why productivity in the United States has grown more slowly in recent years.

_____

_____

_____

_____

THINKING ABOUT AND APPLYING ECONOMIC GROWTH

I. Quality of Life and Economic Growth

One of the issues discussed in this chapter has been the difficulties of using standard measures of economic growth (growth in GNP or growth in GNP per capita) to show changes in the well-being of people. The effects on economic well-being of growth in GNP per capita does not take into account the distribution of income or quality-of-life issues such as pollution. When economic growth increases pollution, most people would agree that people are not really as much better off as the economic growth statistics show. Conversely, increases in the quality of life may not show up in the economic growth figures.

Since the middle 1960s, people have become more concerned about the environment and pollution. One of the ways the U.S. government has responded to this concern is by passing laws requiring businesses to install pollution control equipment. As a result of these laws and other factors, the air and water in most of the United States are substantially cleaner now than they were ten or fifteen years ago. Although most of us would agree that cleaner air and water improve our quality of life, this improvement does not show up in the economic growth statistics. In fact, environmental improvements can result in lower measured economic growth. Let's take a look at the reasons for this.

1. Suppose that the Best-Yet Whatchamacallit Company has saved $1 million. Best-Yet was planning to use the money to buy a machine that would produce an additional $2 million worth of whatchamacallits every year for ten years. However, the government just passed a law requiring Best-Yet to buy $1 million worth

of pollution control equipment to eliminate the horrible-smelling green smoke that the factory emits. Refer back to the chapter on national income accounting and figure out the following:

a. Effect on GNP of purchase of machine:

_____

b. Effect on GNP of purchase of pollution-control equipment:

_____

c. Effect on GNP of an extra $2 million worth of whatchamacallits produced per year:

_____

d. Effect on GNP of elimination of horrible-smelling green smoke:

_____

2. Buying the whatchamacallit machine will _____ (raise, lower) total factor productivity.

3. Buying the pollution control equipment will _____ (raise, lower) total factor productivity.

4. Compare the timing of the decline in TFP growth in the United States and the environmental movement in the United States. Is there any possible connection? If there is, do you think productivity has really slowed down as much as the statistics show?

_____

_____

_____

_____

II. Government Policy and Growth

The "Economically Speaking" section of the chapter explains why government policies that hold down interest rates have adverse effects on economic growth in developing countries. Although low interest rates are intended to make it cheaper for local businesses to invest in new capital goods, they have the effect of drying up the supply of savings, since savers can get a higher return by taking their money out of the country or by making less productive investments on their own. Similar policies are sometimes followed in other economic sectors, with similarly bad results.

For example, many developing countries require farmers to sell their crops to the government, which resells the food to city dwellers. To keep the city dwellers happy, the prices charged for food are set very low, as are the prices paid to farmers. Think about the farmers' opportunity costs of growing food for sale, and predict what is likely to happen to the food supply in countries adopting this policy.

_____

_____

_____

_____

ANSWERS

Quick Check Quiz

Section 1: Defining Economic Growth

1. b; 2. c; 3. d; 4. e
   If you missed any of these questions, you should go back and review pages 460–464 in Chapter 18.

Section 2: The Determinants of Growth

1. b; 2. e; 3. b; 4. e
   If you missed any of these questions, you should go back and review pages 464–468 in Chapter 18.

Section 3: Productivity

1. d; 2. c; 3. c; 4. e
   If you missed any of these questions, you should go back and review pages 468–477 in Chapter 18.

Practice Questions and Problems

Section 1: Defining Economic Growth

1. national income; GNP; GDP
2. compounded
3. c is correct. The growth rate is calculated this way:

$$\text{Growth rate} = \frac{\text{change in real GNP over year}}{\text{real GNP in beginning year}} \times 100$$

$$\text{For Lalaland, growth rate} = \frac{(210 - 200)}{200} \times 100 = 5 \text{ percent}$$

   If you chose answer a, you found the amount of growth, not the growth rate. If you chose answer b, you must have thought that the actual change was the same as the percentage change. If you chose answer d, you used the GNP in the ending year (1988) rather than the GNP in the beginning year (1987). If you chose answer e, you forgot to multiply by 100 to convert the answer into a percentage.

4. b is correct. You should use the rule of 72 to find the length of time to double income. Divide 72 by the percentage growth rate to find the time to double. In this case, 72/3 = 24, or 24 years to double the town's income.

   If you chose answer a, you forgot about the effect of compounding. The rule of 72 is just a shorthand way to look at compound growth. If you chose answer c or d, you need to review Sections 1.a.1 and 1.a.2. If you chose answer e, you multiplied the growth rate times 72 instead of dividing the growth rate into 72.

5. real national income; population
6. a. Aaaland: GDP growth rate: 3 percent
                 GDP per capita growth rate: 3 percent

       Zeeland: GDP growth rate: 5 percent
                 GDP per capita growth rate: 2.4 percent

To calculate the GDP growth rate, see Section 1, question 3 above. To calculate the GDP per capita growth rate, you first need to calculate GDP per capita in both years; then you find the growth rate the same way you found the growth rate for GDP.

Aaaland: GDP per capita in 1985 is 20,000/25 = 800
GDP per capita in 1986 is 20,600/25 = 824

GDP per capita growth rate = (24/800) × 100 = 3 percent

Zeeland: GDP per capita in 1985 is 40,000/40 = 1,000
GDP per capita in 1986 is 42,000/41 = 1,024

GDP per capita growth rate = (24/1,000) × 100 = 2.4 percent

  b. Which country is growing faster depends on which statistic you want to look at. Aaaland's GDP per capita is growing faster, but Zeeland's GDP is growing faster. The size of Zeeland's economy is growing faster, but the average standard of living in Aaaland is growing faster.

7. income distribution
quality of life

Section 2: The Determinants of Growth

1. supply; right
2. labor; capital; natural resources; technology
3. working-age population; participation
4. saving
5. resources; output
6. low levels of education
limited financial resources (capital)

Section 3: Productivity

1. output produced; inputs
2. Total factor productivity
3. 2.6 percent
Growth is growth in TFP plus growth in each resource × that resource's share of national income. For this case, growth = 1 (TFP growth) + .7 (1 percent growth in labor × labor's .7 share of national income) + .9 (3 percent growth in capital × capital's .3 share of national income).
4. patent
5. lower-quality labor force
fewer technological innovations
higher energy prices
shift from manufacturing to service industries

Thinking About and Applying Economic Growth

I. Quality of Life and Economic Growth

1. a. increases GNP by $1 million (Machine is counted in GNP as investment.)
  b. increases GNP by $1 million (Pollution control equipment is counted in GNP as investment.)
  c. increases GNP by $2 million (assuming that the resources used, such as the $1 million in savings, would not otherwise be used elsewhere in the economy)
  d. no effect on GNP (since green smoke is not bought and sold through markets)

2. raise

   Buying the whatchamacallit machine increases output by $2 million and the capital stock by $1 million. Output is in the numerator of the TFP equation, and capital is in the denominator. Since the numerator (the top part) of the ratio increased by more than the denominator (the bottom part), TFP will increase.

3. lower

   Buying the pollution control equipment increases the capital stock but does not increase output (as measured by GNP). Since the numerator is unchanged and the denominator increased, the ratio is smaller: investing in pollution control equipment makes TFP decrease.

4. The timing of the decline in TFP growth matches the timing of increases in investments in pollution control equipment. Although the amount spent on pollution control is not large enough to explain all of the decrease in the growth of TFP, it may account for some of the drop. Since we have a cleaner environment, pollution control equipment is doing something worthwhile, even though it does not show up in the standard economic statistics.

II. Government Policy and Growth

If the price paid for food crops is low enough, farmers will decide to do something else with their resources than grow food crops. They may switch to cash crops sold for export or just take more leisure, growing only enough to feed themselves and their families. Either way, the amount of food produced for sale to city dwellers will drop substantially. The low prices charged to city dwellers will not help them much when there is no food available for sale.

CHAPTER 19
Development Economics

FUNDAMENTAL QUESTIONS
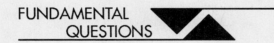

1. How is poverty measured?

Although most of us have an idea of what it means to be poor, measuring poverty is not easy, partly because there are two different ways of looking at poverty. Poverty can be defined in an absolute sense: you are poor if your income is below a specified level. Poverty can also be defined in a relative sense: if your income is much less than the income of those around you, you feel poor. In the United States, for example, the poverty level is calculated by the federal government; in 1988, a family of four was poor if their income was less than $12,675. Most of the people in the world would feel quite well off if they received that high an income.

When comparing countries, the usual measure of people's standard of living is per capita GNP. The World Bank uses a per capita GNP of less than $480 as its standard for poverty. Other measures aim at the quality of life in different countries, using measures such as life expectancy, infant mortality, literacy, and other things that reflect a people's standard of living.

2. Why are some countries poorer than others?

Although the industrialized, "First World" countries have shown that economic growth and development are possible and that countries can maintain a high average standard of living, most "Third World" countries have not been able to follow in their footsteps. Several common factors have been found in many developing countries that help explain their lack of growth. These factors can be grouped into political obstacles and social obstacles.

Political obstacles include a lack of skilled government officials, political instability and risks of **expropriation**, and constraints imposed on governments by special-interest groups. Social obstacles include cultural attitudes that discourage business and entrepreneurial activities, and rapid population growth that can reduce the amount of capital per worker and can divert resources away from uses that promote economic growth.

3. What strategies can a nation use to increase its economic growth?

In terms of trade with other nations, most developing countries have a natural comparative advantage only in **primary products** such as agricultural products and minerals. Countries whose governments have wanted to encourage economic development have tried to shift resources from primary sectors to industrialized, manufacturing sectors in the belief that industrialization is necessary for economic development.

The two basic industrialization strategies followed by developing countries are known as inward-oriented development (followed by most developing countries) and outward-oriented development (followed by South Korea, Taiwan, Hong Kong, and Singapore). Inward-oriented development focuses on **import substitution**: developing a domestic manufacturing sector to produce goods that replace imports. Outward-oriented development focuses on **export substitution**: developing a domestic manufacturing sector that can produce goods for export. In general, the countries that have chosen outward-oriented strategies have been more successful.

4. How are savings in one nation used to speed development in other nations?

    In any country, savings are used to pay for investments in capital goods. Developing countries typically have such low levels of income that saving is difficult if not impossible. In order to buy capital goods, these countries must use other countries' savings. Foreign investment in developing countries can be by private sources or in the form of foreign aid from other governments. Foreign investment can increase economic growth by creating new jobs, transferring modern technology, or stimulating exports.

KEY TERMS

expropriation	dual economy	trade credit
primary product	foreign direct investment	foreign aid
import substitution	portfolio investment	bilateral aid
export substitution	commercial bank loan	multilateral aid
terms of trade		

QUICK CHECK QUIZ

Section 1: The Developing World

1. According to the World Bank, a country is below the poverty level if its per capita GNP is less than
    a. $12,675.
    b. $6,550.
    c. $2,100.
    d. $480.
    e. $155.

2. Which of the following is NOT one of the standard ways to measure the economic progress of a country?
    a. per capita GNP
    b. life expectancy at birth
    c. percentage of the population involved in natural resource production
    d. infant mortality
    e. literacy rate

Section 2: Obstacles to Growth

1. Political obstacles to growth include all of the following EXCEPT
    a. government workers' lack of administrative skills.
    b. political instability.
    c. lack of property rights protection.
    d. control by the military.
    e. pressure from special-interest groups.

2. Social obstacles to growth include all of the following EXCEPT
   a. decision-making systems based on tradition.
   b. a lack of entrepreneurs.
   c. capital shallowing caused by rapid population growth.
   d. reduced savings caused by large numbers of children.
   e. property rights structures that prevent expropriation.

3. Expropriation is
   a. government seizure of assets, typically without adequate compensation to the owners.
   b. government purchase of assets at their market price.
   c. seizure of the government by the military.
   d. restriction of immigration to discourage immigrant entrepreneurs.
   e. restriction of immigration to encourage local entrepreneurs.

4. In many developing countries, entrepreneurs are usually
   a. immigrants or descendants of recent immigrants.
   b. native residents from the traditional leadership groups.
   c. low-ranking members of the military.
   d. members of groups supporting traditional values that discourage change.
   e. people who believe that poverty is a virtue.

Section 3: Development Strategies

1. The economic development strategy aimed at replacing imports with domestically manufactured goods is known as
   a. replacement oriented.
   b. substitution oriented.
   c. inward oriented.
   d. outward oriented.
   e. domestically oriented.

2. The economic development strategy aimed at exporting domestically manufactured goods is known as
   a. replacement oriented.
   b. substitution oriented.
   c. inward oriented.
   d. outward oriented.
   e. domestically oriented.

3. An economy with two sectors that show very different levels of development is called a
   a. dual economy.
   b. double-level economy.
   c. differentiated economy.
   d. split-level economy.
   e. divided economy.

Section 4: Foreign Investment and Aid

1. Which of the following is NOT a form of private foreign investment?
   a. multilateral aid
   b. foreign direct investment
   c. portfolio investment
   d. commercial bank loans
   e. trade credit

2. Which of the following is NOT one of the benefits of foreign investment?
   a. creation of new jobs
   b. transfer of technology
   c. increased earnings from exports
   d. reduced need for education
   e. transfer of information

PRACTICE QUESTIONS AND PROBLEMS

Section 1: The Developing World

1. Poverty can be defined in a(n) _____ sense, for example, by a specified minimum amount of income, or in a(n) _____ sense, for example, by how one's income compares with the average income in one's area.

2. The World Bank uses a _____ of less than $480 as its standard for defining poverty. This standard is a(n) _____ (relative, absolute) measure of poverty.

3. Life expectancy, infant mortality rates, and other similar measures are called _____ measures of economic progress.

Section 2: Obstacles to Growth

1. Obstacles to growth can be grouped into _____ and _____ obstacles.

2. To encourage private investment and economic development, governments must protect

   _____ .

3. _____ is the seizure of private property without compensation by the government.

4. Societies that make decisions based on tradition usually lack _____, who are willing to take risks to gain profits.

5. Explain why each of the following effects of rapid population growth can have a negative effect on economic growth:

   a. capital shallowing: _____

   _____

   b. age dependency: _____

   _____

   c. investment diversion: _____

   _____

Section 3: Development Strategies

1. Most economic development efforts aim at replacing exports of _____ products like minerals or agricultural products with manufactured products.

2. The amount of exports that must be exchanged for some amount of imports is the

   _____ .

3. Inward-oriented development strategies focus on building an _____ (import, export) substitution manufacturing sector.

4. Outward-oriented development strategies focus on building an _____ (import, export) substitution manufacturing sector.

5. Countries using _____ (inward, outward) oriented development strategies have shown higher growth rates.

6. List the four newly industrialized countries that have successfully used outward-oriented development.

   _____

   _____

   _____

   _____

Section 4: Foreign Investment and Aid

1. Foreign _____ (aid, investment) is a gift or low-cost loan made to developing countries from official sources, whereas foreign _____ (aid, investment) comes from private sources.

2. Match the forms of foreign investment with the definitions.

foreign direct investment   portfolio investment
commercial bank loans   trade credit
bilateral aid   multilateral aid

a. _____ : foreign aid that flows from one country to another

b. _____ : the extension of a period of time before an importer must pay for goods

or services purchased

c. _____ : the purchase of a physical operating unit in a foreign country

d. _____ : the purchase of securities

e. _____ : aid provided by international organizations supported by many nations

f. _____ : a loan at market rates of interest, often involving a syndicate of lenders

3. The largest and most important multilateral aid institution is the _____ .

4. The agency that coordinates and plans foreign aid programs in the United States is the

_____ .

5. List three reasons why foreign investment may benefit a developing country.

_____

_____

_____

THINKING ABOUT AND APPLYING DEVELOPMENT ECONOMICS

I. Lessons from the NICs

Before the 1980s, development economists divided the countries of the world into three groups: the *First World*, or the industrialized countries of North America, Western Europe, and Japan; the *Second World* communist countries; and the *Third World*, or the developing nations. Events in the 1970s and 1980s have created a new group, the newly industrialized countries, or NICs, made up of Hong Kong, Singapore, South Korea, and Taiwan. Although not yet as advanced as the First World countries, these four nations seem to have moved their economies out of the developing nation stage into a regime of sustained rapid economic growth. One of the "Economic Insight" sections in this chapter gives some of the history of the NICs. Review that section, and then answer the questions below.

1. What basic strategy did the NICs use to move into sustained economic growth?

_____

_____

_____

_____

2. What groups within the NICs were made worse off (at least temporarily) by this strategy, and why?

_____

_____

_____

_____

3. If the World Bank sent you to be economic advisor to a developing country that had not been successful at economic growth, would you advise following the strategy used by the NICs? What social changes would be necessary before your strategy would work?

_____

_____

_____

_____

II. Foreign Aid: Food or Money?

The "Economically Speaking" section for this chapter looks at world efforts to relieve the effects of famine and also discusses the effects of different forms of aid. Let's look a little more closely at this issue.

The graphs below reproduce the graphs in the section, except that hypothetical numbers have been added to let us go further with the analysis. The left graph shows the effects of giving foreign aid in the form of food; the right graph shows the effects of giving people enough money to buy the same amount of food as they would have received in aid.

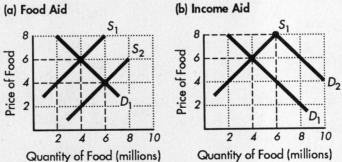

1. On the left graph, the supply shifts to the right by the amount of food given in aid. How much is this?

   Amount of food aid: _____

2. What effects on price and quantity produced did the food aid have on the local farmers? (Hint: Supply curve S_1 shows the amounts supplied by local farmers at different prices.)

   Effect on price: _____

   _____

Effect on quantity produced: _____

_____

3. What effects on price and quantity produced did cash aid have (the right graph) on the local farmers?

Effect on price: _____

_____

Effect on quantity produced: _____

_____

4. Which policy (food aid, cash aid) is likely to encourage farmers to produce more food in the long run?

_____

5. Much foreign aid has been provided to developing countries in the form of various products that they could produce on their own. Use your analysis above to generalize about which foreign aid policy will have more beneficial effects for the receiving country: giving aid in the form of *physical products*, or giving *cash aid* that people in the developing country can spend themselves. _____

6. Which policy (cash aid, physical products) creates more economic benefits for the country that *provides* the aid? _____

ANSWERS

Quick Check Quiz

Section 1: The Developing World

1. d; 2. c

If you missed either of these questions, you should go back and review pages 484–488 in Chapter 19.

Section 2: Obstacles to Growth

1. d; 2. e; 3. a; 4. a

If you missed any of these questions, you should go back and review pages 488–493 in Chapter 19.

Section 3: Development Strategies

1. c; 2. d; 3. a

If you missed either of these questions, you should go back and review pages 494–499 in Chapter 19.

Section 4: Foreign Investment and Aid

1. a; 2. d

If you missed either of these questions, you should go back and review pages 499–503 in Chapter 19.

Practice Questions and Problems

Section 1: The Developing World

1. absolute; relative
2. GNP per capita; absolute
3. quality-of-life

Section 2: Obstacles to Growth

1. political; social
2. private property rights
3. Expropriation
4. entrepreneurs
5. a. An increase in the number of workers leads to a decrease in capital per worker.
   b. When there are many children in a society, resources must be used to support them.
   c. When there are growing numbers of children in a society, investment needs to be used for health care and education facilities, leaving less investment in directly productive uses.

Section 3: Development Strategies

1. primary
2. terms of trade
3. import
4. export
5. outward
6. Hong Kong
   Singapore
   South Korea
   Taiwan

Section 4: Foreign Investment and Aid

1. aid; investment
2. a. bilateral aid
   b. trade credit
   c. foreign direct investment
   d. portfolio investment
   e. multilateral aid
   f. commercial bank loans
3. World Bank
4. U.S. Agency for International Development
5. creation of new jobs
   transfer of technology
   foreign exchange earnings

Thinking About and Applying Development Economics

I. Lessons from the NICs

1. They encouraged the development of manufacturing sectors that could increase exports by competing effectively in the world market.

2. Those groups in society who had previously been protected from import competition were made worse off. Removing restrictions on imports to allow the export sector to develop makes it harder for those groups competing with imports to succeed, whereas under previous approaches they were protected from competition.

3. Yes. The outward-oriented strategy seems to work when the conditions are right. For the outward-oriented strategy to be effective, a country must have a sufficient supply of entrepreneurs and sufficient economic flexibility for the entrepreneurs to make changes. Traditional values and the opposition of groups previously protected must be overcome.

II. Foreign Aid: Food or Money?

1. Amount of food aid: 4 million
   The supply curve is shifted to the right by the amount of the food given in aid. At any price (say 2, for example), the quantity supplied is 4 million more than before.

2. Effect on price: Price dropped from 6 to 4, lowering the price not only for buyers, but also for local farmers.
   Effect on quantity produced: Because the price was lower, fewer farmers could afford to keep producing for sale in the market. The *local* quantity supplied at a price of 4 dropped to 2 million, found from the original supply curve. People had more to eat because of the aid (6 million instead of 4 million), but not as much more as the amount of the aid (4 million), because local farmers had to reduce their output.

3. Effect on price: Price increased from 6 to 8.
   Effect on quantity produced: Because the increase in demand raised the market price, local farmers could supply more to the market. Their output went up from 4 million to 6 million.

4. cash aid (because it encourages an expansion of local production)

5. cash aid (Aid in the form of cash is likely to be better than aid in a form that replaces local production.)

6. physical products
   Look at the situation from the point of view of an American farmer. You have to pay taxes to provide the funds for foreign aid, so will you be better off if the money goes to farmers in the receiving country or if it is used to buy the output of American farmers? When foreign aid is used to buy the products of the giving country, that country receives more benefits, even though such aid is not as worthwhile to the receiving country.

CHAPTER 20*
World Trade Equilibrium

FUNDAMENTAL
QUESTIONS

1. What are the prevailing patterns of trade between countries? What goods are traded?

    Trade occurs because specialization in production, based on **comparative advantage,** leads to increased output. Countries specialize in those products for which their opportunity costs are lower than costs in other nations; countries then trade what they produce beyond their own consumption and receive other countries' products in return.

      The bulk of world trade occurs within the industrialized group of countries; trade between the industrialized countries and developing countries accounts for most of the rest. Canada is the largest buyer of U.S. exports, and Japan is the largest source of U.S. imports. Oil, automobiles, and machinery are the goods that have the largest trading volume, although world trade occurs across a great variety of products.

2. What determines the goods a nation will export?

    A nation exports those goods for which it has a comparative advantage over other nations—that is, those goods for which its opportunity costs are lower than the opportunity costs of other nations. The **terms of trade**—how much of an exported good must be given up to obtain one unit of an imported good—are limited by the domestic opportunity costs of the trading countries.

3. How are the equilibrium price and the quantity of goods traded determined?

    As with most other markets, demand and supply determine the equilibrium price and quantity. For internationally traded goods, the **export supply curve** shows how much countries will be willing to export at different world prices. The **import demand curve** shows how much countries are willing to import at different world prices. Where the import demand curve and the export supply curve intersect is the international equilibrium price and quantity traded.

4. What are the sources of comparative advantage?

    There are two major sources of comparative advantage: productivity differences and factor abundance. Productivity differences come from differences in labor productivity and human capital, and from differences in technology. Factor abundance affects comparative advantage because countries have different resource endowments. The United States, with a large amount of high-quality farmland, has a comparative advantage in agriculture.

      Productivity differences and factor abundance explain most, but not all, trade patterns. Other sources of comparative advantage are human skills differences, product life cycles, and consumer preferences. Consumer preferences explain **intraindustry trade,** in which countries are both exporters and importers of a product. Some consumers prefer brands made in their own country; other consumers prefer foreign brands.

*_Economics_ Chapter 36.

KEY TERMS

absolute advantage   terms of trade   import demand curve
comparative advantage   export supply curve   intraindustry trade

QUICK CHECK QUIZ

Section 1: An Overview of World Trade

1. The bulk of world trade occurs
   a. in the Eastern trading area.
   b. among the developing countries.
   c. among the industrial countries.
   d. between the developing and industrial countries.
   e. between the industrial countries and the Eastern trading area.

2. The United States imports the most from
   a. Canada.
   b. Germany.
   c. Japan.
   d. Mexico.
   e. the USSR.

3. The United States exports the most to
   a. Canada.
   b. Germany.
   c. Japan.
   d. Mexico.
   e. the USSR.

4. The most heavily traded good in the world is
   a. crude petroleum.
   b. airplanes.
   c. automobiles.
   d. televisions.
   e. wheat.

Section 2: An Example of International Trade Equilibrium

1. A nation has an absolute advantage in producing a good when
   a. it can produce a good for a lower input cost than can other nations.
   b. the opportunity cost of producing a good, in terms of the forgone output of other goods, is lower than that of other nations.
   c. it can produce a good for a higher input cost than can other nations.
   d. the opportunity cost of producing a good, in terms of the forgone output of other goods, is higher than that of other nations.
   e. the nation's export supply curve is below its import demand curve.

2. A nation has a comparative advantage in producing a good when
   a. it can produce a good for a lower input cost than can other nations.
   b. the opportunity cost of producing a good, in terms of the forgone output of other goods, is lower than that of other nations.
   c. it can produce a good for a higher input cost than can other nations.
   d. the opportunity cost of producing a good, in terms of the forgone output of other goods, is higher than that of other nations.
   e. the nation's export supply curve is below its import demand curve.

3. The terms of trade are the
   a. price of your country's currency in terms of another country's currency.
   b. price of another country's currency in terms of your country's currency.
   c. amount of an export good that must be given up to obtain one unit of an import good.
   d. amount of an import good that must be given up to obtain one unit of an export good.
   e. amount of imports divided by the amount of exports.

4. The limits on the terms of trade are determined by the
   a. difference between the domestic and world price.
   b. domestic opportunity costs of production within one country.
   c. domestic opportunity costs of production within each country.
   d. ratio of the domestic price to the world price.
   e. ratio of the world price to the domestic price.

5. The export supply and import demand curves for a country measure the
   a. international surplus and shortage, respectively, at different world prices.
   b. international shortage and surplus, respectively, at different world prices.
   c. domestic surplus and shortage, respectively, at different world prices.
   d. domestic shortage and surplus, respectively, at different world prices.
   e. domestic surplus and shortage, respectively, at different exchange rates.

Section 3: Sources of Comparative Advantage

1. The productivity-differences explanation of comparative advantage stresses
   a. differences in labor productivity among countries.
   b. the advantage that comes to a country that is the first to develop and produce a product.
   c. the relative amounts of skilled and unskilled labor in a country.
   d. differences in the amounts of resources countries have.
   e. differences in tastes within a country.

2. The factor-abundance explanation of comparative advantage stresses
   a. differences in labor productivity among countries.
   b. the advantage that comes to a country that is the first to develop and produce a product.
   c. the relative amounts of skilled and unskilled labor in a country.
   d. differences in the amounts of resources countries have.
   e. differences in tastes within a country.

3. The human-skills explanation of comparative advantage stresses
   a. differences in labor productivity among countries.
   b. the advantage that comes to a country that is the first to develop and produce a product.
   c. the relative amounts of skilled and unskilled labor in a country.
   d. differences in the amounts of resources countries have.
   e. differences in tastes within a country.

4. The product-life-cycle explanation of comparative advantage stresses
   a. differences in labor productivity among countries.
   b. the advantage that comes to a country that is the first to develop and produce a product.
   c. the relative amounts of skilled and unskilled labor in a country.
   d. differences in the amounts of resources countries have.
   e. differences in tastes within a country.

5. The consumer-preferences explanation of comparative advantage stresses
   a. differences in labor productivity among countries.
   b. the advantage that comes to a country that is the first to develop and produce a product.
   c. the relative amounts of skilled and unskilled labor in a country.
   d. differences in the amounts of resources countries have.
   e. differences in tastes within a country.

PRACTICE QUESTIONS AND PROBLEMS

Section 1: An Overview of World Trade

1. The country that imports the most from the United States is _____; the country that exports the most to the United States is _____.

2. World trade is _____ (distributed across many products, dominated by only a few products).

3. The product that accounts for the most world trade is _____.

4. Use Table 1 in the text to answer these questions.

   a. Trade within industrial countries accounts for what percentage of world trade?

      _____

   b. Trade within and between industrial and developing countries accounts for what percentage of world trade? _____

Section 2: An Example of International Trade Equilibrium

1. _____ (Comparative, Absolute) advantage is based on the relative opportunity costs of producing goods in different countries.

2. _____ (Comparative, Absolute) advantage occurs when a country can produce a good for a lower input cost than can other nations.

3. The _____ are the amount of an export good that must be given up to obtain one unit of an import good.

4. The _____ (export supply, import demand) curve is derived from the domestic surplus at different world prices.

5. The _____ (export supply, import demand) curve is derived from the domestic shortage at different world prices.

6. The table below shows the number of hours of labor needed to produce a ton of mangos and a ton of papayas in Samoa and in Fiji.

	Samoa	**Fiji**
Mangos	2	6
Papayas	1	2

a. Which country has an absolute advantage in producing mangos? _____

b. Which country has an absolute advantage in producing papayas? _____

c. What is the opportunity cost of 1 ton of papayas in Samoa? _____

d. What is the opportunity cost of 1 ton of papayas in Fiji? _____

e. Which country has a comparative advantage in papayas? _____

f. What is the opportunity cost of 1 ton of mangos in Samoa? _____

g. What is the opportunity cost of 1 ton of mangos in Fiji? _____

h. Which country has a comparative advantage in mangos? _____

i. The limits on the terms of trade are 1 ton of mangos for between _____ and _____ tons of papayas.

7. The graphs below show the soybean markets in the United States and in France (assuming that no other country in the world is involved in trade in soybeans).

a. Before doing any analysis, let's look at the soybean markets in the United States and France. The price in the United States without trade is _____ per bushel; in France it is _____ per bushel. Since market prices reflect opportunity costs, which country has a comparative advantage in soybean production, and should export soybeans?

_____

b. On the "World" graph below, draw in the import demand and export supply curves for the United States and France; then find the equilibrium world price and quantity traded, and the amounts produced and consumed in the United States and France.

(a) United States

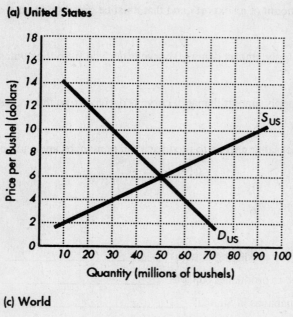

(b) France

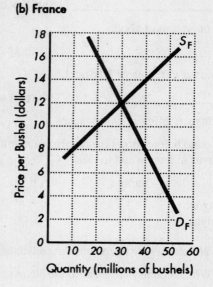

(c) World

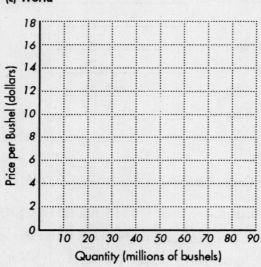

World price: _____

Quantity traded: _____

United States: _____ produced, _____ consumed.

The United States is an _____ (exporter, importer) of soybeans.

France: _____ produced, _____ consumed.

France is an _____ (exporter, importer) of soybeans.

    c. In the problem above, what was the effect of trade on the price of soybeans in the United States and in France?

        United States: _____

        France: _____

Section 3: Sources of Comparative Advantage

1. Name the comparative-advantage theory that matches each explanation of comparative advantage listed below.

    a. _____ : differences in labor productivity among countries

    b. _____ : the advantage that comes to a country that is the first to develop and produce a product

    c. _____ : the relative amounts of skilled and unskilled labor in a country

    d. _____ : differences in the amounts of resources countries have

    e. _____ : differences in tastes within a country

2. The productivity-differences theory of comparative advantage is known as the _____ model.

3. The factor-abundance theory of comparative advantage is known as the _____ model.

4. Differences in consumer tastes within a country explain _____ , in which a country is both an exporter and importer of a differentiated product.

THINKING ABOUT AND APPLYING WORLD TRADE EQUILIBRIUM

I. World Trade Equilibrium

The graphs on the following page show the domestic markets for wheat in the United States, Canada, Argentina, and the USSR. Draw the import demand and export supply curves for the four countries, sum the import demand and export supply curves for the four countries to draw the world import demand and export supply curves on the world graph, find the equilibrium world price and quantity traded, and find the amounts produced and consumed in the four countries.

(a) United States

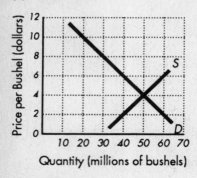

(b) Canada

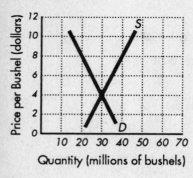

(c) Argentina

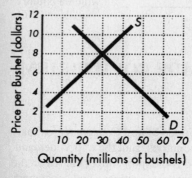

(d) Soviet Union

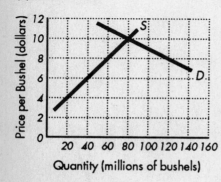

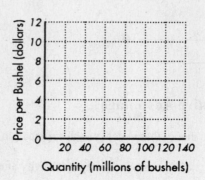

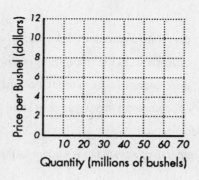

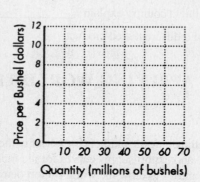

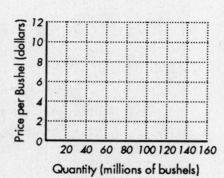

(e) World

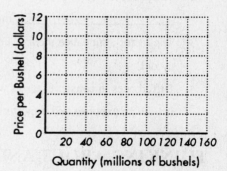

World price: _____

Quantity traded: _____

United States: _____ produced, _____ consumed.

The United States is a(n) _____ (exporter, importer, nontrader) of wheat.

Canada: _____ produced, _____ consumed.

Canada is a(n) _____ (exporter, importer, nontrader) of wheat.

Argentina: _____ produced, _____ consumed.

Argentina is a(n) _____ (exporter, importer, nontrader) of wheat.

USSR: _____ produced, _____ consumed.

The USSR is a(n) _____ (exporter, importer, nontrader) of wheat.

II. Triangular Trade

The "Economically Speaking" section for this chapter discusses the trade imbalance between the United States and Japan and the idea that trade between any two countries need not balance as long as each country's trade with all countries taken together is roughly balanced. Let's look a little further at this idea.

The graphs on the following page show the domestic markets for oranges, bananas, and sugar in Guatemala, Honduras, and Costa Rica. Draw the import demand and export supply curves for the three countries for each product, sum the import demand and export supply curves for each product to draw the world import demand and export supply curves on the world graphs, find the equilibrium world price and quantity traded for each product, the amounts produced and consumed of each product in each country, and the status of each country as an importer, exporter, or nontrader. Sketch the pattern of trade flows among the three countries. (Hint: Look at the picture in the "Economically Speaking" section.)

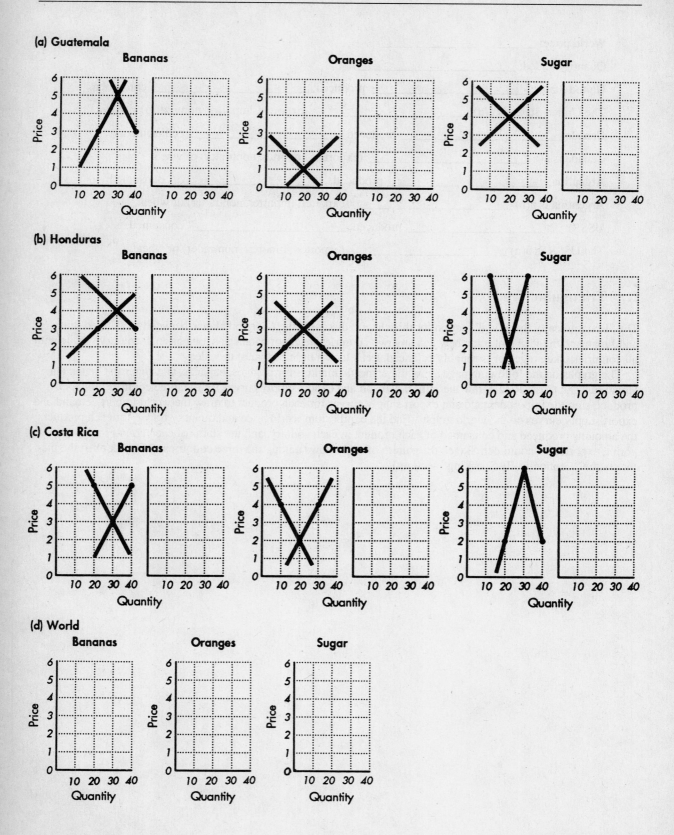

(a) Guatemala

Bananas Oranges Sugar

(b) Honduras

Bananas Oranges Sugar

(c) Costa Rica

Bananas Oranges Sugar

(d) World

Bananas Oranges Sugar

	World Price	**Quantity Traded**
Oranges	$_____	_____
Bananas	_____	_____
Sugar	_____	_____

	Amount Produced	**Amount Consumed**	**Status**
Guatemala			
Oranges	_____	_____	_____
Bananas	_____	_____	_____
Sugar	_____	_____	_____
Honduras			
Oranges	_____	_____	_____
Bananas	_____	_____	_____
Sugar	_____	_____	_____
Costa Rica			
Oranges	_____	_____	_____
Bananas	_____	_____	_____
Sugar	_____	_____	_____

Pattern of trade flows:

ANSWERS

Quick Check Quiz

Section 1: An Overview of World Trade

1. c; 2. c; 3. a; 4. a

If you missed any of these questions, you should go back and review pages 512–515 in Chapter 20 (pages 960–963 in *Economics*, Chapter 36).

Section 2: An Example of International Trade Equilibrium

1. a; 2. b; 3. c; 4. c; 5. c

If you missed any of these questions, you should go back and review pages 515–523 in Chapter 20 (pages 963–971 in *Economics*, Chapter 36).

Section 3: Sources of Comparative Advantage

1. a; 2. d; 3. c; 4. b; 5. e

If you missed any of these questions, you should go back and review pages 523–527 in Chapter 20 (pages 971–975 in *Economics*, Chapter 36).

Practice Questions and Problems

Section 1: An Overview of World Trade

1. Canada; Japan
2. distributed across many products
3. crude oil
4. a. 54.8 percent
   b. 85.5 percent

Section 2: An Example of International Trade Equilibrium

1. Comparative
2. Absolute
3. terms of trade
4. export supply
5. import demand
6. a. Samoa
     Mangos cost only 2 hours of labor in Samoa; they cost 6 hours of labor in Fiji.
   b. Samoa
     Papayas cost only 1 hour of labor in Samoa; they cost 2 hours of labor in Fiji.
   c. 1/2 ton of mangos
     Mangos take twice as much labor time as papayas in Samoa, so you can produce half as many mangos in the same amount of time.
   d. 1/3 ton of mangos
     Mangos take three times as much labor time as papayas in Fiji, so you can produce one third as many mangos in the same amount of time.

e. Fiji

Fiji has the lower opportunity cost: it has to give up only 1/3 ton of mangos to get a ton of papayas, whereas Samoa has to give up 1/2 ton.

f. 2 tons of papayas

Papayas take half as much labor time as mangos in Samoa, so you can produce twice as many papayas in the same amount of time.

g. 3 tons of papayas

Papayas take one-third as much labor time as mangos in Fiji, so you can produce three times as many papayas in the same amount of time.

h. Samoa

Samoa has the lower opportunity cost: it has to give up only 2 tons of papayas to get a ton of mangos, whereas Fiji has to give up 3 tons.

i. 2; 3

7. a. $6; $12; United States

b. **(a) United States**

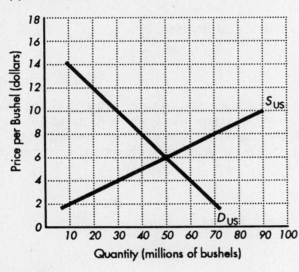

(b) France

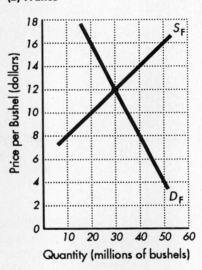

(c) World

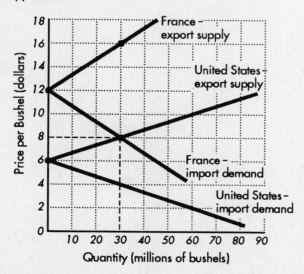

World price: $8
Quantity traded: 30 million
United States: 70 million produced, 40 million consumed; exporter
France: 10 million produced, 40 million consumed; importer

   c. United States: price up from $6 to $8
      France: price down from $12 to $8

Section 3: Sources of Comparative Advantage

1. a. productivity differences
     b. product life cycle
     c. human skills
     d. factor abundance
     e. consumer preferences
2. Ricardian
3. Heckscher-Ohlin
4. intraindustry trade

Thinking About and Applying World Trade Equilibrium

I. World Trade Equilibrium

See solution on page 281.

The domestic prices before trade vary between $4 (United States and Canada) and $10 (USSR). The USSR will begin demanding imports if the world price is below $10; if the price goes below $8, Argentina will also demand imports. The United States and Canada will begin supplying exports if the world price goes above $4; if the price goes above $8, Argentina will also supply exports. The "World" graph shows the amounts these countries will supply (export) and demand (import) at various prices.

World price: $8
Quantity traded: 60 million
United States: 70 million produced, 30 million consumed; exporter
Canada: 40 million produced, 20 million consumed; exporter
Argentina: 30 million produced and consumed; nontrader
USSR: 60 million produced, 120 million consumed; importer

II. Triangular Trade

See solution on page 282.

	World Price	Quantity Traded
Oranges	$2	20
Bananas	4	20
Sugar	4	10

(a) United States

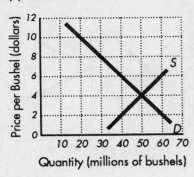

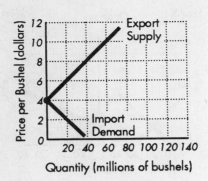

(b) Canada

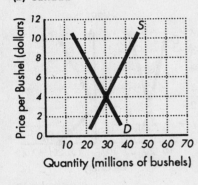

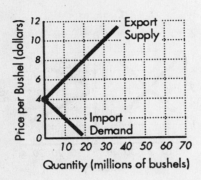

(e) World

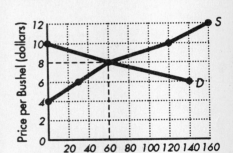

(c) Argentina

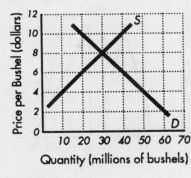

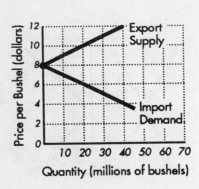

(d) Soviet Union

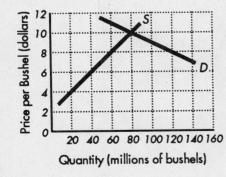

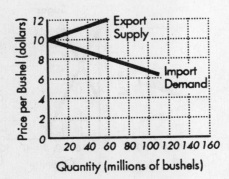

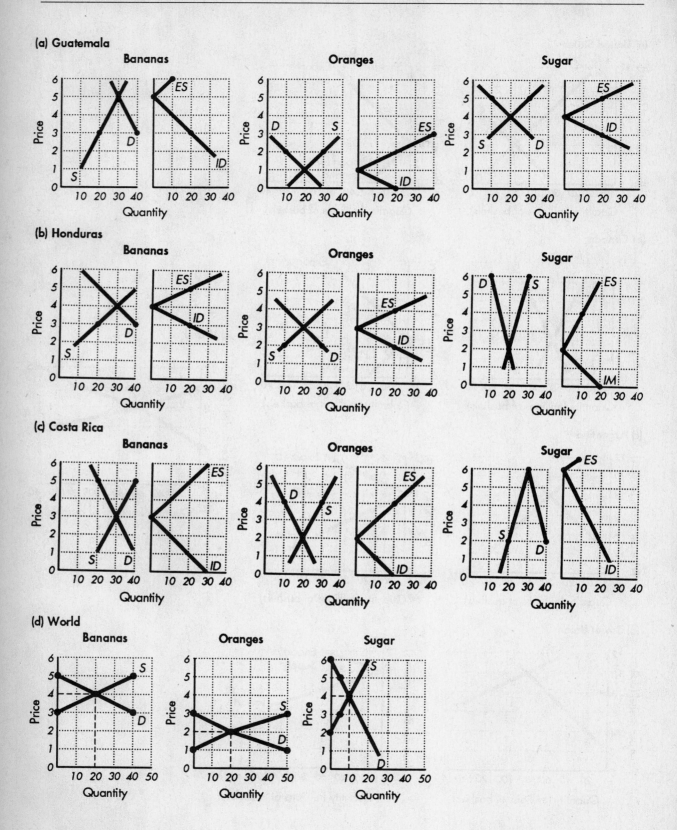

(a) Guatemala

Bananas Oranges Sugar

(b) Honduras

Bananas Oranges Sugar

(c) Costa Rica

Bananas Oranges Sugar

(d) World

Bananas Oranges Sugar

	Amount Produced	Amount Consumed	Status
Guatemala			
Oranges	30	10	Exporter
Bananas	25	35	Importer
Sugar	20	20	Nontrader
Honduras			
Oranges	10	30	Importer
Bananas	30	30	Nontrader
Sugar	25	15	Exporter
Costa Rica			
Oranges	20	20	Nontrader
Bananas	35	25	Exporter
Sugar	25	35	Importer

Pattern of trade flows:

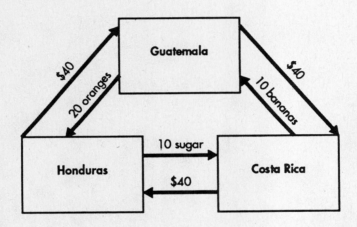

CHAPTER 21*
Commercial Policy

1. Why do countries restrict international trade?

   Most countries follow some sort of **commercial policy** to influence the direction and volume of international trade. Despite the costs to domestic consumers, countries frequently try to protect domestic producers by restricting international trade. Lobbying for trade restrictions is an example of the rent-seeking activities discussed in the chapter on government and public choice.

   To help hide the special-interest nature of most trade restrictions, several arguments are commonly used. These include saving domestic jobs, creating fairer trade, raising revenue through tariffs, protecting key defense industries, allowing new industries to become competitive, and giving **decreasing-cost industries** an advantage over foreign competitors. Although a few of these arguments have some validity, most have little or no merit.

2. How do countries restrict the entry of foreign goods and promote the export of domestic goods?

   Several tactics are frequently used for these purposes. **Tariffs,** or taxes on products imported into the United States, protect domestic industries by raising the price of foreign goods. Quotas restrict the amount or value of a foreign product that may be imported; **quantity quotas** limit the amount of a good that may be imported, and **value quotas** limit the monetary value of a good that may be imported. **Subsidies,** payments made by government to domestic firms, both encourage exports and make domestic products cheaper to foreign buyers. In addition, a wide variety of other tactics, such as health and safety standards, are used to restrict imports.

3. What sorts of agreements do countries enter into to reduce trade barriers to international trade?

   Groups of countries can establish **free trade areas,** where member countries have no trade barriers among themselves, or **customs unions,** where member countries not only abolish trade restrictions among themselves but also set common trade barriers on nonmembers. The United States and Canada established a free trade area in 1987. The best-known customs union is the European Economic Community (EEC), composed of most of the countries in Western Europe. Because they do not include all countries, free trade areas can result in both **trade diversion,** which reduces efficiency, and **trade creation,** which allows a country to obtain goods at lower cost.

Economics Chapter 37.

KEY TERMS

commercial policy	value quota	customs union
decreasing-cost industry	subsidies	trade diversion
tariffs	free trade area	trade creation
quantity quota		

QUICK CHECK QUIZ

Section 1: Arguments for Protection

1. The basic objective of commercial policy is to
   a. promote free and unrestricted international trade.
   b. protect domestic consumers from dangerous, low-quality imports.
   c. protect domestic producers from foreign competition.
   d. protect foreign producers from domestic consumers.
   e. promote the efficient use of scarce resources.

2. Using trade restrictions to save domestic jobs
   a. usually costs consumers much more than the job saved is worth.
   b. usually just redistributes jobs from other industries to the protected industry.
   c. may provoke other countries to restrict U.S. exports.
   d. does all of the above.
   e. does only b and c above.

3. Some arguments for trade restrictions have some economic validity. Which of the following arguments has NO economic validity?
   a. the infant industry argument
   b. the national defense argument
   c. the government revenue creation from tariffs argument
   d. the creation of domestic jobs argument
   e. All of the above have some economic validity.

4. The objective of strategic trade policy is to
   a. protect those industries needed for national defense.
   b. provide domestic decreasing-cost industries an advantage over foreign competitors.
   c. develop economic alliances with other countries.
   d. carefully develop free trade areas to counteract customs unions.
   e. increase government revenues through tariffs.

Section 2: Tools of Policy

1. A tariff is a
   a. tax on imports or exports.
   b. government-imposed limit on the amount of a good that may be imported.
   c. government-imposed limit on the value of a good that may be imported.
   d. payment by government to domestic producers.
   e. payment by government to foreign producers.

2. A subsidy is a
   a. tax on imports or exports.
   b. government-imposed limit on the amount of a good that may be imported.
   c. government-imposed limit on the value of a good that may be imported.
   d. payment by government to domestic producers.
   e. payment by government to foreign producers.

3. A quantity quota is a
   a. tax on imports or exports.
   b. government-imposed limit on the amount of a good that may be imported.
   c. government-imposed limit on the value of a good that may be imported.
   d. payment by government to domestic producers.
   e. payment by government to foreign producers.

4. A value quota is a
   a. tax on imports or exports.
   b. government-imposed limit on the amount of a good that may be imported.
   c. government-imposed limit on the value of a good that may be imported.
   d. payment by government to domestic producers.
   e. payment by government to foreign producers.

5. Which of the following are NOT used to restrict trade?
   a. health and safety standards
   b. government procurement regulations requiring domestic purchasing
   c. subsidies
   d. cultural and institutional practices
   e. All of the above are used to restrict trade.

Section 3: Preferential Trade Agreements

1. An organization of nations whose members have no trade barriers among themselves but are free to fashion their own trade policies toward nonmembers is a
   a. customs union.
   b. trade group.
   c. international cartel.
   d. free trade area.
   e. internation economic alliance.

2. An organization of nations whose members have no trade barriers among themselves but impose common trade barriers on nonmembers is a
   a. customs union.
   b. trade group.
   c. international cartel.
   d. free trade area.
   e. internation economic alliance.

3. Trade diversion occurs when a preferential trade agreement
   a. allows a country to buy imports from a nonmember country at a lower price than that charged by member countries.
   b. reduces economic efficiency by shifting production to a higher-cost producer.
   c. allows a country to obtain goods at a lower cost than is available at home.
   d. reduces trade flows between nonmember countries.
   e. increases economic efficiency by shifting production to a higher-cost producer.

4. Trade creation occurs when a preferential trade agreement
   a. allows a country to buy imports from a nonmember country at a lower price than that charged by member countries.
   b. reduces economic efficiency by shifting production to a higher-cost producer.
   c. allows a country to obtain goods at a lower cost than is available at home.
   d. reduces trade flows between nonmember countries.
   e. increases economic efficiency by shifting production to a higher-cost producer.

PRACTICE QUESTIONS AND PROBLEMS

Section 1: Arguments for Protection

1. The main reason governments restrict foreign trade is to protect _____ producers from _____ competition.

2. Governments can generate revenues by restricting trade through _____; this is a common tactic in _____ (industrial, developing) countries.

3. The argument that new industries should receive temporary protection is known as the _____ argument.

4. Strategic trade policy aims at identifying industries with _____ and giving them an advantage over their foreign competitors.

5. Using trade restrictions to protect domestic jobs usually costs consumers _____ (more, less) money than the jobs are worth to the workers holding them.

6. Trade restrictions usually
   a. create more domestic jobs.
   b. just redistribute jobs within the economy.

Section 2: Tools of Policy

1. Tariffs are _____ on imports or exports. In the United States, tariffs on _____ (imports, exports) are illegal under the Constitution.

2. Quotas can be used to set limits on the _____ or _____ of a good allowed to be imported into a country.

3. When an exporting country agrees to limit its exports of a product to another country, the agreement is known as a _____ .

4. List three barriers to trade besides tariffs and quotas.

_____

_____

_____

5. The graph below shows the U.S. market for tangerines. The world price for tangerines is $10 per bushel. On the graph below, mark the quantity demanded and quantity supplied by U.S. sellers when the price is $10.

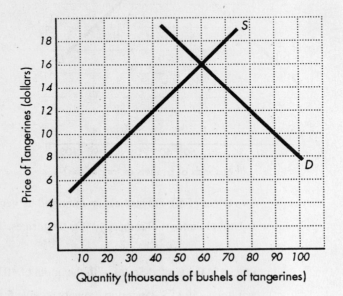

a. If the United States does not restrict imports of tangerines, it will import _____ tangerines at the price of _____ .

b. Suppose the United States imposes a $4 per bushel tariff on imported tangerines. On the graph above, mark the quantity demanded and quantity supplied by U.S. sellers when the price is $14. The United States will then import _____ tangerines at a price of

_____ .

c. With the $4 tariff, _____ tangerines will be produced in the United States, and U.S. growers will receive _____ per bushel.

6. The graph below shows the U.S. market for tangerines again. The world price for tangerines is again $10 per bushel.

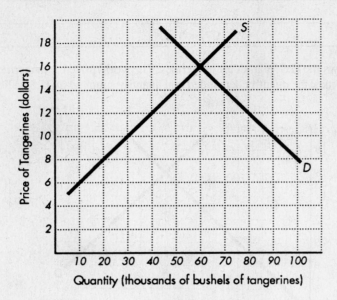

a. Suppose the United States imposes a quota of 40,000 bushels on imported tangerines. On the graph above, mark the price at which the United States will import 40,000 tangerines. The price is

_____ .

b. How many tangerines will be produced in the United States with the quota of 40,000?

_____ What price will U.S. tangerine growers receive for each bushel sold?

_____

Section 3: Preferential Trade Agreements

1. A _____ is a group of nations whose members have no trade barriers among themselves but impose common trade barriers on nonmembers.

2. A _____ is a group of nations whose members have no trade barriers among themselves but have their own trade policies toward nonmembers.

3. The European Economic Community is a _____ . List the six original member countries and the six that joined later.

Original Members	Later Members
_____	_____
_____	_____
_____	_____
_____	_____
_____	_____
_____	_____

THINKING ABOUT AND APPLYING COMMERCIAL POLICY

I.   Rent Seeking in the Textile and Auto Industries

Table 1 in the text shows the costs to consumers and the gains to producers from trade restrictions on various imports into the United States. The "Economically Speaking" section in the text looks at one of those industries—textiles—in detail. Let's explore some of these issues.

1.   Look through Table 1. Can you find any industry for which the benefits of trade restrictions (producer gains) are larger than the costs (total consumer losses)? _____

2.   Let's take a look at some of the reasons why trade restrictions cause net losses to the United States. Flip back to problem 6 in Section 2: the problem with an import quota on tangerines. Before the quota, how much did foreign tangerine growers receive for the tangerines they sold in the United States? _____ After the quota, how much did foreign tangerine growers receive for the tangerines they sold in the United States? _____ Do you think U.S. producers got to keep all the extra money U.S. consumers spent for tangerines after the quota was imposed? Explain.

_____

_____

_____

_____

3.   Look back to Table 1 in your text again, and find the consumer losses and producer gains from trade restraints on automobiles.

Consumer losses: _____

Producer gains: _____

In a good year, auto sales in the United States are around 10 million. How much extra per car are U.S. consumers paying, and how much extra per car are U.S. automakers receiving as a result of trade restraints?

Consumer losses per car: _____

Producer gains per car: _____

4. The most significant restriction on auto imports into the United States has been the voluntary export restraint agreement between the United States and Japan, whereby the Japanese agreed to set a quota on exports of automobiles to the United States and each Japanese automaker was given a specific number of cars that could be exported. Explain why the export quotas help prevent competition among Japanese automakers.

_____

_____

_____

_____

5. Use the ideas you learned in the chapter on government and public choice theory to explain why the U.S. government would encourage restrictions on importing Japanese autos, even though the restrictions cost U.S. car buyers large amounts of money. (Hint: Look at the title of this problem.)

_____

_____

_____

_____

ANSWERS

Quick Check Quiz

Section 1: Arguments for Protection

1. c; 2. d; 3. d; 4. b

If you missed any of these questions, you should go back and review pages 534–540 in Chapter 21 (pages 982–988 in *Economics*, Chapter 37).

Section 2: Tools of Policy

1. a; 2. d; 3. b; 4. c; 5. e

If you missed any of these questions, you should go back and review pages 540–546 in Chapter 21 (pages 988–994 in *Economics*, Chapter 37).

Section 3: Preferential Trade Agreements

1. d; 2. a; 3. b; 4. c

If you missed any of these questions, you should go back and review pages 546–549 in Chapter 21 (pages 994–997 in *Economics*, Chapter 37).

Practice Questions and Problems

Section 1: Arguments for Protection

1. domestic; foreign
2. tariffs; developing
3. infant industry
4. decreasing costs
5. more
6. b

Section 2: Tools of Policy

1. taxes; exports
2. quantity; value
3. voluntary export restraint
4. subsidies
   government procurement
   health and safety standards
5.

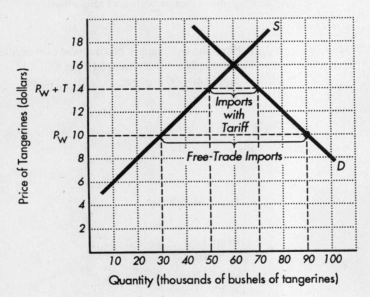

    a. 60,000; $10

At the world price of $10, the United States will demand 90,000 bushels but will produce only 30,000 bushels. The difference (90,000 – 30,000) is how much the United States will import.

    b. 20,000; $14

The tariff raises the price of tangerines in the United States to $14 (the $10 world price + the $4 tariff). At this price, U.S. consumers demand 70,000 tangerines, and U.S. producers supply 50,000, leaving 20,000 to be imported.

    c. 50,000; $14

6.

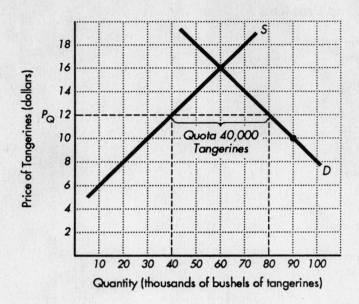

Price of Tangerines (dollars)

Quota 40,000 Tangerines

Quantity (thousands of bushels of tangerines)

a. $12

The quota limits imports to 40,000. From the U.S. supply and demand curves, the price where the difference between U.S. demand and U.S. supply is 40,000 is at $12 per bushel: U. S. consumers buy 80,000 bushels, and U.S. producers supply 40,000 bushels.

b . 40,000; $12

Section 3: Preferential Trade Agreements

1. customs union
2. free trade area
3. customs union

Original Members	Later Members
France	United Kingdom
West Germany	Ireland
Italy	Denmark
Belgium	Greece
Netherlands	Spain
Luxembourg	Portugal

Thinking About and Applying Commercial Policy

I. Rent Seeking in the Textile and Auto Industries

1. no (Except for peanuts, where the gains are estimated to equal the losses, the losses to consumers are larger than the gains to producers.)
2. $10; $12

No; some of the extra money U.S. consumers paid went to foreign sellers of tangerines, who received a higher price.

3. Consumer losses: $5,800,000,000
   Producer gains: $2,600,000,000
   Consumer losses per car: $580
   Producer gains per car: $260

4. Cartels try to raise prices by cutting back output. From the point of view of an individual firm in a cartel, cutting price to expand sales is usually profitable; such cheating contributes to the eventual collapse of most cartels. By using the Japanese government to enforce limits on output, Japanese car makers were able to raise prices without worrying about any cheating their competitors might do.

5. Trade restraints are an example of rent-seeking behavior. Import quotas on automobiles transfer wealth from consumers (a relatively small amount from many car buyers) to automakers and auto workers (a relatively large amount to each one). The cost to car buyers is hidden in the price of the automobile and so does not provoke consumer resentment against politicians who vote for restraints. The automakers and auto workers, of course, know who is responsible for their added wealth and reward cooperative politicians with campaign contributions and votes.

CHAPTER 22*
Exchange-Rate Systems and Practices

1. How does a commodity standard fix exchange rates between countries?

   A commodity standard exists when exchange rates are based on the values of different currencies in terms of some commodity. The **gold standard,** in general use between 1880 and 1914, fixed the value of countries' currencies in terms of how much currency was needed to buy an ounce of gold. Fixing the value of currencies in terms of gold also fixes the relative value of all currencies to each other. For example, if the value of an ounce of gold is 20 U.S. dollars and its value is also 200 Mexican pesos, then a U.S. dollar has the same value as 10 Mexican pesos. As long as countries fix the value of their currencies in terms of some commodity, the relative values of those currencies also stay the same.

2. What kinds of exchange-rate arrangements exist today?

   The gold standard ended with World War I; since then many exchange-rate systems have been tried. At the present time, nations use a variety of exchange-rate arrangements, including fixed exchange rates, freely floating exchange rates, and **managed floating exchange rates.**

3. How is equilibrium determined in the foreign-exchange market?

   Equilibrium is determined in foreign-exchange markets the same way it's determined in other markets: by the intersection of supply and demand curves. The demand for a currency, such as the U.S. dollar, comes from the desire of people in other countries to buy things in the United States; the supply of U.S. currency to the foreign-exchange market comes from U.S. residents' desire to buy things from foreign countries.

4. How do fixed and floating exchange rates differ in their adjustment to shifts in supply and demand for currencies?

   With floating exchange rates, the foreign-exchange market adjusts automatically to shifts in supply and demand, the same way perfectly competitive markets for products adjust. With fixed exchange rates, a government can try to maintain the fixed rate through intervention in the foreign-exchange market, although this is unlikely to work unless the shifts in supply and demand are temporary. A **fundamental disequilibrium** usually requires a currency devaluation.

5. What are the advantages and disadvantages of fixed and floating exchange rates?

   Fixed exchange rates require that a nation match its macroeconomic policies to those of the country or countries to which its currency is pegged; this limits a country's ability to set its own policies. Floating exchange rates allow countries to follow their own macroeconomic policies.

*Economics Chapter 38.

6. What determines the kind of exchange-rate system a country adopts?

Countries can in general choose what kind of exchange-rate system they want to use. The choice seems to depend on four characteristics: how large the country is (in terms of economic output), how **open** the country's **economy** is (how large a fraction of GNP is devoted to international trade), the country's experience with inflation, and how diversified the country's international trade is.

KEY TERMS

gold standard
gold exchange standard
reserve currency
International Monetary Fund
 (IMF)
World Bank
foreign-exchange market
 intervention

equilibrium exchange rates
devaluation
managed floating exchange
 rates
special drawing right
European Monetary System
 (EMS)

appreciate
depreciate
fundamental disequilibrium
speculators
open economy
multiple exchange rates

QUICK CHECK QUIZ

Section 1: Past and Current Exchange-Rate Arrangements

1. Which of the following describes a gold standard?
   a. a currency that is used to settle international debts and that is held by governments to use in foreign-exchange market interventions
   b. an exchange-rate system in which each nation fixes the value of its currency in terms of gold but buys and sells the U.S. dollar rather than gold to maintain fixed exchange rates
   c. the buying or selling of currencies by a government or central bank to achieve a specified exchange rate
   d. the exchange rates that are established in the absence of government foreign-exchange market intervention
   e. a system whereby national currencies are fixed in terms of their value in gold, thus creating fixed exchange rates between currencies

2. Which of the following describes a gold exchange standard?
   a. a currency that is used to settle international debts and that is held by governments to use in foreign-exchange market interventions
   b. an exchange-rate system in which each nation fixes the value of its currency in terms of gold but buys and sells the U.S. dollar rather than gold to maintain fixed exchange rates
   c. the buying or selling of currencies by a government or central bank to achieve a specified exchange rate
   d. the exchange rates that are established in the absence of government foreign-exchange market intervention
   e. a system whereby national currencies are fixed in terms of their value in gold, thus creating fixed exchange rates between currencies

3. Which of the following describes a reserve currency?
   a. a currency that is used to settle international debts and that is held by governments to use in foreign-exchange market interventions
   b. an exchange-rate system in which each nation fixes the value of its currency in terms of gold but buys and sells the U.S. dollar rather than gold to maintain fixed exchange rates
   c. the buying or selling of currencies by a government or central bank to achieve a specified exchange rate
   d. the exchange rates that are established in the absence of government foreign-exchange market intervention
   e. a system whereby national currencies are fixed in terms of their value in gold, thus creating fixed exchange rates between currencies

4. Which of the following describes foreign-exchange market intervention?
   a. a currency that is used to settle international debts and that is held by governments to use in foreign-exchange market interventions
   b. an exchange-rate system in which each nation fixes the value of its currency in terms of gold but buys and sells the U.S. dollar rather than gold to maintain fixed exchange rates
   c. the buying or selling of currencies by a government or central bank to achieve a specified exchange rate
   d. the exchange rates that are established in the absence of government foreign-exchange market intervention
   e. a system whereby national currencies are fixed in terms of their value in gold, thus creating fixed exchange rates between currencies

5. Which of the following describes equilibrium exchange rates?
   a. a currency that is used to settle international debts and that is held by governments to use in foreign-exchange market interventions
   b. an exchange-rate system in which each nation fixes the value of its currency in terms of gold but buys and sells the U.S. dollar rather than gold to maintain fixed exchange rates
   c. the buying or selling of currencies by a government or central bank to achieve a specified exchange rate
   d. the exchange rates that are established in the absence of government foreign-exchange market intervention
   e. a system whereby national currencies are fixed in terms of their value in gold, thus creating fixed exchange rates between currencies

6. The Bretton Woods system
   a. created the International Monetary Fund and the World Bank.
   b. was a gold exchange standard.
   c. used the U.S. dollar as a reserve currency.
   d. tried to maintain exchange rates through foreign-exchange market intervention.
   e. was and did all of the above.

Section 2: Fixed or Floating Exchange Rates

1. Currency appreciation is
   a. a decrease in the value of a currency under floating exchange rates.
   b. an increase in the value of a currency under floating exchange rates.
   c. a decrease in the value of a currency under fixed exchange rates.
   d. an increase in the value of a currency under fixed exchange rates.
   e. resetting the pegged value of a currency.

2. Currency depreciation is
   a. a decrease in the value of a currency under floating exchange rates.
   b. an increase in the value of a currency under floating exchange rates.
   c. a decrease in the value of a currency under fixed exchange rates.
   d. an increase in the value of a currency under fixed exchange rates.
   e. resetting the pegged value of a currency.

3. Which of the following statements about fixed and floating exchange rates is false?
   a. Fixed exchange rates put pressure on a nation to manage its macroeconomic policy in concert with other nations.
   b. Floating exchange rates put pressure on a nation to manage its macroeconomic policy in concert with other nations.
   c. Speculators are more likely to be a problem under fixed exchange rates than under floating exchange rates.
   d. Fixed exchange rates can force a devaluation in the event of fundamental disequilibrium.
   e. Floating exchange rates adjust automatically to changes in demand and supply.

Section 3: The Choice of an Exchange-Rate System

1. Economically, an open economy is one in which
   a. no trade with other countries takes place.
   b. there are no trade restraints.
   c. a large fraction of the country's GNP is devoted to internationally traded goods.
   d. exchange rates are freely floating, with no government intervention in foreign-exchange markets.
   e. other nations may freely invest.

2. Which of the following circumstances would make it likely that a country would choose a fixed exchange rate?
   a. The country is large, in terms of GNP.
   b. The country has an open economy.
   c. The country's inflation experience has diverged from its trading partner's.
   d. The country has a very diversified trading pattern.
   e. Both a and d above would make it unlikely that a country would choose floating exchange rates.

3. Multiple exchange rates
   a. are impossible.
   b. eventually lead to fixed exchange rates.
   c. eventually lead to a gold standard.
   d. have the same effects as taxes and subsidies.
   e. are easier to administer than a single exchange rate.

PRACTICE QUESTIONS AND PROBLEMS

Section 1: Past and Current Exchange-Rate Arrangements

1. From about 1880 to 1914, most currencies were fixed in value in terms of _____.

2. The Bretton Woods agreement of 1944 set up two international financial institutions that are still active today. Name the two institutions that match the descriptions below.

   a. _____: supervises exchange-rate arrangements and lends money to member countries experiencing problems meeting their external financial obligations

   b. _____: makes loans and provides technical expertise to developing countries

3. A _____ is a deliberate decrease in the official value of a currency.

4. Today, the major industrial countries determine the value of their currencies through

   _____

5. The _____ is an artificial unit of account averaging the values of the U.S. dollar, German mark, Japanese yen, French franc, and British pound.

6. The European monetary system maintains _____ (fixed, floating) exchange rates among its member nations and maintains _____ (fixed, floating) exchange rates with the rest of the world.

7. Under a gold standard, if gold is worth $35 per ounce in the United States and 175 francs per ounce in France, how many francs will exchange for $1? _____

8. Under a gold standard, if gold is worth $20 per ounce in the United States and 10 marks per ounce in Germany, how many marks will exchange for $1? _____

Section 2: Fixed or Floating Exchange Rates

1. The U.S. demand for German marks comes from the desire of _____ (U.S., German) citizens for _____ (U.S., German) goods.

2. The U.S. supply of German marks comes from the desire of _____ (U.S., German) citizens for _____ (U.S., German) goods.

3. If U.S. citizens decide that they want to buy more Mercedes automobiles from Germany, the U.S. _____ (demand for, supply of) marks will _____ (increase, decrease).

4. If German citizens decide they want to buy fewer IBM computers from the United States, the U.S. _____ (demand for, supply of) marks will _____ (increase, decrease).

5. The two graphs below show the current U.S. demand for and supply of German marks. The exchange rate between marks and dollars is freely floating.

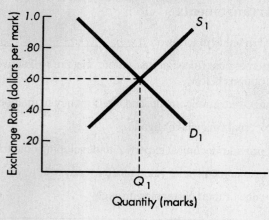 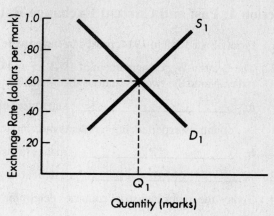

a. What is the current exchange rate, in dollars per mark? _____

b. What is the current exchange rate, in marks per dollar? _____

c. On the left graph, sketch in a new demand or supply curve (whichever is appropriate) that shows the effects of a decrease in the purchase of German BMW automobiles by U.S. residents.

d. Did the dollar appreciate or depreciate relative to the mark? _____ Did the

mark appreciate or depreciate relative to the dollar? _____

e. On the right graph, sketch in a new demand or supply curve (whichever is appropriate) that shows the effects of a decrease in the purchase of Boeing airplanes (made in the United States) by German airlines.

f. Did the dollar appreciate or depreciate relative to the mark? _____ Did the

mark appreciate or depreciate relative to the dollar? _____

Section 3: The Choice of an Exchange-Rate System

1. Countries with fixed exchange rates are likely to be _____ (large, small), to be

(more open, less open), to trade with _____ (many countries, mostly one country),

and to have a _____ (similar, different) inflation history compared with their trad-

ing partners.

2. Some countries use _____ exchange rates to effectively provide subsidies for

favored activities and taxes for activities that are discouraged.

3. Section 3.b in the text, on multiple exchange rates, cites Venezuela as a country that was using multiple exchange rates in 1985. Use the exchange rates listed there to find the costs in Venezuelan bolivars (Bs) of the transactions below.

    a. _____ : $10,000 interest payment on debt owed by a Venezuelan company to Citibank in New York

    b. _____ : $10,000 purchase of drilling supplies by the Venezuelan national oil company

    c. _____ : $10,000 purchase of personal computers by the Venezuelan education agency

    d. _____ : $10,000 purchase of a Chevrolet by a Venezuelan citizen

THINKING ABOUT AND APPLYING EXCHANGE-RATE SYSTEMS AND PRACTICES

I. Stable Exchange Rates and Foreign-Exchange Risk

When we compared fixed and floating exchange rates, one of the important differences was that fixed exchange rates forced countries to adapt their macroeconomic policies and inflation rates to match those of their trading partners. Why would any country want to give up the flexibility of setting its own policies? The "Economically Speaking" section for this chapter gives part of the answer: businesses prefer stable exchange rates because they minimize foreign-exchange risk.

    The next chapter discusses foreign-exchange risk in detail, but we don't need much detail yet. Read through the "Preview" section of the next chapter (the one on foreign-exchange risk), review the "Economically Speaking" section of this chapter, and summarize the arguments for and against a system of fixed exchange rates.

_____

_____

_____

_____

_____

_____

ANSWERS

Quick Check Quiz

Section 1: Past and Current Exchange-Rate Arrangements

1. e; 2. b; 3. a; 4. c; 5. d; 6. e

    If you missed any of these questions, you should go back and review pages 556–562 in Chapter 22 (pages 1004–1010 in *Economics*, Chapter 38).

Section 2: Fixed or Floating Exchange Rates

1. b; 2. a; 3. a

If you missed any of these questions, you should go back and review pages 562–568 in Chapter 22 (pages 1010–1016 in *Economics*, Chapter 38).

Section 3: The Choice of an Exchange-Rate System

1. c; 2. b; 3. d

If you missed any of these questions, you should go back and review pages 568–572 in Chapter 22 (pages 1016–1020 in *Economics*, Chapter 38).

Practice Questions and Problems

Section 1: Past and Current Exchange-Rate Arrangements

1. gold
2. a. International Monetary Fund (IMF)
   b. World Bank
3. devaluation
4. managed floating exchange rates
5. special drawing right (SDR)
6. fixed; floating
7. 5 francs
   It takes 5 times as many francs as dollars to buy an ounce of gold (175 francs per ounce/$35 per ounce), so one dollar would be equivalent to five times as many francs.
8. .5 mark
   It takes .5 times as many marks as dollars to buy an ounce of gold (10 marks per ounce/$20 per ounce), so one dollar would be equivalent to half as many marks.

Section 2: Fixed or Floating Exchange Rates

1. U.S.; German
2. German; U.S.
3. demand for; increase
   The Mercedes factory in Germany wants to be paid in its own currency (marks). U.S. buyers of German products have to buy marks with dollars. Since we want to buy more marks than before, the demand for marks will increase.
4. supply of; decrease
   IBM in the United States wants to be paid in its own currency (dollars). German buyers of U.S. products have to sell marks to get dollars. Since they want to sell fewer marks than before, the supply of marks will decrease.

5.

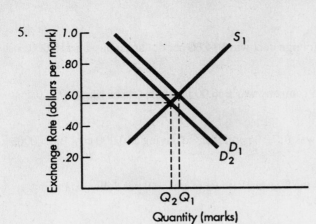

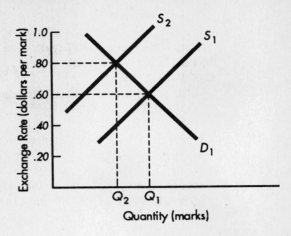

a. .60 dollar per mark

It takes $.60 to buy 1 mark, in dollars per mark. You can read this value from the intersection of demand and supply on the graph.

b. 1.67 marks per dollar

The exchange rate in marks per dollar is the inverse of the exchange rate in dollars per mark: $1/.60 = 1.67$. Exchange rates can be expressed either way around.

c. U.S. buyers of German products are the demanders of marks (they need to buy marks to pay Germans), so the demand curve will shift. If we buy fewer BMWs, the demand for marks will decrease, as shown on the graph above. The size of the shift on the graph does not matter.

d. appreciate; depreciate

It takes fewer dollars now to buy a mark than it did before (.55 dollar per mark instead of .60), so the dollar is more valuable relative to the mark.

It now takes 1.82 marks to buy a dollar (1/.55). It takes more marks now to buy a dollar than before, so the mark is less valuable relative to the dollar.

e. German buyers of U.S. products are the sellers of marks (they need to sell marks to get dollars to pay Americans), so the supply curve will shift. If they buy fewer Boeing airliners, the supply of marks will decrease, as shown on the graph above. The size of the shift on the graph does not matter.

f. depreciate; appreciate

It takes more dollars now to buy a mark than it did before (.80 dollar per mark instead of .60), so the dollar is less valuable relative to the mark.

It now takes only 1.25 marks to buy a dollar (1/.80). It takes fewer marks now to buy a dollar than before, so the mark is more valuable relative to the dollar.

Section 3: The Choice of an Exchange-Rate System

1. small; more open; mostly one country; similar
2. multiple

3. a. Bs43,000

   The exchange rate for interest payments on foreign debt was Bs4.30 per dollar, so buying $10,000 cost Bs43,000 ($10,000 times 4.30).

   b. Bs60,000

   The exchange rate for the national petroleum company was Bs6.00 per dollar, so buying $10,000 cost Bs60,000 ($10,000 times 6.00).

   c. Bs75,000

   The exchange rate for government agencies was Bs7.50 per dollar, so buying $10,000 cost Bs75,000 ($10,000 times 7.50).

   d. Bs144,000

   The exchange rate for other transactions was the free-market rate of Bs14.40 per dollar, so buying $10,000 cost Bs144,000 ($10,000 times 14.40).

Thinking About and Applying Exchange-Rate Systems and Practices

I. Stable Exchange Rates and Foreign-Exchange Risk

Arguments for fixed exchange rates:
1. They reduce foreign-exchange risk, improving the accuracy and efficiency of business decisions.
2. They force discipline in macroeconomic policy making.

Arguments against fixed exchange rates:
1. They reduce macroeconomic policy flexibility.
2. They create difficulties in reacting to shifts in demand and supply.

CHAPTER 23*
Foreign-Exchange Risk and International Lending

1. What is foreign-exchange risk, and how does it affect international traders?

    In the last chapter, we looked at how foreign-exchange rates are determined and how they can change when the international demand or supply of a country's goods changes. For firms importing or exporting products, there is usually some time lag between the date a contract in international trade is signed and the date payment will be made. If exchange rates change during that time, the value of the payment will change.

    For example, let's say that you want to buy a Mercedes-Benz automobile direct from the factory and pick up the car in three months during your vacation in Germany. You will have to pay 150,000 marks when you pick up the car. Today, the **spot exchange rate** is 1.5 marks per dollar: your Mercedes would cost you $100,000 if you paid for it today. But you won't pay for it until three months from now. If the value of the mark depreciates to 2 marks per dollar in three months, you will get a bargain: your Mercedes will only cost you $75,000. But what if the value of the mark appreciates to 1 mark per dollar: now your Mercedes will cost you $150,000. It's hard to make good decisions when you don't know what the price will be.

2. How do the forward, futures, and options markets in foreign exchange allow a firm to eliminate foreign-exchange risk?

    The forward, futures, and options markets in foreign exchange allow a firm expecting to receive or make payments in a foreign currency in the future to change an **open position,** whereby the firm is exposed to foreign-exchange risk, to a **covered position,** whereby the firm knows today what the domestic value of its foreign payment will be in the future.

    Although all three types of markets allow a firm to reduce or eliminate foreign-exchange risk, they work in somewhat different ways. The foreign-exchange forward market is a global market in which any amount of foreign currency is bought and sold for delivery at a future date. The foreign-exchange futures market is an organized market in which standardized contracts for future delivery of some currencies are bought and sold. Foreign-currency options give the purchaser the right to buy or sell a specified amount of currency at a set price on or before a particular date.

3. What caused the international debt crisis?

    Buying and selling products are not the only international economic transactions; international lending and borrowing are also an important source of financing, particularly for developing countries. In the 1970s, many developing countries borrowed large amounts from commercial banks in the industrial countries. In the early 1980s, a global recession led to high interest rates, at the same time reducing the demand for the exports of developing countries. With less earnings from exports and higher loan payments due to high interest rates, many developing countries in Latin America were not able to keep up payments on their loans.

*Economics Chapter 39.

4. What solutions have been proposed for the debt crisis?

A variety of solutions have been proposed. Initially, **debt rescheduling** was used to stretch out payments, with new loans given to help pay the interest on older loans. When financial conditions in the debtor countries did not improve, other possible solutions were considered. Debt buy-backs, debt-for-equity swaps, and debt-for-bonds swaps have all been used in limited cases. The Baker Plan, by which countries would implement free-market reforms in exchange for expanded loans, has not been implemented.

KEY TERMS

spot exchange rate	forward exchange rate	striking price
foreign-exchange risk	call	LIBOR
open position	put	debt rescheduling
covered position		

QUICK CHECK QUIZ

Section 1: Foreign-Exchange Transactions

1. The spot exchange rate is the foreign-exchange rate established today for delivery of a foreign currency
   a. at a specified location.
   b. immediately.
   c. at a specified time in the future.
   d. at some unspecified time in the future.
   e. at some specified time and location in the future.

2. The forward exchange rate is the foreign-exchange rate established today for delivery of a foreign currency
   a. at a specified location.
   b. immediately.
   c. at a specified time in the future.
   d. at some unspecified time in the future.
   e. at some specified time and location in the future.

3. Which of the following describes the forward exchange market?
   a. a market where you can buy the right to buy or sell a specified amount of currency at a set price on or before a particular date
   b. a market where you can buy $1 million or more in foreign currency to be delivered at a specific date in the future
   c. a market where you can buy or sell foreign currency for delivery immediately
   d. a market where you can buy a standardized contract for immediate delivery of some foreign currencies
   e. a market where you can buy a standardized contract for future delivery of some foreign currencies

4. Which of the following describes the spot foreign-exchange market?
   a. a market where you can buy the right to buy or sell a specified amount of currency at a set price on or before a particular date
   b. a market where you can buy $1 million or more in foreign currency to be delivered at a specific date in the future
   c. a market where you can buy or sell foreign currency for delivery immediately
   d. a market where you can buy a standardized contract for immediate delivery of some foreign currencies
   e. a market where you can buy a standardized contract for future delivery of some foreign currencies

5. Which of the following describes the foreign-exchange futures market?
   a. a market where you can buy the right to buy or sell a specified amount of currency at a set price on or before a particular date
   b. a market where you can buy $1 million or more in foreign currency to be delivered at a specific date in the future
   c. a market where you can buy or sell foreign currency for delivery immediately
   d. a market where you can buy a standardized contract for immediate delivery of some foreign currencies
   e. a market where you can buy a standardized contract for future delivery of some foreign currencies

6. Which of the following describes the foreign-currency options market?
   a. a market where you can buy the right to buy or sell a specified amount of currency at a set price on or before a particular date
   b. a market where you can buy $1 million or more in foreign currency to be delivered at a specific date in the future
   c. a market where you can buy or sell foreign currency for delivery immediately
   d. a market where you can buy a standardized contract for immediate delivery of some foreign currencies
   e. a market where you can buy a standardized contract for future delivery of some foreign currencies

7. A call option
   a. gives you the right to sell currency at a certain price.
   b. gives you the right to buy currency at a certain price.
   c. is a contract requiring you to buy a specified amount of currency at the future spot price.
   d. is a contract requiring you to sell a specified amount of currency at the future spot price.
   e. gives you the choice of either buying or selling currency at a specific time in the future.

8. A put option
   a. gives you the right to sell currency at a certain price.
   b. gives you the right to buy currency at a certain price.
   c. is a contract requiring you to buy a specified amount of currency at the future spot price.
   d. is a contract requiring you to sell a specified amount of currency at the future spot price.
   e. gives you the choice of either buying or selling currency at a specific time in the future.

Section 2: The International Debt Problem

1. Which of the following is NOT among the causes of the international debt problem?
   a. increases in LIBOR
   b. decreased demand for exports because of global recession in the early 1980s
   c. loans with variable interest rates
   d. careless lending to countries that were involved in regional wars
   e. increases in the U.S. prime rate

2. Which of the following is NOT true of the Baker Plan for dealing with developing countries' debt problems?
   a. It is named after James Baker, who was the U.S. Treasury Secretary.
   b. Government intervention in the economies of developing countries would be expanded.
   c. Countries would continue to receive new loans.
   d. Developing countries would emphasize free markets.
   e. Economic changes in the developing countries were expected to lead to improved growth and eventual repayment of all loans.

3. Which of the following has NOT been one of the ways proposed or used to reduce developing countries' debt?
   a. debt buy-backs
   b. debt-for-equity swaps
   c. the Baker Plan
   d. debt-for-bonds swaps
   e. complete debt forgiveness

PRACTICE QUESTIONS AND PROBLEMS

Section 1: Foreign-Exchange Transactions

1. When you are waiting to buy foreign currency in the future in the spot market, you have a(n) _____ (open, covered) position and _____ (are, are not) exposed to foreign-exchange risk.

2. You can eliminate foreign-exchange risk by using the _____, _____, or _____ markets in foreign exchange. When you use these markets, you can convert an open position into a _____ position.

3. In the foreign-currency options market, a call option gives you the right to _____ (buy, sell) currency at a certain price, and a put option gives you the right to _____ (buy, sell) currency at a certain price. The price at which currency can be bought or sold in this market is called the _____ .

4. Match the following descriptions with the three types of foreign-exchange markets.
   a. The _____ market trades the rights to buy and sell foreign currency in the future.

   b. The _____ market trades standardized contracts to buy or sell foreign currency for delivery in the future.

   c. The _____ market is for large-scale buying and selling of foreign currency for future delivery at a price set today.

5. In late February 1990, the Red Cedar Shingle Company ordered 2,000,000 cedar shingles from a Canadian lumber company; the shingles cost 1 Canadian dollar (C$) each. The shingles were scheduled for delivery and payment in September 1990.

a. What was the cost of the shingles in U.S. dollars when the order was placed? (Figure 1 in the text has the exchange rate you need; use the Wednesday rate.) _____

b. If the exchange rate changes so that a Canadian dollar is worth .87 U.S. dollar when the order is delivered, what will be the cost of the shingles in U.S. dollars then? _____

c. To avoid foreign-exchange risk, the Red Cedar Shingle Company plans to use the forward exchange market. Assuming there were no service charges, what was the cost of C$2,000,000 on Wednesday, February 21, 1990, for delivery 180 days later? (Figure 1 in the text has the information you need; use the Wednesday rate.) _____

d. If Red Cedar uses the foreign-exchange futures market, how many Canadian-dollar contracts will it need to buy? _____ Ignoring the commissions charged in the futures market, what was the cost in U.S. dollars of using September futures contracts to buy C$2,000,000? (Figure 2 in the text has the information you need; use the settle price.) _____

6. In late February 1990, the Yellow Cedar Shingle Company ordered 500,000 cedar shingles from a Canadian lumber company; the shingles cost 1 Canadian dollar (C$) each. The shingles were scheduled for delivery and payment in March 1990.

a. What was the cost of the shingles in U.S. dollars when the order was placed? (Figure 1 in the text has the exchange rate you need; use the Wednesday rate.) _____

b. If the exchange rate changes so that a Canadian dollar is worth .80 U.S. dollar when the order is delivered, what will be the cost of the shingles in U.S. dollars then? _____

c. Why can't the Yellow Cedar Shingle Company use the forward market to avoid foreign-exchange risk?

_____

d. If Yellow Cedar uses the foreign-exchange futures market, how many Canadian-dollar contracts will it need to buy? _____ Ignoring the commissions charged in the futures market, what was the cost in U.S. dollars of using March futures contracts to buy C$500,000? (Figure 2 in the text has the information you need; use the settle price.) _____

e. If Yellow Cedar uses the foreign-exchange options market, how many Canadian-dollar contracts will it need to buy? _____ Will it buy put or call options? _____ If Yellow Cedar would be satisfied with an exchange rate of US$.83 = C$1.00, how much would an option ensuring it would pay no more than $.83 cost? (Figure 3 in the text has the information you need.) _____

f. If Yellow Cedar would be satisfied with an exchange rate of US$.835 = C$1.00, how much would an option ensuring it would pay no more than $.835 cost? (Figure 3 in the text has the information you need.) _____

Section 2: The International Debt Problem

1. The developing-country debt crisis began when Mexico was unable to _____.

2. The main cause of the debt crisis was a combination of rising _____ and worldwide _____.

3. During the 1982–1985 period, the initial response to debt-repayment problems was _____, which extended payments and offered new loans.

4. Variable-interest-rate loans to developing countries based interest rates on the U.S. _____ or on _____, the rate charged for loans between major banks in London.

5. In a _____, the lender agrees to eliminate the debt in exchange for immediate payment of less than the face value of the debt.

6. In a _____ swap, a private firm buys a country's debt for less than face value and sells the debt back to the developing country in exchange for an ownership position in a firm in the developing country.

7. In a _____ swap, new debtor-country bonds are exchanged for existing commercial-bank debt.

THINKING ABOUT AND APPLYING FOREIGN-EXCHANGE RISK AND INTERNATIONAL LENDING

I. Debt-Reduction Strategies: Debt Buy-Backs

Section 2.b.2 in the text and the "Economic Insight" section entitled "Buying Back Bolivian Government Debt" look at one way that developing countries have reduced their debt. Bolivia, for example, offered to buy back some of its debt to commercial banks at a price of 11 cents for each dollar of debt.

1. How much debt did banks buy back from Bolivia, and how many dollars did Bolivia pay?

   _____

   _____

2. What did the banks gain from selling Bolivian debt for a small fraction of the amount Bolivia owed?

   _____

   _____

   _____

   _____

3. Bolivia had made no payments on its debt for the four years before the buy-back offer. Why did Bolivia use some of its foreign aid to buy back its debt, instead of just keeping on paying nothing? (Hint: Look at the "Economic Insight" article entitled "Country Risk.")

_____

_____

_____

_____

II. Debt-Reduction Strategies: Debt-for-Equity Swaps

Section 2.b.3 in the text discusses debt-for-equity swaps, including a 1986 swap involving Mexico, Nissan Motors, and U.S. commercial banks.

1. What did Nissan gain from the swap?

_____

_____

_____

_____

2. What did Mexico gain from the swap?

_____

_____

_____

_____

3. What did U.S. banks gain from the swap?

_____

_____

_____

_____

III. Debt-Reduction Strategies: Debt-for-Bonds Swaps

Section 2.b.4 examines another method of reducing developing country debt, swapping commercial bank debt for government bonds. The text section analyzes a 1987 Mexican debt-for-bonds swap. Let's apply that analysis to a hypothetical debt-for-bonds swap.

1. Suppose that Brazil offers to swap $5 billion of its commercial bank debt for Brazilian bonds, using U.S. Treasury bonds as collateral; Brazil has made no payments on its debt for several years. If Brazil offers to swap the debt for bonds at a rate of 70 cents per dollar, the commercial banks will get bonds worth how much? _____

2. Why would the banks be willing to make the swap?

_____

_____

_____

_____

3. How does the swap help Brazil?

_____

_____

_____

_____

IV. Clipping the Wings of "Flight Capital"

This chapter's "Economically Speaking" section examines the phenomenon of "capital flight" from Latin American countries, of wealthy investors in these countries sending their money to places like the United States or Switzerland for investing rather than investing the money in their own countries. One key to a permanent solution to the international debt problem is to encourage people in developing countries to invest their money "at home" rather than in other countries. Read over the "Economically Speaking" section, list the factors mentioned there that motivate capital flight, and explain what parts of the Baker Plan would be helpful in discouraging capital flight.

_____

_____

_____

_____

_____

_____

ANSWERS

Quick Check Quiz

Section 1: Foreign-Exchange Transactions

1. b; 2. c; 3. b; 4. c; 5. e; 6. a; 7. b; 8. a

If you missed any of these questions, you should go back and review pages 578–586 in Chapter 23 (pages 1026–1034 in *Economics*, Chapter 39).

Section 2: The International Debt Problem

1. d; 2. b; 3. e

If you missed any of these questions, you should go back and review pages 586–594 in Chapter 23 (pages 1034–1042 in *Economics*, Chapter 39).

Practice Questions and Problems

Section 1: Foreign-Exchange Transactions

1. open; are
2. forward; futures; options; covered
3. buy; sell; striking price
4. a. options
   b. futures
   c. forward
5. a. $1,668,400

   The Wednesday spot exchange rate from Figure 1 was .8342 U.S. dollar for 1 Canadian dollar. Red Cedar was buying 2 million shingles at C$1 each, or C$2 million of shingles. To find the value in U.S. dollars, multiply the C$2 million times .8342 US$ per C$.

   b. $1,740,000

   Multiply C$2 million times .87 US$ per C$. This increase shows the effects of foreign-exchange risk.

   c. $1,634,800

   The 180-day forward exchange rate was .8174 US$ per C$, so the cost to Red Cedar was C$2 million times .8174.

   d. 20 contracts; $1,631,000

   The Canadian-dollar futures contracts in Figure 2 are for C$100,000, as listed in the figure on the Canadian Dollar line. To cover the C$2 million purchase, Red Cedar needs to buy 20 contracts (C$2 million/C$100,000 per contract).

   The settle rate in the futures market was .8155 for September contracts. This is the cost in US$ per C$ bought, so the cost of futures contracts for C$2 million is C$2 million times .8155 US$ per C$ (not including commissions).

6. a. $417,100

   The Wednesday spot exchange rate from Figure 1 was .8342 U.S. dollars for 1 Canadian dollar. Yellow Cedar was buying 500,000 shingles at C$1 each, or C$500,000 of shingles. To find the value in U.S. dollars, multiply the C$500,000 times .8342 US$ per C$.

   b. $400,000

   Multiply C$500,000 times .80 US$ per C$. Foreign-exchange risk can work to a buyer's benefit if the exchange rate falls. Converting an open exchange position to a covered exchange position avoids foreign-exchange risk but also prevents any gains from changes in exchange rates.

   c. The forward market deals only in transactions of $1 million or more.

   d. 5 contracts; $415,700

   The Canadian-dollar futures contracts in Figure 2 are for C$100,000, as listed in the figure on the Canadian Dollar line. To cover the C$500,000 purchase, Yellow Cedar needs to buy 5 contracts (C$500,000/C$100,000 per contract).

   The settle rate in the futures market was .8314 for September contracts. This is the cost in US$ per C$ bought, so the cost of futures contracts for C$500,000 is C$500,000 times .8314 US$ per C$ (not including commissions).

   e. 10 contracts; call options; $2,350

   The Canadian-dollar options contracts in Figure 3 are for C$50,000, as listed in the figure on the Canadian Dollar line. To cover the C$500,000 purchase, Yellow Cedar needs to buy 10 contracts (C$500,000/C$50,000 per contract).

Call options give you the right to buy foreign currency: you can "call" the money and it comes to you. Put options give you the right to sell foreign currency: you can "put" the money into the market.

To avoid paying more than US$.83 for C$1, Yellow Cedar should buy call options with a strike price of .83. The cost of the March call option with a strike price of .83 is listed as .47 cent per C$, or US$.0047 per C$. To cover C$500,000 would cost $2,350 (C$500,000 times .0047).

f. $1,250

To avoid paying more than US$.835 for C$1, Yellow Cedar should buy call options with a strike price of .83 1/2. The cost of the March call option with a strike price of .83 1/2 is listed as .25 cent per C$, or US$.0025 per C$. To cover C$500,000 would cost $1,250 (C$500,000 times .0025).

Section 2: The International Debt Problem

1. make its debt payments on schedule
2. interest rates; recession
3. debt rescheduling
4. prime rate; LIBOR
5. debt buy-back
6. debt-for-equity
7. debt-for-bonds

Thinking About and Applying Foreign-Exchange Risk and International Lending

I. Debt-Reduction Strategies: Debt Buy-Backs

1. The article says that the banks sold back $270 million of debt. If they received 11 cents per dollar, they received $29.7 million ($270 million times .11).
2. Bolivia had not been making payments on the debt and might never pay back any of the debt. Through the buy-back, the banks received some money back and removed the uncertainty about the value of the debt.
3. By reducing the amount of its debt and demonstrating its willingness to make at least partial payment, Bolivia probably increased its credit worthiness and its ability to borrow in the future. Also, with the amount of debt reduced, Bolivia has a better chance of being able to pay off its other creditors.

II. Debt-Reduction Strategies: Debt-for-Equity Swaps

1. Nissan received $54 million in pesos to pay for expanding its factories in Mexico at a cost of only $40 million, so Nissan got a $54-million factory for $40 million, saving $14 million.
2. Mexico paid off $60 million of debt at a cost of $54 million, using its own currency instead of some of its limited supply of U.S. dollars. Also, Mexico has an expanded Nissan factory that generates more jobs in Mexico; without the swap, Nissan might have decided to build the factory in another country.
3. As with debt buy-backs, banks receive at least some payment on their loans. Getting $40 million back on $60 million in loans is better than getting nothing back.

III. Debt-Reduction Strategies: Debt-for-Bonds Swaps

1. $3.5 billion ($5 billion times .70)
2. Once again, a bird in the hand is worth two in the bush. Being sure you receive at least partial payment (guaranteed by the U.S. Treasury bonds in this case) is better than receiving no payment at all.
3. By reducing the amount of its debt, Brazil can improve its credit worthiness and increase its chances of paying off other creditors.

IV.   Clipping the Wings of "Flight Capital"

Factors that motivate capital flight:
> avoidance of high inflation rates
> high taxes
> economic mismanagement and political instability
> higher interest rates abroad
> possible expropriation
> overvalued exchange rates

Elements of the Baker Plan:
> stimulate economic growth through continued lending
> restructure economies to emphasize free markets
> de-emphasize government intervention in markets
> de-emphasize government subsidies
> de-emphasize government enterprises

The objective of the Baker Plan was to create local economies that have a foundation of economic efficiency and that will provide long-term growth. The Baker Plan would, if successful, not only enable the debtors to eventually repay their debts, but also create local economic conditions that would encourage local investment, removing many of the incentives for capital flight. A stable, growing local economy should create lower inflation and competitive interest rates and exchange rates. De-emphasizing the role of government in markets should reduce taxes and economic mismanagement, as well as the fear of expropriation.